**Empire in D

Empire in Denial

The Politics of State-building

DAVID CHANDLER

Pluto Press

LONDON • ANN ARBOR, MI

First published 2006 by Pluto Press
345 Archway Road, London N6 5AA
and 839 Greene Street, Ann Arbor, MI 48106

www.plutobooks.com

British Library Cataloguing in Publication Data
A catalogue record for this book is available from the British Library

ISBN   0 7453 2429 0 hardback
ISBN   0 7453 2428 2 paperback

Library of Congress Cataloging in Publication Data applied for

10   9   8   7   6   5   4   3   2   1

Designed and produced for Pluto Press by
Chase Publishing Services Ltd, Fortescue, Sidmouth, EX10 9QG, England
Typeset from disk by Stanford DTP Services, Northampton, England
Printed and bound in the European Union by
Antony Rowe Ltd, Chippenham and Eastbourne, England

Contents

For Debi and Aiden

Acknowledgements

This book would not have been possible without the support of my wife Bonnie and the patience of my children, Harvey and Oliver, who had to contend with the strange and 'unfair' concept that when Daddy was at home he was also sometimes still 'at work'.

Having the time to engage in writing is necessary but, of course, not sufficient; it is the engagement with and development of the ideas which matter. To the extent that this book has been able to open up the theme of international state-building and pose new questions with regard to the reshaping of international relations, the work is a product of collective engagement in a number of international forums and working groups, including those organised in conjunction with: the British Academy (Grants for Joint Projects with South Eastern Europe); International Studies Association (ISA); European Consortium for Political Research (ECPR); British International Studies Association (BISA); Political Science Association (PSA); Military Centre for Strategic Studies (CeMISS), Rome; Royal Institute for International Relations (RIIR-KIIB), Brussels; International Institute for Strategic Studies (IISS), London; Cambridge International Studies Association, Cambridge University; Institute of Ideas; Institute for European Studies (IES), Vrije Universiteit, Brussels; Italian Institute for International Studies (IPSI), Milan; Centre for Applied Policy Research (CAP), University of Munich; Balkan Forum, Federal Foreign Office, Berlin; Department of Politics, University of Limerick; Goodenough College, London; School of Oriental and African Studies (SOAS), University of London; Institute of Commonwealth Studies, University of London; the Sovereignty And Its Discontents (SAID) working group; and the International Relations discussion group at the Centre for the Study of Democracy, University of Westminster.

There are many individuals who have provided feedback, assistance, ideas and, of course, critique without whom the arguments would without doubt be less developed, these include: Rita Abrahamsen; Josie Appleton; William Bain; Christopher Bickerton; Didier Bigo; Berit Bliesemann de Guevara; Giovanna Bono; Alan Bullion; Simon Chesterman; Jarat Chopra; Philip Cunliffe; Barbara Delcourt; Mark Duffield; Alastair Fraser; Alex Gourevitch; Philip Hammond; Graham Harrison; James Heartfield; Volker Heins; Tara McCormack; Brendan

O'Neill; David Ost; Roland Paris; John Pender; Jonathan Pugh; Vanessa Pupavac; Deepayan Basu Ray; Julian Reid; Ian Richardson; Wim van Meurs; and Dominik Zaum. Last but not least I would like to thank my ever supportive commissioning editor at Pluto Press, Anne Beech.

An earlier version of Chapter 2 was prepared as a research paper, 'Post-conflict State-building: Phantom States and Fragile Empires', for the Centre for Military and Strategic Studies (CeMiSS), Rome, and the Foreign Policy Studies Institute (ISPI), Milan, research project on 'Asymmetry, Terrorism and Preventive War: The Crisis of the Form of War and the Collapse of International Society'. Chapter 3 is an amended version of 'Potemkin Sovereignty: Statehood without Politics in the New World Order', forthcoming in *The Monist*, Vol. 90, No. 1 (2007) 'Sovereignty' issue. Chapter 4 is a revised version of 'The "Other-regarding" Ethics of Empire in Denial', forthcoming in Volker Heins and David Chandler (eds) *Rethinking Ethical Foreign Policy: Pitfalls, Possibilities and Paradoxes* (London: Routledge, 2006). Chapter 5 is a revised and updated version of 'Governance: The Unequal Partnership' published in Wim van Meurs (ed.) *South Eastern Europe: Weak States and Strong International Support, Prospects and Risks Beyond EU Enlargement*, Vol. 2 (Opladen: Leske & Budrich/Bertelsmann Foundation, 2003), pp. 79–98. Chapter 6 is an amended version of 'State-building in Bosnia: The Limits of "Informal Trusteeship"', forthcoming in the *International Journal of Peace Studies*, Vol. 11, No. 1, 2006. Chapter 7 is a revised version of 'Building Trust in Public Institutions? Good Governance and Anti-corruption in Bosnia-Herzegovina', forthcoming in *Ethnopolitics*, Vol. 5, special issue on Bosnia, 2006. Chapter 8 is an amended version of 'The Problems of "Nation-building": Imposing Bureaucratic Rule From Above', published in the *Cambridge Review of International Affairs*, Vol. 17, No. 3, 2004, pp. 577–91.

List of Abbreviations

ACTG	Anti-Corruption and Transparency Group
APRM	African Peer Review Mechanism
BiH	Bosnia-Herzegovina
CAFAO	Customs and Fiscal Assistance Office
CARDS	Community Assistance for Reconstruction, Development and Stabilisation
CFSP	Common Foreign and Security Policy
CoM	Council of Ministers
CPA	Coalition Provisional Authority
DEI	Directorate of European Integration
DFID	Department for International Development
DPI	Democratization Policy Institute
EBRD	European Bank for Reconstruction and Development
ESI	European Stability Initiative
EU	European Union
FBiH	Bosnian Federation
FRY	Federal Republic of Yugoslavia
GAO	General Accountancy Office (US Congress)
HDZ	Croatian Democratic Community (*Hrvatska Demokratska Zajednica*)
HIPC	Highly Indebted Poor Country
HLSG	High Level Steering Group
ICB	International Commission on the Balkans
ICG	International Crisis Group
ICISS	International Commission on Intervention and State Sovereignty
IFI	international financial institution
IMF	International Monetary Fund
IPTF	International Police Task Force
KM	Convertible Mark
MCA	Millennium Challenge Account
MDG	Millennium Development Goals
MUP	Ministry of Internal Affairs
NATO	North Atlantic Treaty Organisation
NEPAD	New Partnership for Africa's Development
NGO	non-governmental organisation

OECD	Organisation for Economic Cooperation and Development
OHR	Office of the High Representative
OSCE	Organisation for Security and Cooperation in Europe
PDP	Party of Democratic Progress (*Partija Demokratskog Progresa*)
PIC	Peace Implementation Council
PPA	participatory poverty assessment
PRGF	Poverty Reduction and Growth Facility
PRSP	Poverty Reduction Strategy Paper
PSIA	poverty and social impact analysis
RS	Republika Srpska
SAA	Stabilisation and Association Agreement
SAp	Stabilisation and Association process
SAP	Structural Adjustment Programme
SDA	Party of Democratic Action (*Stranka Demokratska Akcija*)
SDS	Serbian Democratic Party (*Srpska Demokratska Stranka*)
SEE	South Eastern Europe
SFOR	(NATO) Stabilisation Force
SP	Stability Pact
SPACI	Stability Pact Anti-Corruption Initiative
SPSEE	Stability Pact for South Eastern Europe
TI	Transparency International
UK	United Kingdom
UN	United Nations
UNDP	United Nations Development Programme
UNHCR	United Nations High Commissioner for Refugees
UNMIBH	United Nations Mission in Bosnia-Herzegovina
UNMIK	United Nations Mission in Kosovo
US	United States
USAID	United States Agency for International Development

1

Introduction: Empire in Denial

State-building – constructing or reconstructing institutions of governance capable of providing citizens with physical and economic security – is widely held to be one of the most pressing policy questions facing the international community today. Those concerned with such issues cross the political spectrum. They include political realists who argue that there is more to fear from failing states than from conquering ones. They also embrace activists who see the dysfunction of state institutions as lying at the heart of the global poverty trap. Indeed, it is the intersection of these concerns on the part of the security and development communities that has made state-building a core policy focus across the policy agendas of major Western states, international institutions and international non-governmental organisations (NGOs).

For some commentators, the focus on capacity-building states and encouraging country ownership of poverty reduction strategies and Millennium Development Goals (MDGs) is potentially empowering for non-Western states and their citizens, many of whom are currently excluded from the new globalising order. For others, the language of capacity-building and empowerment merely hides the traditional practices of empire or even extends them in new regulatory forms.

This book will challenge both the above positions. It analyses how state-building practices constitute highly invasive forms of external regulation but argues that these therapeutic and empowering practices cannot be fully understood merely as mechanisms designed to enforce the self-interests of Western actors. Instead, state-building forms of regulation are considered, in the context of Empire in Denial, as attempts by Western states and international institutions to deny the power which they wield and to evade accountability for its exercise.

This introductory chapter highlights the centrality of state-building to international relations today and then locates this book in relation to existing debates and discussion on state-building and introduces the framework of Empire in Denial, contrasting the theoretical approach developed in this book with traditional Left and

Foucauldian approaches to current forms of external international regulatory control. It then provides an overview of the chapters which follow.

STATE-BUILDING

In the discourse of poverty reduction and international development, state-capacity has, over the last decade, become central to international concerns and 'enhancing the capacity of African states has risen to the top of the continent's development agenda' (Léautier and Madavo, 2004: v). These concerns, and policy interventions in response to them, are highlighted in the World Bank's *World Development Report 1997: The State in a Changing World* and in the 2000 follow-up study, *Reforming Public Institutions and Strengthening Governance: A World Bank Strategy* (WB, 1997; 2000). The UK government's 2005 Commission for Africa report argues that failures in state capacity have been the central barrier to development in the continent (CFA, 2005: 14). The UN Millennium Project expert panel, directed by Jeffrey Sachs, suggests that the central problem faced by poor and heavily indebted states is weak governance, caused not so much by 'corrupt' governments but those that 'lack the resources and capacity to manage an efficient public administration' (UNMP, 2005b: 113). The World Bank's perspective has become an international consensus, upheld by all the leading Western governments, including the United States, and the United Nations.

In the current discourses of international security, state-building is seen as central to address the threats posed by weak states, which can harbour terrorists, drug traffickers and international criminal networks and therefore export instability, refugees, crime and terror. The 2002 US National Security Strategy sums up the prevalent fears in its assertion that: 'America is now threatened less by conquering states than we are by failing ones' (NSS, 2002: Section 1). For US Secretary of State, Condoleezza Rice:

Today ... the greatest threats to our security are defined more by the dynamics within weak and failing states than by the borders between strong and aggressive ones. Weak and failing states serve as global pathways that facilitate the spread of pandemics, the movement of criminals and terrorists, and the proliferation of the world's most dangerous weapons. Our experience of this new world leads us to conclude that the fundamental character of regimes matters more today than the international distribution of power. (Rice, 2005)

Stephen Krasner and Carlos Pascual argue ominously that state weaknesses 'constitute structural threats akin to dead leaves that accumulate in a forest. No one knows what spark will ignite them, or when. Over the long run, the only real way to create lasting peace is to promote better governance' (Krasner and Pascual, 2005: 155). According to Francis Fukuyama, 'state-building is one of the most important issues for the world community because weak or failed states are the source of many of the world's most serious problems, from poverty to AIDS to drugs to terrorism' (Fukuyama, 2004: ix). Robert Rotberg does not exaggerate in arguing that state-building has 'become one of the critical all-consuming strategic and moral imperatives of our terrorized time' (Rotberg, 2004b: 42).

It seems that no international policy or strategy document can be complete without the focus on state-building as a key objective: in August 2004 the US government established a state-building department, the Office of the Coordinator for Reconstruction and Stabilization (USOCRS, 2005); in February 2005 the UK government's Strategy Unit report *Investing in Prevention – An International Strategy to Manage Risks of Instability and Improve Crisis Response* viewed state-building as a key part of its 'partnerships for stability' agenda (UKSU, 2005); in March 2005, at the High Level Meeting of the Organisation for Economic Cooperation and Develoment (OECD) Donor Assistance Committee in Paris, the Ministers of Development of OECD countries agreed to a set of 'Principles for Good International Engagement in Fragile States' with a 'focus on state-building as the central objective' (OECD, 2005: 8); in the same month the Commission for Africa report welcomed the fact that more than a quarter of bilateral aid to Africa was already being channelled directly into state capacity-building (CFA, 2005: 136); in September 2005 the UN world summit agreed on the establishment of a proposed Peace-Building Commission to coordinate international activity in this area (UN, 2005b: §97–105).

The task of international state-building has rapidly assumed a central role in the foreign policy concerns of Western states and in the organisational remits of international institutions. International policy practices in relation to state-building go well beyond the post-conflict transitional processes in places such as Bosnia, Kosovo, East Timor, Afghanistan and Iraq. State-building practices of external support for governance capacity now extend to most of the countries in the world. Practically every international engagement between international institutions and non-Western states includes forms of conditionality which relate to the internal governance mechanisms of non-Western states. This is especially true of international agreements for development aid and debt relief assistance, for example under programmes of debt reduction under the G8, the UN's Millennium Development Goals and the World Bank's Poverty Reduction Strategies.

The United States government under George W. Bush has been keen to stress the importance of the export of state-building assistance, not just to postwar Afghanistan and Iraq but to large regions of the world, including the Middle East, Africa and Eastern Europe. Since January 2004, US external assistance for state-building poor and indebted countries has taken place under the Millennium Challenge Account (MCA) initiative where increased international aid is delivered on the basis of allowing greater external assistance for good governance and state institutional capacity-building. Bush has requested $3 billion from Congress for the MCA in 2006 and has pledged to increase annual funding to $5 billion in the future (MCA, 2005). The World Bank and the International Monetary Fund have shifted their focus away from traditional approaches to development, which stressed external conditionality, towards state capacity-building and good governance in order to assist in the development of national ownership strategies of poverty reduction. The European Union's central foreign policy focus has been on its enlargement to the East this process has involved state-building through the integration process and the EU has played a crucial role in managing the transitional status of the quasi- and full-protectorates of Bosnia-Herzegovina and Kosovo and is leading the process of 'member state-building' with the accession of the Balkan states to the Stabilisation and Association process (SAp) (ICB, 2005: 14). The UN has made the agenda of external state-building its own in the organisational support given to the new, much more interventionist, practices of 'human security' and the merging of the concerns of security and development throughout the 1990s, given focus in the central role of state-building in the delivery of the Millennium Development Goals.

However, despite the focus of attention on the question of external engagement with the domestic governing mechanisms of non-Western states, there has been little theoretical engagement with state-building as a policy framework, either in terms of the state-building actors, with leading Western states and international institutions at the forefront, or in terms of the consequences for the objects of these practices, non-Western states.

Problem-solving and critique

State-building has generally been addressed, in a dry and technical way, as a question of the development of the international expertise necessary to increase the effectiveness of external regulatory intervention into 'failed' post-conflict states or potentially failing or fragile non-Western states. These states are deemed to have 'capacity problems' which are held to prevent them from adequately dealing with the complex problems arising in the economic, social and political management of their societies. It is 'they' who have the problem, but in an interconnected world their problems are seen as increasingly necessary for 'us' to address, either for self-interested security reasons or as a result of our ethical duties and responsibilities towards others. The problematic of state-building is therefore that of how Western governments, policy-makers and civil society activists can resolve the wide-ranging problems facing the citizens and governments of the non-Western world.

This approach could be seen as a problem-solving approach in terms of the critical theory perspective developed by Robert Cox and others (Cox, 1981). The focus on the technical problems facing international administrative assistance has led to a large number of 'lessons learned' reports which repeat generic nostrums of preparedness, early intervention, strategic planning, international coordination, the importance of the rule of law, the integration of military and civic agencies, the problems of relying overly on elections, the need to develop strategies to deal with 'spoilers' and to integrate and encourage more moderate political forces, to support civil society initiatives, establish early gains to win the confidence of people in international assistance, deal with health, education, HIV/AIDS awareness, post-conflict demobilisation, etc. (see, for example, Zartman, 1995; UN, 2000; Cousens and Kumar, 2001; CSDG, 2003; Dobbins et al., 2003; Maley, Sampford and Thakur, 2003; Milliken, 2003; Rotberg, 2004a; Chesterman, Ignatieff and Thakur, 2005a). The bulk of the state-building research has focused on the high-profile cases where there has been direct international administrative control in post-conflict situations. Less empirical work has, so far, been done on the impact of external strategies of capacity-building and good governance linked with EU enlargement or with governance reforms linked with development aid and debt reduction.

One striking aspect of the literature is the highly depoliticised nature of the discussions of state capacity-building, where concerns of stability and regulation are discussed in a narrow technical and functionalist framework (see Goureritch, 2004; Bøås and Jennings, 2005). The functionalist approach is probably best summed up in Roland Paris' critical view that in post-conflict situations there should be 'Institutionalization before Liberalization' (Paris, 2004). 'Institutionalization', i.e. the focus on institutional capacity-building, such as that of the judiciary, police and the civil service, is considered to be an essential prerequisite for self-government, i.e. 'Liberalization'. The functional capacity of state institutions is privileged over their representational or policy-making autonomy and increasingly understood in technical and administrative terms (see further, Chapter 3).

The understanding of state-building and the external capacity-building of institutions in highly technical and functionalist terms has gone hand in hand with the problematisation of traditional perspectives of sovereignty as self-government and political autonomy. For some commentators, the coexistence of external administrators with elected governments has proved problematic, revealing the limitations to external assistance which cannot assume the controlling powers of past empire. For Fukuyama, the problem of encouraging good governance and strengthening capacity, without direct forms of rule, remains a problematic 'circle to be squared' (Fukuyama, 2004: 164). Michael Ignatieff has condemned 'empire lite' for occupying an untenable middle ground, neither providing the prolonged external assistance and control necessary to transform weak states and societies, nor allowing self-government (Ignatieff, 2003: 126). Other commentators have argued that the internationalisation of sovereign state functional responsibilities is the way forward, and concepts of 'neo-trusteeship', 'guided sovereignty' and 'shared sovereignty' have increasingly been proffered as a way of bridging the gap between the functional demands deemed necessary and the lack of non-Western state capacity (see, for example, Krasner, 1999; 2004; Keohane, 2002; 2003; Fearon and Laitin, 2004).

This book seeks to take a step back from the problem-solving approaches which dominate the publications in this field to consider why state-building approaches have become so central to the agendas of Western states and international institutions. It seeks to consider what state-building discourses and practices reveal about the actors engaged in them and more broadly what they say about our changing perceptions of the importance of political engagement and the political sphere itself. What is it that leads Western states and international institutions to reinterpret economic, social and political problems in other parts of the world as questions which are largely amenable to technical administrative solutions? How can it be that today it seems that the answer to every problem from security threats to human rights to development is now that of good governance and the export of external advisers and capacity-builders? Can new external forms of regulation which seek to strengthen and empower and capacity-build non-Western states and their citizens achieve their stated aims if they view the state in narrow technical and functional terms?

If these are new forms of the exercise of Western power, of the needs of the market, or of empire, then what is it that drives Western states and international institutions to draw on the language of capacity-building and empowerment rather than the traditional discourses of democracy and the market? This shift in the forms of legitimisation of international regulatory controls seems to call for some explanation when it appears that international institutions have a much freer hand and are under less critical pressure than during the geopolitical divide of the Cold War. If the shifting focus to therapeutic and bureaucratic forms of empowerment and capacity-building is a result of the problems that Western institutions have in establishing their own legitimacy, what is the cause of this?

The questions raised by external state-building initiatives go to the heart of the nature of politics today. The consensus that most people in the world can be governed better with support from external experts and capacity-builders highlights the diminished view of the importance of politics, of the importance of self-government and political autonomy. When it appears that the solutions to the problems of security, development and human rights are amenable to resolution through therapeutic, legal, administrative and bureaucratic means and are not political questions, then the role or necessity of politics is clearly put to question.

There is little doubt that many advocates of current state-building approaches view state sovereignty and representative government to be as much a problem as an asset when it comes to developing the essential mechanisms of administrative management and good governance necessary to ensure 'pro-poor' policies and social inclusion. This book locates the shift away from traditional approaches to international politics and towards post-political regimes of empowerment and capacity-building in the post-Cold War crisis of confidence facing Western political elites – this crisis of self-belief means that the exercise of power is fraught with denial. For this reason, it is to Empire in Denial which we now turn.

EMPIRE IN DENIAL

Today empire is in denial. Power is exercised in a way which is transforming international relations and the relations between non-Western states and their societies. But the actors who wield this power seek to deny accountability for its exercise. European Commission bureaucrats who negotiate Stabilisation and Association process agreements with prospective EU members in the Balkans argue that they are merely facilitators, encouraging applicant governments to take up the EU *acquis*. The EU is keen to stress that it is working in partnership with potential applicants to the East and is keen to give them 'country ownership' of the state capacity-building process (EC, 2001a: 7). World Bank and IMF advisers who work through the Poverty Reduction Strategy Papers (PRSPs), necessary as a condition for the extension of international credits, grants and debt relief, argue that the documents are 'country-owned' and that they merely 'endorse' them (Rowden and Irama, 2004: 7). Leading Western governments have joined the international financial institutions (IFIs) in insisting that their role is merely to 'support policy leadership by developing countries without imposing our views' (DFID, 2005: iii).

Even where the power of empire is exercised in a traditional way, through invasion and occupation, there is a denial of power and responsibility. The 2003 US-led invasion of Iraq was marked by bans on the coalition forces raising national flags and the rapid removal of the Stars and Stripes when it was displayed by victorious US forces; victory parades were also banned in New York and London (Grigg, 2003; *New York Times*, 2003; Watt, 2003; White, 2003). If this was a victory it was one which the coalition forces felt uncomfortable celebrating. The Iraqi occupation was also an occupation in denial with the rapid and closely guarded handing back of Iraqi sovereignty in June 2004. Empire is also in denial in the protectorates of Bosnia and Kosovo. In Bosnia there is the pretence that Bosnia is an independent state negotiating with – rather than run by – the EU. In Kosovo there is the pretence that the future status of the province will be decided in internationally mediated talks between Belgrade and Pristina, rather than by agreement between the US and the EU.

Why should empire be so coy about its new found freedoms with the end of the Cold War? Perhaps there is the embarrassment that so much power has been literally handed to Western states and international institutions with the implosion, rather than the defeat, of the Soviet alternative? The pluralist post-World War II framework of the United Nations Charter has been replaced, literally overnight, by a new hierarchy of Western power. Yet this hierarchy has not been formalised in the way that empire was in the past. In fact, the new framework of domination has been built on the basis of the denial of Western power and responsibility. The new administrators of empire talk about developing relations of 'partnership' with subordinate states, or even of African 'leadership', at the same time as instituting new mechanisms of domination and control. Gone is the language of Western dominance and superiority; replaced by the discourses of 'capacity-building' and 'empowerment' in the cause of the non-Western Other. It seems that Western states are unhappy to bear the responsibilities for power, which the end of the Cold War has opened up. They are eager to deny that they have any interests or deciding influence at the same time as instituting new mechanisms of regulation which artificially seek to play up the authority, rights and interests of those subordinate to them.

This book will suggest that while Empire in Denial may sound nicer than the brash hubris and overt racism of the imperial past, it is, in its formulation, no less elitist and patronising and, in its consequences, no less divisive, destabilising and restricting. At the heart of Empire in Denial is the post-Cold War project of state-building. Where traditional forms of imperial domination were defined on the basis of their denial of political rights to statehood, Empire in Denial makes a fetish of the state form and the formal separation of Western-dominated policy-making processes from the political process within non-Western states. We are witnessing the development of a new set of practices which fill the old forms of state sovereignty with a new political content. In fact, it suggests that the practices of Empire in Denial are much more invasive than those of nineteenth-century empire, preventing the establishment of strong links between non-Western states and their societies and resulting in the phenomenon of 'phantom states' whose governing institutions may have extensive external resourcing but lack social or political legitimacy.

Through the transformation of the institution of sovereignty the division between the sphere of domestic government and international governance has been blurred and the external influence of major Western powers and international institutions has been extended at the same time as Western institutions have been formally distanced from responsibility. Empire in Denial, unlike more direct forms of colonial rule, exercises power without the drawback of overt or transparent mechanisms of political accountability. The traditional rights of state sovereignty, those of self-government and non-intervention, have been increasingly undermined. Yet, at the same time the shell of sovereignty – the state form – especially international legal sovereignty, formal independence in international law, has been emphasised. Not only has sovereignty been extended to the creation of new states, such as in Yugoslavia and the former Soviet Union, but the rights and responsibilities of sovereign governments have been increasingly stressed. Non-Western states sign up to international legal agreements and are members of international institutions, such as the United Nations. On the surface, the post-Cold War UN framework of sovereign equality appears to be intact but, underneath the formal trappings of independence, non-Western state governments have been opened up to a wide range of external regulatory controls and direct intervention under the rubric of state capacity-building.

It is clear that Empire in Denial is not the lack of Western intervention and regulation, suggested by historian Niall Ferguson's use of the term in his book *Colossus* (2004: 29) or his *Chronicle Review* article (2003) of the previous year. Here Ferguson is referring to what he sees as America's lack of long-term or sustained interest in the international sphere. He argues that it is punching below its weight considering that: 'Its defense budget is 14 times that of China and 22 times that of Russia', much greater than the more activist Britain ever enjoyed over any potential rivals (2003). In Ferguson's reading, America is an empire but currently lacks the historical, cultural and economic desire to act as one:

the empire that rules the world today is both more and less than its British begetter. It has a much bigger economy, many more people, a much larger arsenal. But it is an empire that lacks the drive to export its capital, its people, and its culture to those backward regions that need them most urgently and that, if they are neglected, will breed the greatest threats to its security. It is an empire, in short, that dare not speak its name. It is an empire in denial. (2003)

In this book, the concept of Empire in Denial attempts to capture the new forms of international regulation of non-Western states and societies: the fact that the new forms of international control attempt to evade responsibility and accountability for the exercise of power. It poses the question of why the exercise of power takes the form of the abnegation of self-interest in the professed concern to empower and capacity-build others. Empire is not in denial because it is not regulating enough (in fact, there is much more regulatory control attached to aid, trade and institutional relations than ever before) but because the political power of decision-making elites seeks to clothe itself in non-political, therapeutic or purely technical, administrative and bureaucratic forms.

The politics of empire

There are essentially two ways in which power and domination have traditionally been understood to be exercised in the international sphere – those of formal empire and informal empire. Formal empire refers to the denial of the right to self-government – analogous to the denial of formal civil and democratic rights in the domestic sphere. Formal empire is therefore one of hierarchy rather than equality and relies on force and coercion rather than consent. Informal empire refers to the informal relations of domination understood to operate in the socio-economic sphere of market relations, in which underdeveloped 'peripheral' and 'semi-peripheral' states are dependent on and exploited by the 'core' developed industrialised nations (see, for example, Wallerstein, 1974). This relationship is analogous to the inequalities between social classes, i.e. between capitalists who own the means of production and workers who own merely their labour power. These inequalities are not maintained by coercion but through the worker's freedom. In the words of Karl Marx: 'This sphere [of exchange] within whose boundaries the sale and purchase of labour-power goes on, is in fact a very Eden of the innate rights of man. There alone rule Freedom, Equality, Property and Bentham' (Marx, 1954: 172). It is the free reproduction of capitalist social relations, which compel and reproduce subordination through market compulsion rather than the direct use of governing power.

Empire was traditionally understood as the direct domination of other territories which were dependent and lacked the right of self-government: the right of sovereignty. Not so long ago this was a respectable form of rule. In Britain, for the first half of the twentieth century (from 1904 onwards) Empire Day was celebrated as a major social event with street parties and school commemorations. Celebrated on the 24 May (Queen Victoria's birthday), Empire Day was initiated by Edward VII to celebrate 'the magnificence and power of the Empire' (BECM, 2003). In the second half of the twentieth century, the British and other European empires were undermined with around a hundred territories gaining independent sovereign status, for example: India, 1947; Indonesia, 1949; Morocco, 1956; Tunisia, 1956; Ghana, 1957; Congo, 1960; Cyprus, 1960; Burundi, 1962; Rwanda, 1962; Jamaica, 1962; Uganda, 1962; Kenya 1963; Singapore, 1965; Angola, 1975; Mozambique, 1975; Zimbabwe, 1980. When the United Nations was formed in 1945, 750 million people – almost a third of the world's population – lived under empire. There were 51 signatories to the UN's Charter; at the time of writing there are 191 members. The extension of the membership of the UN reflects the universalising of the rights of state sovereignty and the decolonisation process in the second half of the last century.

In formal terms, little has changed with the end of the Cold War. The first post-Cold War decade from 1990 to 2000 was officially declared by the United Nations General Assembly as the International Decade for the Eradication of Colonialism. In 2001, the UN proclaimed the Second Decade for the Eradication of Colonialism. A small number of non-self-governing territories remain: by far the largest is Western Sahara, followed by the French administered New Caledonia and the British dependency of the Falkland Islands, the remainder being small island territories from US administered Guam with 500 square kilometres to British administered Pitcairn of 5 square kilometres. In 1994 the UN's Trusteeship Council fell into abeyance; its tasks were held to be completed with the independence of the remaining trust territories of the Pacific Islands (Palau) previously administered by the US.

This formal renunciation of empire and the universalising of the state form came under increasing international pressure in the 1990s. By the late 1990s it appeared that a new international hierarchy was overturning the UN framework of state sovereignty. Debates about the failures of humanitarian intervention in Somalia, Bosnia and Rwanda led to greater external engagement in Kosovo and East Timor. State sovereignty was not just under pressure in relation to demands for external military intervention in the cause of humanitarian concerns. In 2001, the declaration of the Global War on Terror after 9/11 seemed to strengthen the legitimacy of international intervention and, as a consequence, US-led wars of 'regime change' followed in Afghanistan and Iraq.

However, high-profile international military interventions in the 1990s and early 2000s in Somalia, Bosnia, Kosovo, East Timor, Afghanistan and Iraq have not resulted in the prolonged denial of the formal rights of state sovereignty. All these territories remained, became, or are in the process of becoming self-governing with formal recognition by the UN. In the case of Kosovo, formal sovereignty lies with Serbia, despite the de facto administrative control of the UN Mission. In the case of East Timor, the Indonesian government consented to the independence referendum and the presence of UN mandated forces and independence was formally recognised in 2002. In Bosnia, where external administrative control has existed since the Dayton peace agreement in 1995, it should be noted that the territory maintained its sovereign status and that the government formally consented to external administrative regulation. Afghanistan was not formally subject to external rule, while in Iraq the postwar Coalition Provisional Authority (CPA) had the retrospective recognition of the UN and formally handed back sovereign authority the following year.

Empire has not returned in formal terms, yet a new hierarchical and interventionist order has led to an upsurge in discussion of empire in recent years. Many of these commentators suggest that we are entering a new age of empire. US military and ideological predominance, since the end of the Cold War, is seen to be enforcing the hegemony of neoliberal ideas and rejecting the international law of the UN Charter era. The US-led war in Iraq and the postwar resistance and instability are argued to lay bare the dynamics of a new era of power politics. The US is held to be the global hegemon, acting on behalf of international capital and instituting a new universal empire, enforcing the power of the market over elites which refuse to cooperate with international financial institutions.

In this framework, it is the informal mechanisms of empire which are stressed and which are bolstered by the use of US power as a coercive force. Michael Hardt and Antonio Negri (2001), David Harvey (2003), Michael Mann (2003) and Ellen Meiksins Wood (2003), among others, have focused on empire based on the power of capital rather than formal territorial control and the denial of sovereignty. The first theorists to do so were John Gallagher and Ronald Robinson in their famous 1953 article, 'The Imperialism of Free Trade', in which they argued that 'informal empire' was much more important to Britain than the power gleamed from colonial rule (Gallagher and Robinson, 1953). Making the comparison between forms of British foreign domination in the mid and late nineteenth century, they argued that there was little difference between domination through formally denying sovereignty and domination through the power of Britain's market strength:

Throughout, British governments worked to establish and maintain British paramountcy by whatever means best suited the circumstances of their diverse regions of interest. The aims of the mid-Victorians were no more anti-imperialist than their successors', though they were more often able to achieve them informally; and the late-Victorians were no more 'imperialist' than their predecessors, even though they were driven to annex more often. British policy followed the principle of extending control informally if possible and formally if necessary. To label the one method 'anti-imperialist' and the other 'imperialist', is to ignore the fact that whatever the method British interests were steadily safeguarded and extended. (Gallagher and Robinson, 1953)

This formulation then understands empire to include relations of domination which do not require the extra-economic compulsion of colonial rule. William Appleman Williams made similar points with regard to the American empire (see, for example, Williams, 1964). Empire, understood as the denial of sovereignty – formal state independence – was seen as the second best option, one only to be pursued if capitalist interests are threatened by rival powers or local resistance. In this reading, the extension of sovereign rights to self-government and the process of decolonisation in the wake of World War II, demonstrated the power of capital and the lack of inter-imperialist rivalry under US domination. Justin Rosenberg, for example, argues that the extension of sovereign rights cannot be understood without taking into account the extension of market relations, and the social power of capital, which made colonial rule unnecessary for the extraction of an economic surplus. He makes the point thus:

it is this formal disjuncture (between public and private political realms) which explains part of the paradox of sovereignty ... It explains how we can see simultaneously an enhanced territorial differentiation between states together with an unprecedented porousness and interdependence ... [I]t becomes increasingly apparent that in realism [international relations theory] reality is standing on its head. Realists tell us that the modern international political system is different because it is a states-system organized by anarchy rather than an empire organized by centralized command. However, ... [i]t means the rise of a new kind of empire: the empire of civil society. (Rosenberg, 1994: 131)

The 'civil society' of equal sovereign states conceals the capitalist social relations that reproduce and reinforce Western hegemony, thereby making empire invisible in formal terms (see also Kiely, 2005: 139). It is the informal mechanisms of market inequality which mean that non-Western states have little choice but to accept discriminatory trade regulations or to accept the conditions set by the World Bank and the IMF in order to gain access to loans or development aid. What appears formally to be a relationship between two contracting partners is in effect a product of the hierarchy of power. For the critics of informal mechanisms of empire, the formalities of international law and rights of sovereign equality are a sham, in the same way as the freedoms of domestic political and legal equality hide the realities of class power.

Today, relations of hierarchy in the international sphere cannot easily be captured in terms of the formal empire of the coercive denial of sovereign rights to self-government nor by the informal empire of the equal contractual relations of the market. The new regulatory forms of Empire in Denial seek to deny any direct political control and to reinforce the formal legal status of sovereignty. However, these practices are much more interventionist than those based on contractual relations enforced by market dependency. The hierarchy of power and external dependency of states on external aid or debt relief is not concealed, through the equality of legal contract, but emphasised as the premise upon which the empowering and capacity-building exercises of international state-building are legitimised.

In recognition of the more interventionist models of international regulation, which neither rely on market relations nor on the direct usurpation of state sovereignty, some commentators have adapted a Foucauldian framework of governmentality to explain the exercise of Western power (see Foucault, 1991; Dean, 1999). Governmentality is understood as an alternative framework to either the direct coercion of formal empire or the *laissez-faire* of the social power of capital. Here intervention takes forms which appear to be consensual rather than coercive, through which the technologies and practices of domination simultaneously produce or constitute the subjects being dominated through the discursive practices and frameworks of knowledge, meaning, norms and values. This framework appears particularly useful in the attempt to understand why Western power should attempt to construct frameworks of non-Western state policy ownership and seek to engage in what appears to be deeply interventionist strategies of social engineering in the encouragement of civil society participation in the policy process.

Mark Duffield has argued that interventionist programmes of capacity-building demonstrate that 'liberal governance has a radical mission to transform societies as a whole, including the attitudes and beliefs of the people within them' (Duffield, 2001: 258). He argues that capacity-building tied to development aid and debt relief has become a 'relationship of government: a set of technologies having the power to reorder the relationship between people and things to achieve desired aims' (Duffield, 2003: 292). The apparently self-effacing ethics of empowering and assisting the poor in fact facilitate external interference in non-Western states, positing the need for an external interlocutor and thereby legitimising external regulation; establishing 'a will to govern', a framework and set of practices of intervention (Duffield, 2003: 294). For Duffield, these new forms of external governmentality have opened up non-Western states to 'metropolitan monitoring, intervention and regulation unprecedented since the colonial period' in an attempt to regulate the unrest and resistance generated by the failures of the market (2003: 308). It is the emerging threat to international stability arising from the failure of previous World Bank and IMF structural adjustment policies that has made underdevelopment appear to be a security threat and has driven the merging of the development and security discourses in the desire to control and regulate the peripheral states of the 'borderlands'.

Other commentators, who have focused more narrowly on international regulation in African states, for example, David Craig and Doug Porter (2002), Rita Abrahamsen (2004, 2005) and Alastair Fraser (2005), also argue that state capacity-building and country ownership of development strategies through the Poverty Reduction Strategy Papers and participatory poverty assessment (PPA) exercises can best be understood as technologies of social control. For Craig and Porter the state-building approach taken by the World Bank's PRSPs and other development funding frameworks attempt to 'generate a level of global to local integration, discipline and technical management of marginal economies, governance and populations unprecedented since colonial times' (2002: 4). The internationalisation of poverty reduction strategies has transformed the mechanisms of international regulation, especially:

in terms of how poverty is linked with global surveillance, subordination and undermining of local governance dynamics, the removal from public scrutiny of key choices and decisions, and the diversion of energies from the pressing task of designing appropriate domestic poverty and growth strategies. (Craig and Porter, 2002: 5)

For Craig and Porter, these new forms of surveillance and control are necessary to legitimise the neoliberal agenda of international institutions by engaging civil society groups who tend to be 'the primary agents of dissent' (2002: 8). Fraser similarly argues that the IFIs have come to see participatory forms of capacity-building as a potential solution to the crisis of structural adjustment policies and as a way of influencing the values and behaviour of country governments and civil society actors (2005: 322). He argues that the emphasis on giving ownership to states, and particularly on empowering the poor, strengthens external interventionist bureaucratic mechanisms: '"Bottom-up conditionality" thus paradoxically legitimates increasing intervention and implies insulating political processes from the majority of the population' (Fraser, 2005: 329). For Fraser, the World Bank has been forced to 'burrow deeper and deeper into the fabric of African political communities' in order to prevent opposition to its neoliberal agenda and has shifted from disciplining governments to disciplining populations through the projects of participatory inclusion (2005: 336–7).

Drawing on a similar approach, Abrahamsen argues that state-building and the new partnership frameworks are mechanisms through which the governing elites of Africa come to internalise the neoliberal values of global governance. Capacity-building is therefore about the disciplined inclusion of non-Western governments and the poor in the global order. Through the discipline of country ownership and participatory involvement, the state-building agenda in Africa comes replete with a multitude of new mechanisms for monitoring, evaluating and auditing behaviour and the policy choices of recipient countries. These mechanisms help to reshape the participants' image of themselves and to engender new forms of conduct and new kinds of 'self-managed' subjectivities (Abrahamsen, 2004: 1463).

On a descriptive level it seems that the theorists of governmentality have a clearer insight into the new mechanisms of regulation, which could be held to constitute today's politics of empire, than traditional Left approaches. Yet, it is not clear from the analysis why non-Western governments and their poor need to be disciplined in such a way today. It would seem that there are few alternatives to the agendas put forward by the World Bank and the IMF and that there is much less demand for any non-market alternative than there was during the Cold War, when at least it was possible to gain economic aid from the Soviet Union. It would appear that non-Western countries are in a much worse position to bargain with or to oppose the will of international institutions than in the past and face relatively little opposition from within their own societies to the projects and funding offered by the international donors.

Empire in Denial

The three perspectives of empire outlined above all start from the assumption that the forms which the regulation and enforcement of empire take can only be understood by considering the instrumental interests of the Western actors. For Marxists, these interests are vital geostrategic or economic interests which can be safeguarded informally, through the dictate of the market, and, if necessary, through direct coercive intervention and the negation of sovereign rights. For Foucauldians, these vital interests, of maintaining neoliberal market conditions and social stability, necessitate more complex forms of intervention, aimed at the regulation of societies as well as governments. The thesis outlined in this book is that the state-building practices described well by Foucauldian theorists are those of Empire in Denial. It suggests that these new forms of external regulation are driven less by the desire to extend and enforce Western power than they are by the desire to deny it.

Foreign policy, the projection of power externally, often tells us more about the foreign policy actor than any external object. It is not only power which is projected but a certain framework of ideas and values and political purpose. To this extent, social constructivist theorists in international relations are right to argue that the interests of any actor cannot be separated from their political identities (for example, Wendt, 1992). Social constructivism has become increasingly dominant in the academic literature because it appears to capture the fluidity of interests since the end of the Cold War. There seems to be no clear framework of international ordering to replace that of the geopolitical division which ended in 1989. Despite the US's dominance in military terms, America has not been able to shape a new order comparable to that of the post-World War II institutional order based on the UN and the Bretton Woods institutions (Reus-Smit, 2004: 2; see also Bacevich, 2002; Kupchan, 2002). The dominant discourse is one of powerlessness in the face of globalisation or the threats of global warming or acts of terror.

It would be no exaggeration to say that approaches to the international sphere have never been less future-orientated than today. It seems that the end of superpower competition has left the remaining power exhausted, without a mission or a sense of purpose. There is little doubt that the absence of great power conflict appears to have removed a framework of meaning in which the international sphere was highly politicised. Niall Ferguson makes the point that the lack of any international project poses the risk that, rather than the choice being between 'realist' views of 'unipolarity' or 'multipolarity', there is a real risk of a 'generalized impotence – or, if you like, apolarity' (2004: 296). When those with power lack a clear framework through which to exercise it, then as French theorist Zaki Laïdi writes:

Power – understood in its widest sense – is conceived and experienced less and less as a process of taking over responsibilities, and more as a game of avoidance ... Social actors avoid taking on their own responsibilities or some responsibilities because, in the absence of a framework of meaning, responsibilities are measured only in cost terms. (1998: 13)

Without a cause, a sense of purpose or political meaning it is difficult to engage in the life of society, in political life in its broadest sense. This problem is felt particularly acutely by governments and policy-makers who experience their power more often as an embarrassment or a cost, rather than as an opportunity. It seems to be the lack of perceived legitimacy that drives government policy-making, rather than the confidence of a popular mandate (Bunting, 2006). Rather than claiming the rights of power, most governments seem to be happier when they are disclaiming them, seeking to devolve policy-making responsibilities either to regional and local authorities or to higher bodies such as the European Union or international institutions. The dynamic of politics seems to be one of avoidance of responsibility. This is because taking on responsibility depends upon having a conviction in a political goal. It is only a strong conviction in the political ends of a policy that enables governments and societies to bear the costs of achieving it. Today, Western political elites lack a strong political vision and therefore have a transformed perception of and relationship to political power. They seek to reject, rather than welcome, the responsibilities of power. This book argues that it is this rejection of responsibility which is driving the state-building dynamic and which has taken the therapeutic ethos of empowerment and capacity-building from the margins to the mainstream.

State-building as social inclusion

The clearest example of the avoidance of political responsibility is possibly the politics of social inclusion. The theme of social inclusion, with its security concerns of crime and social concerns of welfare, is the nearest domestic parallel to the international state-building discourse. In the focus on social inclusion, governments create their own agenda there are no popular movements for social inclusion and there is no clear definition of social inclusion or exclusion. Despite the fact that tackling social exclusion has been a central theme of the UK Blair governments (the social exclusion unit was launched by Tony Blair in 1997) the British government's Communities Minister, David Miliband, set out a definition of social exclusion for the first time in November 2005, defining those adults as socially excluded who experienced five or more or a range of ten problems, ranging from unemployment and the lack of educational requirements to poor mental or physical health (Ward, 2005). Social exclusion is not a political concept and not a self-chosen designation, it is a category created by government advisers and professional experts, in effect creating an artificial political constituency of policy legitimisation and at the same time constituting an object of social regulation through a discourse of empowerment.

The politics of social inclusion are the opposite of traditional politics. Firstly, there are no interests involved; there is no appeal to a particular social or political constituency. Social inclusion is beyond the politics of contestation; social inclusion is based on meeting the needs of the excluded, of empowering them through inclusion. The policy focus is on those without power, there can be no accusation that policy is led by government self-interest or those of its supporters or rich donors. Secondly, there is no ideological or political content, the politics of social inclusion are not about social change or transformation, they are based on pragmatism, on results-based policy-making; policy-making in this area is the task of policy professionals in association with the advocacy groups which represent the needs of the excluded social groups. In many ways the capacity-building of the socially excluded is little different to the state-building practices of international institutions, which are seen to be above politics and led by technical and administrative expertise.

However, the clearest connection with state-building is in the broader rejection of responsibility in the politics of social inclusion. With social inclusion there appears to be an ambitious and radical agenda of tackling poverty, improving access to education, improving mental health facilities, improving housing opportunities, etc., but, in fact, the complex and interdependent nature of the problems alleged to cause social exclusion means that the focus is shifted away from a transformative social agenda to the problems facing a minority of the population with multiple problems and towards individualised or localised assistance. The focus on the socially excluded like the international state-building focus on the poor is part of an agenda which, in fact, insists that little can be done about social problems on a macro-level. The radical claims are based on making the poor or socially excluded the focus of policy not on any broader social agenda of transformation.

For example, the UN adviser and Millennium Development Project director, central to the 'Making Poverty History' initiative, Jeffrey Sachs, argues that to meet the goal of 'ending poverty' by 2005 would mean nobody having to live on less than $1 a day. However, with the average American already living on about $114 per day and the average Briton on $83 per day, it is clear that the focus is merely on the most extreme levels of poverty, much less ending poverty or overcoming the wealth and income gap between the rich and poor (Ben-Ami, 2005; Sachs, 2005; see also Kiely, 2005: 103–5). This rejection of social transformation puts the focus on technocratic solutions to alleviate the suffering of the poorest sections of society (Ben-Ami, 2005; Kiely. 2005: 104); on the coping strategies of the socially excluded; and on the professional assistance, training and capacity-building necessary to empower them. This is the politics of the evasion of responsibility, a shift from government as policy actor to government as therapeutic empowerer (see, for example, Nolan, 1998).

It is true that policy practices of social inclusion exercise power over those groups designated as excluded and often constitutes, or gives purchase to, group identities on the basis of these needs and provides a basis upon which advocates can give them voice. However, it does not follow that the desire to regulate or to constitute these constituencies of need was the motive or goal of these practices (see also Campbell, 1998a: 8). It could be argued that the practices of the politics of social inclusion are a product of governments' attempts to deny their power and responsibility and that the regulation of the excluded can be seen as a by-product of this, an unintended consequence, rather than the principal aim. This brief analysis of the domestic discourse of social inclusion – highlighting how the capacity-building and empowerment agenda is driven by governments' desire to promote themselves as 'caring' or 'concerned' while avoiding the responsibilities of delivering on any larger or more ambitious social programmes – is intended merely as an analogy. It does, however, reflect the analytical approach that will be taken in the following chapters which will draw out how the international discourse of state-building reflects the more complex process of the evasion of the responsibilities of power in the international sphere.

STRUCTURE OF THE BOOK

The following chapters draw out the policy drives and the consequences of Empire in Denial as it is expressed in the politics of state-building. The next three chapters focus on the dynamics of Western policy-making. Chapter 2 locates the state-building consensus in policy shifts in response to the 1990s decade of humanitarian intervention and considers the differences and continuities with previous interventionist policies. It then goes on to analyse the changing definition and understanding of state sovereignty, considering how it has been reformulated in terms of capacity rather than rights, illustrating the discussion with a consideration of Stephen Krasner's 'unbundling' of sovereignty and the International Commission on Intervention and State Sovereignty (ICISS) *Responsibility to Protect* report's view of sovereignty as 'responsibility' (ICISS, 2001a). It then introduces the case study of Bosnia as a leading example of the trend towards Empire in Denial, highlighting the EU's evasion of responsibility through the state-building framework.

In 'The Governance of Government', Chapter 3 questions the privileging of governance over government in Western approaches to state-building which tend to assume that economic, social and political problems of non-Western states can be addressed through the external capacity-building agenda. This approach marks a shift in the understanding of state–society relations and is one which places much less emphasis on how societal pressures and demands are constitutive of stable and legitimate institutional mechanisms. This chapter questions this approach and considers how this shift in the understanding of the non-Western state has been shaped by current understandings of war and conflict, and how the prioritisation of governance has fitted with critical and post-positivist trends in academic thinking in international relations and security studies.

Chapter 4 argues that since the end of the 1990s we have witnessed an ethical convergence of concern for the Other, in both national foreign policy and international financial institutional frameworks, which has given ideological coherence to Empire in Denial. Today, it would appear that Western states and international institutions have taken postmodern ethics to heart in their claims to be acting on the basis of their 'responsibilities to the Other' rather than being guided by self-interest. The chapter then analyses how these discursive ethical practices separate power from political subjects in three ways. Firstly, by casting external policy-makers (Western states and international institutions) as powerless and disinterested actors. Secondly, by internationalising the domestic policy-making mechanisms of non-Western states, thereby undermining the capacity of state sovereignty to demarcate an 'inside' and an 'outside'. Thirdly, by transforming the political sphere of non-Western states through recasting policy in needs-based terms which necessitate a technical consensus, objectifying the Other as the political subject but one without agency.

The following two chapters draw out this process with a particular emphasis on EU enlargement and external regulation in Bosnia, which has been central to experiments in international state-building. Chapter 5 focuses on the EU's attempts to deny its east European empire through experimenting with member state-building through the enlargement process; particularly with regard to the South Eastern European states after the establishment, in 1999, of a range of new state capacity-building frameworks for EU integration, including the Stabilisation and Association process and the Stability Pact for South Eastern Europe (SPSEE). It considers how these mechanisms have operated and the language of empowerment, partnership and pedagogy embedded in them.

Chapter 6 expands the analysis of the EU's denial of its power in the Balkan region, focusing particularly on the informal trusteeship of Bosnia and tracing the changing forms of Empire in Denial. The chapter highlights a shift in the portrayal of empire in 2000, which reflected the experiences of the exposed and increasingly illegitimate nature of international administerial rule as powers accumulated under the Office of the High Representative (OHR) with little sense of purpose or framework for their exercise. Since 2000, the EU has sought to give greater direction to the running of Bosnia through the enlargement process and has sought to downplay the role of the international administration, gradually Europeanising the state structures of Bosnia through the work of the Directorate of European Integration (DEI). Bosnian state-building has since assumed the central characteristics of similar internationalised governance regimes in non-Western states, where there is no longer a line of demarcation between domestic and external policy-making, leaving the EU able effectively to negotiate with itself on Bosnia's accession programme.

The following two chapters focus more closely on the impact of international state-building practices on the ground, considering how the policy techniques of evading Western accountability – highlighted in the core state-building policy practices of anti-corruption and the rule of law – impact on the subject societies. Chapters 7 and 8 highlight how, rather than strengthening state institutions, capacity-building approaches have the effect of weakening the relationship between state institutions and societies, producing a tendency towards phantom states which exist more on paper than in reality. These chapters analyse how this process works through reorientating state institutions around external agendas while the focus on administrative and technical frameworks severs institutions from the political and social demands emanating from their societies.

These chapters focus on Bosnia as the central case study, where these practices have been pushed further than in other states and therefore reveal more clearly the limitations of anti-corruption initiatives and the rule of law as central levers in the state-building policy armoury of Empire in Denial. Chapter 7 considers the development and implementation of the internationally coordinated anti-corruption strategy. The Bosnian experience allows anti-corruption strategy, and the good governance agenda informing it, to be assessed and analysis to be made regarding the impact of external management programmes, designed to strengthen collective state institutions in post-conflict states, such as Bosnia. The chapter suggests that the focus on corruption acts as an excuse for Western policy failures by blaming government officials and cultural factors for their consequences while anti-corruption initiatives tend to replace political justifications for policy with bureaucratic ones, undermining the political process.

A second technique of Western evasion is considered in Chapter 8: the focus on the rule of law. It is suggested that Empire in Denial seeks to evade the responsibilities of power through the establishment of an independent framework or code of law. The assumption that law can exist independently of political power, that law can provide its own legitimacy, is shown to be a misplaced one. Paradoxically, in seeking to hide behind the law, Empire in Denial gives the law a content which separates it from domestic social processes. In the phantom states, which are the products of these practices, the law takes arbitrary and often irrational forms, freed from the constraints of the political process. This paradox is drawn out in examples from Iraq and Bosnia which illustrate how this process tends to weaken and discredit the rule of law rather than strengthen it. Chapter 9 concludes the book, briefly drawing out six theses on phantom states and Empire in Denial.

2
State-building States
without Sovereignty

State-building – the development of international mechanisms aimed at addressing cases of state collapse or at shoring up failing states – is increasingly becoming the dominant framework for the international regulation of non-Western states. This chapter seeks to examine the development, content and consequences of the state-building discourse. Locating state-building as a response to the consequences of the 1990s decade of humanitarian intervention, it engages with changing theoretical approaches to state sovereignty, which redefine sovereignty as state capacity rather than as political independence; recasting intervention as strengthening sovereignty rather than undermining it. Today this intervention often no longer appears as external coercion but as an internal matter of administrative assistance for good governance or institutional capacity-building. The consequences of this move are also considered and it is suggested that state-building non-Western states without self-government will result in the institutionalisation of weak states which have little relationship with their societies and lack legitimate authority.

The focus on state capacities and institutions seems to herald a shift away from the 1990s when new, more interventionist, norms were heralded which challenged the fundamental rights of state sovereignty – those of self-government and non-intervention. These rights took their clearest institutional form in the UN Charter framework of international law which emphasised the rights of peoples to self-government (Article 1.2), the sovereign equality of member states (Article 2.1), and the principle of non-intervention – outlawing the threat or use of force (Article 2.4) (UN, 1945). Throughout the Cold War, successive judgments of the International Court of Justice upheld these rights to self-government and denied the existence of any legitimate grounds for external intervention, even on the basis of 'humanitarian' or 'human rights' justifications (Chandler, 2002a: 157–66).

After the end of the Cold War, the focus appeared to shift to an emphasis on the rights of individuals, often posed counter to the rights of states. States were no longer seen to be the primary security referent and state sovereignty was not considered to be an absolute barrier to external intervention. There was extended military intervention in Iraq, to protect the Kurds and Marsh Arabs after the 1991 Gulf War, and external military intervention for humanitarian purposes in Somalia (in 1992–93) and Bosnia (1993–95); the high point of this new focus on individuals rather than states was the NATO-led international intervention over Kosovo in 1999.

Today, the state is once more at the centre of security concerns. It now appears that states, particularly those that have been marginalised by the world economy or weakened by conflict, can no longer be ignored or isolated. In the aftermath of 9/11 – where the failure of the Afghan state to control its borders and the activities of its citizens was held to have opened the way for Al Qaeda's operations – the state is no longer viewed from a mainly negative perspective. Non-Western states now appear less obviously as objects of opprobrium and are more likely to be fêted by international institutions and leading Western states, offering programmes of poverty reduction, capacity-building, democratisation and good governance.

This chapter questions the vision of the state which is being placed at the centre of international security and development policy-making. The following section puts the state-building discussion in the context of current problems in conceptualising the role of states and in response to the 1990s decade of humanitarian intervention. Further sections then lay out specific problems which highlight the corrosive nature of current policy practices in this area. Firstly, that the redefinition of sovereignty, central to the state-building framework, facilitates the erosion of ties linking power and accountability, enabling international interveners to distance themselves from the policies they promote. Secondly, that they do not work; states without the capacity for self-government will always be weak and lacking in legitimate authority, the policy agenda focuses on bureaucratic, administrative mechanisms, which can only institutionalise current divisions between the West and the non-West and is unable to overcome the social and political divisions of post-conflict states.

FROM THE 'RIGHT TO INTERVENE' TO STATE-BUILDING

The discussion of state-building – of international mechanisms to capacity-build weak states – seems, at face value, to herald a return to traditional frameworks of international relations. This chapter suggests that this focus on a familiar political form should not obscure what is, in effect, a radical transformation of the mechanisms of international regulation. Everyone seems to be agreed that states are not what they used to be. As Fukuyama notes, 'for well over a generation, the trend in world politics has been to weaken stateness', this trend has been particularly marked since the end of the Cold War (2004: 161). It is only in the context of current uncertainties and ambiguities over the role and purpose of the non-Western state that we can understand the novel processes at the heart of state-building policy and practice.

In the 1990s it seemed clear that states were losing their capacities rather than gaining them. For many commentators, this was a positive development (Rosenau and Czempiel, 1992; Archibugi, Held and Kohler, 1998; Linklater, 1998). Across the board of social theory, from historical sociology to postmodern international relations, states were increasingly cast as problems rather than solutions. Charles Tilly's work was regularly drawn on to argue that states were merely government-run protection rackets based on the repression and exploitation of their citizens in the interest of criminal or self-interested elites (Tilly, 1985). Postmodernists drew on the work of Foucault to argue that Clausewitz's famous dictum should be inverted to reveal the illegitimacy of the liberal democratic state and understand 'politics as the continuation of war by other means' (Foucault, 2003). David Campbell, Mary Kaldor and others argued that it was the state-orientated perspective of the international community that encouraged many post-Cold War conflicts, such as the Bosnian war (Campbell, 1998b; Kaldor, 1998).

In this context, the post-1990s focus on the state, rather than on alternative forms of international governance, might seem to be an unexpected development. Some commentators have explained this by suggesting that the new focus on state capacity is a reaction against the humanitarian intervention policies of the 1990s which were held to have underestimated the importance of states for maintaining international stability (for example, Malone, 2005: xv). One example of interventionist policies that is often held to have been counterproductive in this context is that of international aid provision which bypassed state institutions establishing parallel bureaucracies and encouraging a brain drain from the underpaid state sector (see for example, Ghani, Lockhart, Carnahan, 2005: 10). The Commission for Africa report argues that state-building policies should 'stand in marked contrast to the approach in the 1980s and much of the 1990s, when aid was often used to try to compensate for poor governance, simply ignored governance issues, tried to force policies on reluctant countries, or aimed primarily at advancing the economic or political interests of the donor' (CFA, 2005: 94):

Aid conditionality has had a bad reputation in the past. The IFIs have tried to specify in detail the policies that recipient countries must adopt, even when these conditions have been ill-suited to the local political, economic and social context and have been unlikely to be implemented ... It is far more productive to focus on transparency and accountability. This approach allows the recipient country to choose its own course for development – an approach that history shows is most effective – while at the same time increasing the probability that the choice is made by society as a whole, rather than a few leaders. (CFA, 2005: 374)

It seems that conditionality and external coercion have been rejected for their negative effects, although it should be noted that this assessment is one which international institutions only highlighted at the end of the 1990s. It is now not unusual for commentators to argue that the result of 1990s humanitarian and human rights interventions has been the 'sucking out' of state capacity as core state functions have been taken over by UN agencies, international institutions and international NGOs, undermining the legitimacy and authority of non-Western states (for example, Ignatieff, 2003; Fukuyama, 2004: 139; ESI, 2005: 10).

There is little doubt that international policy intervention in the 1980s and 1990s tended to bypass or reduce the non-Western state's administrative and political institutional capacity, through giving coercive powers of conditionality to international financial institutions which: imposed fiscal regimes cutting the state's role in the economy and service provision; implemented discrete projects run independently by international agencies and NGOs; and often dictated policy outcomes through tying aid to donor goods and services. However, this chapter suggests that the criticisms of 1990s interventionist policies have less to do with unease over the limited success of the policies promoted than the fact that the mechanisms of regulation placed the onus and political responsibility on the Western interveners.

The key element of these interventions was their overtly external and coercive nature. The relations of authority were transparent; nowhere more so than in aid conditionality where international financial institutions specified detailed policies which the recipient countries had to accept. It was clear that, in these cases, non-Western states, particularly those in the Balkans and Africa, were more accountable to international policy-makers than to their own people. With the end of the Cold War, increasingly interventionist regimes of international regulation clearly exposed the power wielded by Western states and international institutions. Once relations of sovereign equality were openly brought into question through aid conditionality and human rights intervention, the question was sharply posed of Western responsibility.

This was most strikingly raised in the Balkans, where individual Western states and the EU, UN and other international institutions played a major role in overseeing the fragmentation of the Yugoslav state, making key decisions on recognition and republic boundaries. The result of this process of being drawn directly into conflict prevention was the unwieldy international protectorates of Bosnia, since 1995, and Kosovo, since 1999, which left intervening institutions exposed (so much so that the UN was reluctant to assume similar responsibilities in Afghanistan and Iraq).

Bearing this context in mind, this chapter suggests that the new international institutional focus on the non-Western state has little to do with a desire for strong non-Western states, or a new found confidence in non-Western governing elites. Rather, it is driven by Western elites' desire to avoid political responsibility for their relationships with large areas of the world. The fact that state-building is not driven by the need to strengthen non-Western states is highlighted by the strong consensus among those engaged in the field that strong states are deeply problematic; that state capacities should not include the traditional 'right to do what they will within their own borders'.

William Zartman, for example, argues that 'weak/soft' states are no worse than 'strong/hard/brittle' states – while weak states cannot exercise adequate authority over the domestic arena, strong states exercise too much authority and tend to marginalise other voices from civil society (Zartman, 2005). Robert Rotberg agrees that there is a 'special category of weak state: the seemingly strong one' and that the number of states in this category has grown rapidly in recent times (Rotberg, 2004b: 5). States that are resistant to external engagement in their affairs, which cling to traditional ideas of 'Westphalian sovereignty, referring to the exclusion of external actors from domestic authority configurations' are seen to be problematic (Krasner, 1999: 9; see also Keohane, 2002; 2003; Fearon and Laitin, 2004; Krasner, 2004).

In fact, the more one investigates the capacity-building literature the more ambiguity creeps into the claims that states are being capacity-built by external interveners. The first thing that is clear is that the aim is not to create states as classically understood, as self-governing, independent and autonomous political subjects.

This chapter argues that today's discussion of 'bringing the state back in', in the policy discussions of state failure and state-building, can be better understood as a radical extension of the practices of the 1980s and 1990s which internationalised the domestic policy-making sphere of non-Western states (see, for example, Jackson, 2000; Straw, 2002a; 2002b). The key difference, with the overtly interventionist approach of the 1990s, is that the emphasis is now on the non-Western state rather than those states and institutions doing the intervening. The transition away from justifying and holding intervening powers to account was presaged by the ICISS *Responsibility to Protect* report, published in December 2001, and formulated prior to 9/11.

In this widely cited report, the ICISS proposed a shift in language away from the 'human-centred' framework of a 'right to intervention' and towards a 'state-centred' framework of the 'responsibility to protect'. Whereas the right of intervention put the emphasis on the international interveners to justify and legitimise their actions, the responsibility to protect sought to avoid this 'attention on the claims, rights and prerogatives of the potentially intervening states' (ICISS, 2001a: 16). The responsibility to protect seeks to off-load responsibility onto the non-Western state at the same time as these states increasingly lose their policy-making authority.

The ICISS report successfully set out to shift the terms of the debate, and has facilitated the evasion of any clarification of the competing rights of state sovereignty and of those of intervening powers, by arguing that state rights of sovereignty can coexist with external intervention and state-building. The report spells out that, in its view, 'sovereignty then means accountability to two separate constituencies: internally, to one's own population; and internationally, to the community of responsible states' (ICISS, 2001b: 11). As the ICISS co-chairs note, this shift changes 'the essence of sovereignty, from control to responsibility' (Evans and Sahnoun, 2002: 101). The major implications which this shift would have for accountability (a power which is accountable to another, external, body clearly lacks sovereign authority – the capacity for self-government) have been consistently played down by the report's authors and academic commentators. Robert Keohane, for example, disingenuously argues that the ICISS report is not at all 'devaluing' sovereignty, merely that it is 'reinterpreting' it, to bring the concept more into line with the modern world (Keohane, 2003: 276).

Rather than the 1990s debate, where international intervention was posed in terms of a clash of competing rights – the 'right of intervention' against the 'right of state sovereignty' – today the language is one of 'shared responsibilities' and 'new partnerships'. Where the non-Western state was the subject of overtly coercive external intervention it is now more likely to be the focus of supportive, empowering, and capacity-building practices and new modalities of surveillance. The product of this change has been the enthronement of the state-building discourse as the framework for discussing Western regulation of and intervention in non-Western states.

This shift in the language of the Western projection of power reflects both the new relations of subordination with the end of the bi-polar world and at the same time the desire of Western institutions to reject direct accountability and distance themselves from political responsibility for 'zones of instability'. The state-building framework seeks to obfuscate and confuse relations of power and accountability which stood clearly exposed in the 1990s as a fundamental clash of rights. The *Responsibility to Protect* report, in emphasising the responsibilities of the non-Western state, heralded the shift towards state-building as a policy of both intervention and evasion. The contradictions involved in this process are highlighted in the irony that states are alleged to be being 'built' at the same time as they increasingly lose the key attribute of sovereignty: self-government.

STATES WITHOUT SOVEREIGNTY

Sovereignty in international relations signifies political and legal autonomy: constitutional independence. It is a legal concept which is unconditional and indivisible. As Robert Jackson summarises:

[It is] legal in that a sovereign state is not subordinate to another sovereign but is necessarily equal to it by international law ... Absolute [unconditional] in that sovereignty is either present or absent. When a country is sovereign it is independent categorically: there is no intermediate condition. Unitary [indivisible] in that a sovereign state is a supreme authority within its jurisdiction. (1990: 32)

Prior to decolonisation in the last century, the sovereign state form was only one of several kinds of international status. Under European colonialism territorial entities took the form of 'colonies', 'protectorates', 'mandates', 'trust territories' or 'dominions' (Jackson, 1990: 33). What these various forms had in common was formal legal subordination to a foreign power; they were a denial of sovereignty. There is nothing inevitable or natural about the sovereign state form or about its universalisation in the twentieth century, in the wake of World Wars I and II (Morgenthau, 1970: 258–61; Wight, 1979: 23).

Few people engaged in the field would argue that the international state-building of the non-Western state is based on the desire to create or support traditional sovereign entities. This can be seen clearly in practice in the cases of international engagement in Bosnia, Afghanistan, the handing over of sovereignty in Iraq, and moves to make Kosovo an independent state in 2006, and more broadly in the UN and G8 proposals for state capacity-building in Africa. The sovereign state forms are held up but sovereignty is being redefined – or 'unbundled' in Stephen Krasner's phraseology (1999) – emphasising the importance of the legal shell of the state form while abandoning its political content of self-government and autonomy.

This is done in three ways: firstly, by redefining sovereignty as a variable capacity rather than an indivisible right, thereby legitimising a new hierarchy of variable sovereignty and undermining the UN Charter principle of sovereign equality; secondly, by redefining sovereignty as a duty or responsibility rather than a freedom, legitimising external mechanisms of regulation, held to enhance sovereignty despite undermining the traditional right of self-government or autonomy; and, thirdly, by exaggerating the formal importance of international legal sovereignty so that this formal shell then facilitates the repackaging of external domination as partnership or country ownership and the voluntary contract of formally equal partners.

Sovereignty as capacity?

The most important challenge to traditional conceptions of sovereignty has been the conflation of the formal political and legal right to self-government (an absolute quality) with the question of state capacity (a variable quantity), usually formulated in terms of good governance. The conception of sovereignty as a capacity, rather than as a formal legal right to self-government and international legal equality, creates a structure of a 'continuum' of sovereignty or a hierarchy of sovereignty where some states are considered to be more sovereign than others. This approach was notably developed by Robert Jackson, with his conception of 'quasi-states' (Jackson, 1990). For Jackson, the sovereignty granted to postcolonial states was artificial. Not because they were often still under the influence of their former colonial rulers, but because many of these states did not have the capacity to regulate and control their societies to the same extent as states in the West. Jackson argued that these states possessed 'de jure' sovereignty, formal international legal rights, but lacked 'de facto' sovereignty, the capacity to govern domestically.

This idea of the 'unbundling' of sovereignty into its different attributes was popularised by Stephen Krasner in his 1999 book *Sovereignty: Organized Hypocrisy*. In his more recent work, he has focused on sovereignty as a 'bundle' of three separate attributes: 'domestic sovereignty', the capacity of domestic governance structures; 'Westphalian/Vattelian sovereignty', i.e. self-government or political autonomy; and international legal sovereignty, formal juridical independence (Krasner, 2004: 87–8). Krasner uses the problem of weak state capacity to argue that self-government should not be a barrier to international intervention. Whereas in the 1990s intervention would have been posed as a conflict between human rights (or the right of intervention) and the right of state sovereignty (self-government and autonomy), in Krasner's terminology there is no conflict with sovereignty because human rights would be protected if governments possessed adequate governing capacity (domestic sovereignty):

Honoring Westphalian/Vattelian sovereignty ... makes it impossible to secure decent and effective domestic sovereignty ... To secure decent domestic governance in failed, failing, and occupied states, new institutional forms are needed that compromise Westphalian/Vattellian sovereignty for an indefinite period. (2004: 89)

The discovery that the formal legal equality of sovereignty hid the inequality of state capacities was not a new one. The same problem, although to a lesser extent, is present in domestic politics, where equality at the ballot box or under the law in liberal democracies does not necessarily ameliorate social and economic inequalities between individuals. In the domestic context, of course, relatively few people would argue that these inequalities should mean that formal political and legal equalities should be abandoned. In the international sphere, the existence of vast inequalities of power was one of the reasons that state sovereignty, held to be unconditional and indivisible, was the founding principle of international society. It was only on the basis of formally upholding the equality and autonomy of states, and the sovereign rights of non-intervention, that postcolonial societies could be guaranteed the rights to self-government. UN General Assembly declarations during the Cold War regularly asserted that differences in state capacity could never be grounds for undermining the rights of state sovereignty.

The affirmation that differences in capacity were no justification for the inequality of treatment as sovereign equals was confirmed most notably in the UN General Assembly Declaration on the Granting of Independence to Colonial Countries and Peoples of 14 December 1960 (Resolution 1514 (XV)) which proclaimed that: 'all peoples have the right to self-determination; by virtue of that right they freely determine their political status and freely pursue their economic, social and cultural development' and that 'inadequacy of political, economic, social or educational preparedness should never serve as a pretext for delaying independence' (UN, 1960). This was passed in the General Assembly by a vote of 89 to 0, with 9 abstentions. Even the colonial powers were unwilling to reject it (Jackson, 1990: 77). This was followed by the Declaration on the Inadmissability of Intervention in the Domestic Affairs of States and Protection of their Independence and Sovereignty of 21 December 1965 (Resolution 2131 (XX)) and the Declaration on Principles of International Law Concerning Friendly Relations and Co-operation among States in Accordance with the Charter of the United Nations of 24 October 1970 (Resolution 2625 (XXV)). The latter declaration made it clear that: 'All States enjoy sovereign equality. They have equal rights and duties and are equal members of the international community, notwithstanding differences of an economic, social, political or other nature' (UN, 1970).

By associating sovereignty with a sliding scale of capacities, rather than political and legal rights of equality, not only is a new international hierarchy legitimised but intervention can be framed as supporting sovereignty at the same time as it is undermining the rights of self-government. This inversion of the concept of 'sovereignty' is formulated in the clearest terms in the UK Overseas Development Institute working paper report 'Closing the Sovereignty Gap'. In this report, by Ashraf Ghani, Clare Lockhart and Michael Carnahan, sovereignty is understood in functional rather than political or legal terms:

The consensus now emerging from global economic, military and political institutions signals that this gap between de jure sovereignty and de facto sovereignty is the key obstacle to ensuring global security and prosperity. The challenge is to harness the international system behind the goal of enhancing the sovereignty of states – that is, enhancing the capacity of these states to perform the functions that define them as states. Long-term partnerships must be created to prepare and then implement strategies to close this sovereignty gap. (2005: 4)

Here sovereignty is no longer conceived of as a right to self-government. Sovereignty is merely a capacity which can be enhanced or, presumably, weakened. The therapeutic conflation of external intervention for the purposes of capacity-building with enhancing state sovereignty and independence is central to the state-building discourse. In Africa, where state capacity is held to be a fundamental concern for external powers engaged in supporting a multitude of empowering projects, headlined by the UN's Millennium Development Goals, these governance interventions have gone furthest (see for example the Sachs report (UNMP, 2005b) and Tony Blair's Commission for Africa report (CFA, 2005: Chapter 4)).

If sovereignty is defined as the capacity of non-Western states for good governance there would seem to be little wrong in external institutions implementing strategies for long-term engagement in these societies in order to enhance their sovereignty. In fact, governments which resisted this external assistance could, in the Orwellian language of international state-builders, be accused of undermining their own sovereignty. The key to the success of this conceptual conflation is not in its legitimisation of external intervention (already accepted in the 1990s) but in its portrayal of external regulation as somehow empowering or strengthening non-Western states. Here is the virtuous circle for intervening powers, one that was not possible in the post-conflict interventions of the 1990s: the more intervention there is the more the target state is held to be responsible and accountable for the consequences of these practices.

Sovereignty as responsibility?

The second shift articulated by the advocates of state-building as empowerment is the assertion that non-Western states have the responsibilities of sovereignty rather than the rights of sovereignty. What these responsibilities consist of is not held to be a decision made solely by the citizens of the state or their representatives, but one made in 'partnership' with external bodies. Rather than being a barrier to external interference, sovereignty becomes a medium through which non-Western states and societies become integrated into networks of external regulation. International regulatory mechanisms of intervention are legitimised, firstly through the role of international institutions in deciding the content of the responsibilities of sovereignty, and, secondly, through holding states to external account for 'failings' in the exercise of sovereignty (now discussed in the language of responsibility/capacity).

Sovereignty as responsibility enables a new consensual or partnership approach to state-building. Non-Western states are in a poor position to resist new international mechanisms of regulation which come replete with carrots of international aid, trade privileges, debt forgiveness, or integration into international organisations, in return for external support for governance reforms and institutional capacity-building. State-building or sovereignty-building involves non-Western states being firmly embedded in international institutional frameworks, over whose decision-making processes they have little influence. For the UK Overseas Development Institute, the focus on strengthening sovereignty entails a much more interventionist role by external institutions:

We define a sovereignty or state-building strategy as ... the alignment of the internal and external stakeholders ... In order to design and implement state-building strategies, the operation of the current international system must be reorientated towards a model where partnership and co-production of sovereignty becomes the aim of both national leaders and international partners. (Ghani, Lockhart and Carnahan, 2005: 13)

This 'co-production of sovereignty' follows the strategies adopted by the European Union towards Balkan states from 2000 onwards where international partnerships enmeshing applicant states in a network of international institutional processes were coordinated through the Stability Pact (SP), the Stabilisation and Association process, the Community Assistance for Reconstruction, Development and Stabilisation programme (CARDS), and the 'European Partnership' process. The prospect of future EU membership was explicitly offered to Albania, Bosnia, Croatia, Macedonia and the Federal Republic of Yugoslavia (FRY) at the Feira European Council in June 2000. At this point the EU shifted away from external conditionality and towards state-building in the Balkan region, initiating a project of 'reforming and reinventing the state in South Eastern Europe' (ESI, 2001a: 18) (see further, Chapter 5).

This shift from external relations of aid and trade conditionality to partnership in domestic governance is symbolised by the dropping of the term 'Balkans' by international institutions, as too 'negative' and 'hegemonic', and its replacement by 'South Eastern Europe' (SEE) symbolising that this is a joint project of partnership, addressing 'European problems' with 'European solutions' (see, for example, *Balkanologie*, 1999; Hatzopoulos, 2005). The EU argued that it was well placed to assist these states in developing governance capacity which was identified as not just their main barrier to progress but also an area where the EU held a vital 'comparative advantage' and could 'provide real added value' (EC, 2001a: 9). This engagement in domestic policy-making is held to have 'both pedagogical and political' benefits for the candidate states (EU, 2001: IIIc). Despite talking up the partnership between international institutions, the EU and prospective member states, the state-building process has been directed by close cooperation between the EU and international financial institutions which together have provided 'an effective means of focusing authorities' minds on essential reforms and of engaging with them in a sustained way to secure implementation' (EU, 2001: IIIc).

Since 2000 the concept of state-building through international partnerships to enhance governance capacities has increasingly replaced external pressures. Where the incentive of European membership is not available, a wide range of other governance partnerships has been established around acceptance that the core problem of non-Western states is that of state capacity and that the solution lies with the shared responsibilities of both the non-Western state and international institutions. The general rule of thumb appears to be that the greater the inequalities at play in the relationship between non-Western states and international institutions the more grandiose the language of partnership. As would be expected, it is in relation to Africa that the rhetoric and reality are most out of step. Here the language is of 'African leadership' and an entirely 'new kind of partnership' not based on inequality and hierarchy but on 'mutual respect and solidarity' (CFA, 2005: 17). The UN Millennium Development Goals project, following and extending the country ownership approach of the interventionist World Bank Poverty Reduction Strategies, requires that states engage in far-reaching governance reform and open up every area of domestic policy-making to international scrutiny and involvement. The responsibilities or leadership or ownership lie with the domestic state but their partners (or joint stakeholders) decide the policies:

The host country should lead and own the effort to design the MDG strategy, drawing in civil society organizations; bilateral donors; the UN specialized agencies, programs, and funds; and the international financial institutions, including the IMF, the World Bank, and the appropriate regional development bank. The contributions of the UN specialized agencies, programs and funds should be coordinated through the UN Country Team, and the UN Country Team should work closely with the international financial institutions. (UNMP, 2005b: 53)

The 'host country' books the meeting rooms but the 'guests' come along with the policy frameworks. These external policy prescriptions closely tie international aid to new institutional frameworks of regulation and monitoring. In effect this transforms external assistance from being a subject of international relations, between states, to one of domestic politics, of management and administration. This radical transformation in the relationship between non-Western states and international institutions is highlighted forcefully by the Commission for Africa report which stresses that it is: 'not simply recommending throwing money at the problems' but is recommending a 'fundamental change in the way in which aid works' (CFA, 2005: 94).

Once international financial institutions have a more direct role in the *internal* governance mechanisms of non-Western states, aid is much less likely to be based on overt external regulation in the form of *external* conditionality. Graham Harrison usefully highlights the 'post-conditionality' regimes of international financial institutions in states like Tanzania and Uganda, where the influence of external donors is better conceived not as a 'strong external force' but as 'part of the state itself', through direct involvement in policy-making committees (2001: 669; see also Harrison, 2004). The undermining of sovereign autonomy and the enmeshing of subject states in international institutional frameworks fundamentally blurs the lines of accountability and control and the relationships of power behind these mechanisms. The relationship between Western institutions and non-Western states is a highly coercive one which forces these states to cede their sovereign powers to external institutions; the fiction of partnership then relies heavily on an exaggeration of the importance of international legal sovereignty.

International legal sovereignty?

Today, despite the new interventionist consensus and the international attention given to failing states and the lack of governance capacities in zones of instability, there is surprisingly little support for the return of international protectorates and direct external administrations. Only a small number of commentators argue that states should, in fact, be allowed to fail and more capable neighbours allowed to directly govern these territories (for example, Herbst, 2004) or that the UN Security Council should establish new international trusteeships (Helman and Ratner, 1993).

Intervening powers and international institutions seem to have a particularly strong desire to preserve the formal trappings of sovereignty. The contradictory desire to intervene but also to avoid political responsibility is most sharply posed in questions of military intervention, such as post-9/11 regime change in Afghanistan and Iraq. Few acts are as fundamentally undermining of sovereignty as the external removal of a state's government. Yet, no sooner have intervening actors destroyed sovereignty than they are talking up its fundamental importance and pledging to restore authority to local actors at the soonest possible moment. State-building is the process of negotiating these contradictory drives towards intervention and away from responsibility for outcomes.

Leading US policy advisers and international think tanks are increasingly singing from the same hymn sheet, suggesting that international regulation should no longer be seen in the old ways. In fact, the maintenance of formal sovereignty is at the heart of new approaches to 'neo-trusteeship' (Fearon and Laitin, 2004), 'pooled sovereignty' (Keohane, 2002), or 'shared sovereignty' (Krasner, 2004). In the words of Krasner:

Shared sovereignty would involve the engagement of external actors in some of the domestic authority structures of the target state for an indefinite period of time. Such arrangements would be legitimated by agreements signed by recognized national authorities. National actors would use their international legal sovereignty to enter into agreements that would compromise their Westphalian/Vattellian sovereignty [self-government/autonomy] with the goal of improving domestic sovereignty [governing capacity]. One core element of sovereignty – voluntary agreements – would be preserved, while another core element – the principle of autonomy – would be violated. (2004: 108)

The key difference between new forms of external regulation – neo-trusteeship or, the even more user-friendly, shared sovereignty – and traditional notions of a trust or protectorate is that, today, the subordinated territory will formally be a contracting legal equal. International legal sovereignty is maintained while political autonomy – self-government – is given up. The Bosnian peace agreement at Dayton in 1995 is the classic example of the voluntary surrender of sovereignty; the neo-trusteeship was legitimised not through war and coercive power but through international legal agreement; through the signature of the Bosnian parties (Chandler, 2005b).

Law and reality no longer coincide when considering the location of sovereign power and authority (see Yannis, 2002: 1049). Kosovo, for example, is, at the time of writing, formally part of the state of Serbia-Montenegro, but again the lack of fit between the formal location of sovereignty and external mechanisms of regulation makes discussions of final status hard to resolve as decision-making authority lies neither with the elected Kosovo government in Pristina nor with the Serbian government in Belgrade. Afghanistan and Iraq have the juridical status of independent states despite their dependence on the political and security role of the US. The artificial nature of these regimes is highlighted by the fact that their governments' writs seldom extend outside the protected security zones of the capitals. The restrictions on the Iraqi interim government's authority has meant that the formal transfer of Iraqi sovereignty from the US-led Coalition Provisional Authority to an Iraqi government in June 2004 did not reflect any change in the real relations of authority (see, for example, Klein, 2005).

Here we have states without sovereignty. States exist on paper, in terms of juridical status, for example, as members of the United Nations, with national flags, and maybe their own currencies, but not as independent political subjects capable of self-government. The states which are the products of international state-building are more like 'phantom states' than real ones. As Robert Keohane argues:

We somehow have to reconceptualize the state as a political unit that can maintain internal order while being able to engage in international co-operation, without claiming the exclusive rights ... traditionally associated with sovereignty ... The same institutional arrangements may help both to reconstruct troubled countries that are in danger of becoming 'failed states', and to constrain the autonomy of those states. (2003: 277)

Keohane suggests that state-building can establish the 'institutional arrangements' which are capable of taking responsibility for maintaining order ('domestic sovereignty') but without giving rise to rights of self-government ('Westphalian sovereignty'). He recommends an exit strategy for Kosovo, for example, where there is a shift from existing trusteeship status, which could be called 'nominal sovereignty', to 'limited sovereignty' with external powers able to override domestic authorities, to a final stage of 'integrated sovereignty' where the state is locked into international institutions able to override domestic authorities (2003: 296–7). This would resolve the problem of Kosovo's independence as it would never achieve independence beyond the purely formal trappings of statehood: 'Westphalian sovereignty ... is simply bypassed in the movement from limited to integrated sovereignty' (2003: 297).

His proposals are strikingly similar to those later advocated by the International Commission on the Balkans. The commission's April 2005 report, *The Balkans in Europe's Future*, talks about Kosovo's 'independence without full sovereignty', to be followed by 'guided sovereignty' with 'reserve powers' for the EU and a final stage of 'full and shared sovereignty' (ICB, 2005: 18–23). Here state-building is held to be able to build a new type of state; one which has 'sovereignty' but is still in essentially the same position that it was when it was formally a protectorate. The difference being that formal accountability has been shifted back to the non-Western state.

James Fearon and David Laitin suggest a similar approach arguing that a return to traditional forms of sovereignty is not the solution, but instead that the transfer of power in cases of post-conflict intervention and regime change should be 'not to full sovereignty but rather as a state embedded in and monitored by international institutions' (2004: 42). Krasner argues the point even more openly in his support for the concept of 'shared' sovereignty, which similarly uses 'sovereignty' as a means for enabling external regulation. Here, international legal sovereignty allows non-Western states to enter into 'partnerships' which informally violate their sovereign rights:

For policy purposes, it would be best to refer to shared sovereignty as 'partnerships'. This would more easily let policymakers engage in organized hypocrisy, that is, saying one thing and doing another. Shared sovereignty or partnerships would allow political leaders to embrace sovereignty, because these arrangements would be legitimated by the target state's international legal sovereignty, even though they violate the core principle of Westphalian/

Vattellian sovereignty: autonomy ... Shared sovereignty or partnerships would *make no claim to being an explicit alternative to conventional sovereignty*. It would *allow actors to obfuscate* the fact that their behaviour would be inconsistent with their principles. (2004: 108, emphasis added)

It is this 'obfuscation', hiding the transformed nature of non-Western state sovereignty while maintaining international legal sovereignty, which enables international institutions to present themselves as facilitating partners in a shared project rather than as coercive external powers. Robert Cooper, focusing particularly on the enlargement policies of the European Union, describes this as a new conflict-free 'postmodern' or 'voluntary' form of imperialism (Cooper, 2003). Mark Leonard argues that unlike the old imperialism based on conflict and overt subordination, the EU is completely transforming states from the inside, rather than ruling them from above, for example: 'Europe is changing all of Polish society, from its economic policies and property laws to its treatment of minorities and what gets served on the nation's tables' (Leonard, 2005: 6).

The more sovereignty is 'voluntarily' shared between target states and international institutions, coercive external conditionality is exchanged for internal forms of 'enhanced surveillance' through the reporting mechanisms generated by the good governance requisites of openness and transparency enforced by international institutions (CFA, 2005: 376). Policy advisers can no doubt see the gains to be made in enabling Western governments to talk about sovereignty and accountability in non-Western states, while avoiding political responsibility for their actions and policy prescriptions. However, while sovereignty can be 'unbundled' as a heuristic device there is little evidence that conceiving the non-Western state in purely administrative and bureaucratic terms, as a conduit for external policy, is necessarily a recipe for success. States without sovereignty are not easy to capacity-build.

PHANTOM STATES AND EMPIRE IN DENIAL

States that are not designed to be independent political subjects in anything but name are a façade without content. States without sovereignty may have technically sound governance and administrative structures on paper but the atrophied political sphere hinders attempts to cohere post-conflict societies and overcome social and political divisions. The states created, which have international legal sovereignty but have ceded policy-making control to international institutions, are phantom states because their lack of self-government prevents them from being recognised or legitimised as embodying a collective expression of their societies. The states of Afghanistan, Iraq and Bosnia, for example, may have formal sovereignty and elected governments but their relationship of external dependency means that the domestic political sphere cannot serve to legitimise the political authorities or cohere their societies. This form of state-building is, in fact, even more corrosive of the authority of the non-Western state than earlier policies which sought to bypass or marginalise the state.

Bosnia is possibly the clearest case of a new type of state being built through this process of distancing power and political responsibility. To all intents and purposes Bosnia is a member of the European Union; in fact more than this, Bosnia is the first genuine EU state where sovereignty has in effect been transferred to Brussels. The EU provides its government; the international High Representative is an EU employee and the EU's Special Representative in Bosnia. This EU administrator has the power to directly impose legislation and to dismiss elected government officials and civil servants. EU policy and 'European Partnership' priorities are imposed directly through the Directorate of European Integration (see, for example, the 280-page document outlining the timetable for implementing the EU's medium priorities, BiH DEI, 2005). The EU also runs the police force, taking over from the United Nations at the end of 2002, and the military, taking over from NATO at the end of 2004, and manages Bosnia's negotiations with the World Bank. One look at the Bosnian flag – with the stars of the EU on a yellow and blue background chosen to be in exactly the same colours as used in the EU flag – demonstrates that Bosnia is more EU-orientated than any current member-state (see further, Poels, 1998). However, the EU has distanced itself from any responsibility for the power it exercises over Bosnia; formally Bosnia is an independent state and member of the United Nations and a long way off meeting the requirements of EU membership.

After ten years of state-building in Bosnia there is now a complete separation between power and accountability (see Chandler, 2005a). This clearly suits the EU which is in a position of exercising control over the tiny state without either admitting it into the EU or presenting its policy regime in strict terms of external conditionality. Bosnia is neither an EU member nor does it appear to be a colonial protectorate. Bosnia's formal international legal sovereignty gives the appearance that it is an independent entity, voluntarily engaged in hosting its state capacity-building guests. Questions of aligning domestic law with the large raft of regulations forming the EU *acquis* appear as ones of domestic politics. There is no international forum in which the contradictions between Bosnian social and economic demands and the external pressures of Brussels' policy prescriptions can be raised.

However, these questions are not ones of domestic politics. The Bosnian state has no independent or autonomous existence outside of the EU partnership. There are no independent structures capable of articulating alternative policies. Politicians are subordinate to international institutions through the mechanisms of governance established which give EU bureaucrats and administrators the final say over policy-making. The Bosnian state is a phantom state; but it is not a fictional creation. The Bosnian state plays a central role in the transmission of EU policy priorities in their most intricate detail. The state here is an inversion of the sovereign state. Rather than representing a collective political expression of Bosnian interests – expressing self-government and autonomy, 'Westphalian sovereignty' in the terminology of state-builders – the Bosnian state is an expression of an externally driven agenda.

The more Bosnia has been the subject of external state-building, the less like a traditional state it has become. Here, the state is a mediating link between the 'inside' of domestic politics and the 'outside' of international relations, but rather than clarifying the distinction it removes the distinction completely. The imposition of an international agenda of capacity-building and good governance appears internationally as a domestic question and appears domestically as an external, international matter. Where the sovereign state clearly demarcated lines of policy accountability, the state without sovereignty blurs them. In fact, political responsibility for policy-making disappears with the removal of sovereignty.

In this context, domestic politics has no real content. There is very little at stake in the political process. For external state-builders, the subordination of politics to bureaucratic and administrative procedures of good governance is a positive development. In functional terms they argue that sovereignty, and the political competition it brings with it for control of state power, is a luxury that non-Western states often cannot afford. Keohane argues that many non-Western states are 'troubled societies' plagued by economic, social and ethnic divisions which mean that elections can be highly problematic 'winner-takes-all' situations. In these states, unconditional sovereign independence is a curse rather than a blessing and conflict can be prevented by enabling 'external constraints' on autonomy in exchange for institutional capacity-building (2002: 755–6; see also Paris, 2004: 187–94).

Post-conflict states, such as Bosnia, stand in desperate need of a state-building project which can engage with and cohere society around a shared future-orientated perspective (see also Bickerton, 2005b, who expands this argument to Eastern European accession states more generally). What Bosnia has received is external regulation which has, in effect, prevented the building of genuine state institutions which can engage with and represent social interests. Phantom states are an inevitable product of the technical, bureaucratic and administrative approach exported by international state-builders. Where weak or post-conflict states stand in need of socially engaging state-based projects of development and transformation they are subject to external forms of domination which are uniquely unsuited to the task. It is the problems of the state form in the West that explain why there should be such a mismatch between need and policy prescription in the state-building approach.

Western states may sometimes appear to be happy with the traditional imperialist rhetoric of Great Power responsibility but are quick to recoil from any practical consequences of this. Despite the rhetoric of Great Power responsibility, the resulting ideological, legal and political forms are those of a rush to reject imperial responsibility. It is this dynamic which is essential to understanding the novel features of twenty-first century state-building. State-building can best be grasped as a product of the exhaustion of the political process in the West. Government is increasingly seen as a matter of law and administration, rather than politics; as a matter of bureaucratic competence rather than political struggle. The projection of Western power abroad reflects the lack of any 'big ideas' or mobilising political project. This lack of transformative purpose can be seen in the focus on the processes of state-building rather than its ends.

International state-builders seek to focus on legal, administrative and bureaucratic processes rather than broader problems of social and economic transformation. Good governance, transparency, inclusion, and alignment with the EU *acquis communautaire* stand in as a weak substitute for any imperial 'reordering of the world' (see, for example, Leonard, 2005: 36–45). Even the international financial institutions, such as the World Bank and the International Monetary Fund, are encouraged to drop earlier aspirations towards development and economic growth and to focus more narrowly on non-Western state frameworks of transparency and accountability (CFA, 2005: 374).

Traditional empire was confident in its ability to transform and improve societies being intervened in. Today's Empire in Denial is a fragile one, asserting power and influence but desiring to hide behind forms of formal sovereignty. The new international language of 'good governance', 'capacity-building', 'empowerment', 'partnership' and 'ownership' symbolises the politics of denial and evasion which mark every aspect of the state-building discourse.

CONCLUSION

State-building does not seek to universalise the state form – as in the period of decolonisation – but rather to conceal the disintegration of this form under the interventionist pressures of the post-Cold War international order. The promise that state-building holds out to international intervening powers is that of distancing themselves from the consequences of the collapse of the UN Charter framework of state sovereignty and non-intervention. In a world where the Great Powers had more confidence in themselves and were able coherently to project a sense of purpose, it is unlikely that there would be such a demand for distance and the perceived need to create fictional partners and phantom states to bear the political responsibilities of the post-Cold War order.

The lack of willingness of major Western states to take up the responsibilities of power, to be held to account for their interventions in the international arena, is resulting in a highly destabilising process where power and responsibility are increasingly separated. The following two chapters expand further on how state-building practices flow from an attempt to evade the responsibilities of power. Chapter 3 considers evasion in terms of how the state-building discourse reposes the problems of the non-Western state in technical and administrative terms, allowing the exercise of Western influence to be presented in the language of democracy promotion and capacity-building. Chapter 4 extends the discussion in a consideration of how the understanding of foreign policy-making and practice has been transformed by the substitution of self-interests with the needs of the Other.

3

The Governance of Government

International state-building has become central to international policy concerns and has marked a clear shift in international thinking, spurred by the leadership of the United States and the European Union. Today's approaches insist on the regulatory role of international institutions at the same time as emphasising the importance of external guidance and international capacity-building at the local level. This privileging of 'governance' over 'government' is based on the assumption that the political process in non-Western states can be externally influenced through the promotion of institutional changes introduced at the state level and pays less attention to how societal pressures and demands are constitutive of stable and legitimate institutional mechanisms. This chapter questions this approach and analyses the transformation in the assessment of the importance of the societal sphere. It considers how this shift has been shaped by current understandings of war and conflict, and how the prioritisation of governance has fitted with critical and post-positivist trends in academic thinking in international relations and security studies.

George W. Bush's second term inauguration speech on 20 January 2005 may well be looked back upon as marking the historical rejection of realism in post-Cold War United States foreign policy. Far from being deterred by the debacle in Iraq, the US administration has embraced the state-building agenda of exporting democracy and strengthening states' capacity for good governance in much more strident tones than that achieved by the Clinton administration's earlier forays into this domain (Bush, 2005). The guiding principles of the Bush administration mark a substantial rejection of realist approaches guided by narrow views of national self-interest. The desire for an apparently more activist and interventionist foreign policy in order to encourage other governments to reform and the willingness, if necessary, to intervene in the cause of 'liberty and freedom' confirms that questions of post-conflict state-building and international attempts to prevent and manage the consequences of state failure are set to remain at the top of the international policy agenda.

In the words of George W. Bush, the needs of US national security are dependent upon the meeting of the needs for liberty and security of those elsewhere and therefore call for an activist foreign policy based on the promotion of good governance and democracy: 'The survival of liberty in our land increasingly depends on the success of liberty in other lands. The best hope for peace in our world is the expansion of freedom in all the world' (Bush, 2005). In the similar words of Bush's Secretary of State, Condoleezza Rice:

Implicit within the goals of our statecraft are the limits of our power and the reasons for our humility. Unlike tyranny, democracy by its very nature is never imposed. Citizens of conviction must choose it – and not just in one election. The work of democracy is a daily process to build the institutions of democracy: the rule of law, an independent judiciary, free media and property rights, among others. The United States cannot manufacture these outcomes, but we can and must create opportunities for individuals to assume ownership of their own lives and nations. Our power gains its greatest legitimacy when we support the natural right of all people, even those who disagree with us, to govern themselves in liberty. The statecraft that America is called to practice in today's world is ambitious, even revolutionary, but it is not imprudent. (Rice, 2005)

This shift towards a seemingly neo-Wilsonian internationalism – articulated by the US administration in the wake of World War I, with the establishment of the League of Nations – was immediately welcomed by liberal commentators, albeit warily, and as the UK liberal broadsheet, the *Observer*, editorialised: 'If it had been John Kerry, the words would have been heard as a welcome return to reality and an indication that the US wanted to engage with the rest of the world rather than retreat into isolation' (*Observer*, 2005). By the end of 2005 there was a much more cohered attempt to highlight the progressive potential of neoconservative foreign policy with the London-based Social Affairs Unit's publication of *The Times* columnist Oliver Kamm's *Anti-totalitarianism: The Left-wing Case for a Neoconservative Foreign Policy* in October (Kamm, 2005) and the November 2005 Westminster launch of the Henry Jackson Society with cross-party support for a similar foreign policy position.

This proclaimed shift away from narrow national security towards concerns for others fits much more easily with European sensibilities, and the European Union has for some years worked towards a similar international projection of power based on the interests of others rather than self-interest, as can be seen in the formulation of European Common Foreign and Security Policy (CFSP). For example, Javier Solana, the EU High Representative for the CFSP, has argued that European states' unique capacities to overcome national interests and cooperate peacefully through democratic institutions gives the EU a similar capacity to export freedom, democracy and good governance to the near (and not so near) abroad (Solana, 2003). This idea of the 'real added value' that EU expertise and guidance can offer states outside the European Union has been central to the legitimisation of a wide range of 'democracy-exporting' mechanisms through the EU accession and the Stabilisation and Association processes (EC, 2001a: 9; see further, Chapter 5).

Whereas in the post-1945 era of decolonisation there was an assumption that state-building could not be accomplished by external powers but depended on state sovereignty and political solutions decided by local actors – that, in fact, democracy promotion and state-building meant less external regulation – today there is an opposite starting point. Today's international state-building and democracy-promoting approaches insist much more strongly upon the regulatory role of international institutions and suggest that, without external guidance and capacity-building, locally derived political solutions are likely to be problematic. There is a clear assumption that there are right and wrong approaches to the problems of government – there is good governance and by implication bad or wrong governance – the assertion of a new 'political correctness' is one which seeks to legitimise the external regulation of states on the basis of empowering them.

One consequence of this is that the frameworks of good governance, overseen and regulated by international bodies, are increasingly seen to take precedence over the domestic political processes of *government*. Governance is a term which gives priority to the framework of regulatory controls, or the 'rules of the game', established at an institutional level; government, on the other hand, expresses the importance of the political process, 'the game itself', played out and mediated at a societal level (see further, for example, Fudulu, 2003). This privileging of governance over government is based on the assumption that the political process can be influenced by institutional changes introduced at the state level and pays less attention to how societal pressures and demands are constitutive of stable and legitimate institutional mechanisms.

In terms of state-building, democracy and political autonomy are then seen to be the end goal, rather than crucial aspects of the process of state capacity-building itself, downplaying the centrality of broad social engagement in the political process. By political process, I am referring to the process of social engagement in the making of policy and in the legitimation of government; the existence of a public sphere, through which the state's relationship with society is cohered. This takes place at a variety of levels and through a number of different mechanisms from media discussion, public debate and civil society engagement to more formal political campaigning and the party competition for representation. It is through these mechanisms that individual interests and concerns coalesce and a broader social and political consensus is developed and expressed.

Despite the emergence of this new normative framework of international regulation of, and intervention in, the domestic affairs of states, there is a concern – even in leading policy-making circles – that the development and assessment of the effectiveness of international practices in democracy promotion and state-building has lagged far behind the rapidly growing policy practice in this area (for example, CSDG, 2003; Dobbins et al., 2003; Lund, 2003). This chapter seeks to analyse the most striking, and potentially the most worrying, aspect of current international state-building policy practices: the distancing of external administrative control from the domestic political process. The following sections consider this transformation in the assessment of the importance of the political sphere for state-building, consider how this shift in perspective has been shaped by a changed – and depoliticised – understanding of war and conflict, and how the prioritisation of governance over government has fitted with critical and post-positivist trends in academic thinking of international relations and security studies.

STATE-BUILDING WITHOUT POLITICS?

Prior to the end of the Cold War, the domestic political process was generally understood as key to the creation of stable and viable states. Samuel Huntington's pioneering late 1960s study, *Political Order in Changing Societies*, was regarded as the leading contribution to political development studies during the last 30 years of the twentieth century (Huntington, 1968). Huntington's work was a response to the prevailing orthodoxy of 1950s modernisation theorists who focused on the importance of economic reform at the expense of political and institutional concerns. His concern was not the creation of states which had the stamp of international approval, because the ruling clique supported the policies of those in power in Washington, nor was he trying to design the perfect constitution for export around the world, with a bill of rights and a separation of powers and human rights protections. For Huntington, the key to state stability was a political question of building a domestic consensus, a sense of political community, and establishing a government with popular legitimacy. Huntington argued that bureaucratic rule or government by isolated cliques may be able to produce stability in simple preindustrialised societies but that modernisation and democratic, participatory societies depended on the strengthening and institutionalisation of the political sphere.

Political institutions could only cohere society if they emerged out of existing social forces, if they represented real interests and real clashes of interests which then led to the establishment of mechanisms and organisational rules and procedures which were capable of resolving those disagreements (Huntington, 1968: 11). It was the links between political institutions, political parties and individuals which were considered key to strengthening the state, both institutionally and in terms of its popular legitimacy. Although seen as a conservative by many commentators today, Huntington is worth returning to by those who argue that international administrators can draw up all the necessary legislation for state-building, democracy promotion and post-conflict reconciliation. He argued that powerful rulers would always be tempted to bypass the political sphere and present themselves as able to solve problems without the need for politics:

Inevitably a ruling monarch tends to view political parties as divisive forces which either challenge his authority or greatly complicate his efforts to unify and modernise his country ... The modernizing monarch necessarily sees himself as the 'Patriot King' who is 'to espouse no party, but to govern like the common father of his people'. (Huntington, 1968: 403)

The desire of those with power to legitimise their authority on the basis of being above politics and instead being a direct representative of the public interest will sound familiar to anyone who has read the statements of the succession of internationally appointed administrators charged with state-building and democracy-promotion in the Balkans. Bosnia's High Representative Carlos Westendorp saw the Bosnian Presidency, Council of Ministers (CoM) and Parliamentary Assembly as 'painfully cumbersome and ineffective' when compared to the alternative possibility of the swift signature of his administrator's pen (OHRB, 1997c). Westendorp thrived on being the unaccountable judge of his own policy-making, arguing that: 'You do not [have] power handed to you on a platter. You just seize it, if you use this power well, no-one will contest it' (Rodriguez, 1998). Lord Paddy Ashdown, who ran the OHR until January 2006, used very similar phraseology, for example, in his inaugural speech of May 2002, stating:

I have concluded that there are two ways I can make my decisions. One is with a tape measure, measuring the precise equidistant position between three sides. The other is by doing what I think is right for the country as a whole. I prefer the second of these. So when I act, I shall seek to do so in defence of the interests of all the people of Bosnia and Herzegovina, putting their priorities first. (Ashdown, 2002)

For Lord Ashdown, as for his predecessors, rather than facilitating consensus-building between the three main political parties – representing Bosnian Muslims, Bosnian Serbs and Bosnian Croats – his own personal perspective of 'what I think is right' was held to coincide directly with the interests of the population as a whole (see Chandler, 2002b).

This high-handed approach, which has marked the ten years of international regulation in the tiny postwar Bosnian state, is at the centre of the state-building dilemma discussed here: the dilemma that imposing good governance policy practices, alleged to be in the interests of all, inevitably means restricting the importance of the political sphere of political party competition and policy-making by elected representatives. This dilemma is increasingly posed today when international actors have adopted state capacity-building as the core mechanism of regulation of and intervention in large areas of the world. The imbalance of power between intervening actors and those on the ground has meant that while this dilemma has been acknowledged, there is currently little thought given to the problems caused by this marginalisation of the domestic political sphere. For international administrators and policy-makers, it is well nigh inconceivable that local actors could be better placed to take their own societies forward without the assistance of international 'experts'.

For the international state-builders in Washington, London and Brussels, the unguided domestic political process is held to be a problem for strengthening state-capacity rather than central to it. To return to Huntington:

The administrator opposed to parties accepts the need to rationalize social and economic structures. He is unwilling, however, to accept the implications of modernization for broadening the scope of popular participation in politics. His is a bureaucratic model; the goal is efficiency and the elimination of conflict. Parties simply introduce irrational and corrupt considerations into the efficient pursuit of goals upon which everyone should be agreed. (1968: 404)

For Huntington, the point is that attempting to bypass the domestic political sphere is essentially counterproductive. While kings and bureaucrats, who understand their legitimacy as existing independently of society, are resistant to acknowledging it, historically, the engagement of the public in the political process, through party formation and competition in particular, has been crucial to binding society beyond its disparate component social groups, and to creating a broad social loyalty to a state-based project which transcends parochial and particularist groupings (1968: 405). Against predemocratic, hierarchical approaches of interest coalition, which institutionalise social fragmentation through patronage or the grant of private rights, modern democratic states rely on the autonomy of the political process. The contest for representation thereby forces political parties and interest coalitions to overcome the fragmented nature of their societies and build links between different social constituencies. The more restricted the political sphere is, the less responsibility and accountability elected representatives have and the less likelihood there is of political institutions being able to build social bonds in divided societies (see further, Chapter 7).

Huntington's defence of the autonomy of the political sphere is rarely seen as relevant to today's policy practices of institutional capacity-building. In fact, where his 1960s work is referred to, his points about the importance of strong state institutions are taken out of context and these institutions are seen as being able to develop in isolation from real political processes. A leading example of this latter approach is that of Roland Paris in his influential book, *At War's End*, published in 2004. Paris critiques the 'liberal peace' thesis on the basis that international policy, which sees a market economy and liberal democracy as the two preconditions for a stable peace, misunderstands the process of transition from war to peace. Paris argues that it is necessary to have 'Institutionalization before Liberalization', i.e. to focus on strong institutions, the rule of law and human rights protections before giving post-conflict societies the right to have a say in their own affairs. He argues that the political process of democratic competition in a weak or failing state, or one making a transition from war to peace, is likely to be counterproductive. This is because party political competition is based on the idea of a conflict of interests. This process tends to exacerbate conflict and tension in society rather than ameliorating it, in a context where fragile or failing states do not have the social, economic and legal mechanisms necessary for ensuring that conflicts can be managed and contained.

Paris argues that democracy is fine for developed stable states but is destabilising for states which are failing or are making the transition from war to peace. He asserts that elections are important – the goal is the promotion of democracy after all – but to achieve this end, elections must come second to state-building processes instituted from the top-down. The process of political reconciliation and the development of a shared sense of political community should precede competitive elections: 'Peacebuilders should proceed with elections only when there is evidence that "moderate parties" ... have sufficient popular support ... to prevail over "immoderate" parties' at the polls' (2004: 189–90). This interventionist project attempts to postpone self-government until good governance is guaranteed without external assistance. This is held to be a long and complex process.

This latter task is to be undertaken through a number of means: civil society-building; the encouragement of cross-cutting links and interests; international attention to educational curricula from primary school through to university level; the strict control and regulation of the media; trauma counselling and other therapeutic practices; and through punishing political parties or elected representatives held to be 'obstructing' progress. Clearly this state-building agenda is an ambitious one, but one that in many ways reflects the existing policy practices of international institutions, states and non-governmental organisations on the ground in many parts of the world (see, for example, UN, 2000; ICISS, 2001a).

Before engaging in a more extended discussion about the efficiency of such interventionist measures (in Chapters 7 and 8), the point to be stressed is the increasingly commonplace assumption that democracy is good for the Western powers but the tutelage of capacity-building ('the export of democracy') is better for the many states judged to be 'under stress', at 'risk of failure' or in post-conflict 'recovery'. This assumption rests on a much more negative view of the role of the political process.

The argument that it is possible to create the institutional framework of a strong and stable state before liberalisation – i.e. opening up the political process to democratic competition – suggests that states and citizens can be capacity-built and empowered by correct practices of external regulation. The assumption is that the problems of politics can be resolved outside the realm of the political, in the realms of law, social policy and administration. The potential irrationality of the desire to externally manage non-Western states through internationalising state institutions in isolation from the domestic society is captured well in the RAND Corporation recommendations for Iraq, which suggested that rather than coopting existing Iraqi institutions, the sounder approach was that of a 'root and branch overhaul of state and political structures', involving 'the creation of wholly new organizations at the local and national levels and the recruitment, training, and management of new staff' (Dobbins et al., 2003: 205). It would seem, as Alejandro Bendaña notes, that 'good governance or state-building ... has deep ideological presumptions which purport to offer technical solutions to what in essence are political problems' (Bendaña, 2004; see also Demmers et al., 2004).

It is this view of 'peace without politics' that imbues much of the current discussion around state-building practice which aspires to democratic ends (see Chandler, 2005a). In Bosnia, Kosovo, Iraq and other parts of the world, international administrators argue that the rule of law and even 'respect for democracy' must be developed before elected representatives can assume unassisted political authority. In the wake of the US-led Iraq occupation, Bosnia's High Representative Paddy Ashdown toured Western capitals arguing that the rule of law had to precede elections and political liberalisation (see Ashdown, 2003b; 2003c). This view of 'sequencing', which relegates the political process behind that of law, policing and administration, inverts the traditional understanding of the modern rule of law, derived from liberal democratic contract theory of consent, in contrast to the arbitrary and unaccountable rule-making of elites (see further, Chapter 8). While laws could be issued by right-wing or Soviet-style dictatorships, that also had the prisons and the police to enforce them, these societies were not understood to be operating under the rule of law as law did not derive from popular consent but from the power of coercion. The assertion that the rule of law should come before political liberalisation heralds a fundamental critique of one of the cornerstones of liberal democratic theory.

This is the dilemma of exporting state capacity-building practices. Democracy understood as premised on good governance, the rule of law and the protection of human rights leaves little room for the autonomy or self-determination of those to whom democracy is being brought. As Jarat Chopra and Tanja Hohe note in their survey of international state-building intervention:

Excluded from the equation, extraordinarily, were the people of the country. The subculture of UN missions – their leadership, and much of their staff, was rooted in a diplomatic habit, relating institution to institution or at most talking to a minority elite. Civilian bureaucrats were not as accustomed as some militaries to interacting with the local population in their operations. That asocial form of alienation was tenable in limited types of intervention, but it was disastrous when assisting or acting as a governing authority attempting to build capacity for a self-sustaining state. (Chopra and Hohe, 2004: 290)

It is ironic that governance reforms, legitimised through the discourses of capacity-building and empowering others, tend to marginalise the capacity for choice of those who are the ostensible subjects of these claims. The export of democracy in the context of the low expectations, and indeed perceived dangers, of political autonomy has meant that democracy promotion is increasingly seen as an ongoing process of regulation and international control rather than one of 'liberation' or independence. Because liberation in this instance is a grant of power rather than the recognition of a claim of autonomy, the export of democracy has gone hand-in-hand with greater regulatory controls by international institutions or regulation by ad-hoc groups of self-selecting coalitions of the willing, such as the G8, the Contact Group, the Stability Pact or the Peace Implementation Council (PIC) (the ad hoc coalition to whom Bosnia's 'international' High Representative is accountable).

WAR WITHOUT POLITICS?

The new international dispensation for a range of forms of external intervention undermining the sovereignty of non-Western states has been reinforced by a tendency for international theorists and international security actors to understand the problems of non-Western states in moral rather than political terms. For example, internal conflicts in the non-Western world have been increasingly understood as crimes to be judged and righted rather than as political conflicts to be mediated (see the excellent discussion in Columbo,

2004). Kalevi Holsti captured this new perception of conflict as 'wars of the third kind' where non-Western actors fought, not for social and political interests, as traditionally understood, but for a desire for different community boundaries and a strengthening of a particularist identity. He makes a fundamental assertion that these conflicts cannot be dealt with by traditional international approaches to handling interstate conflict: 'In these wars, ordinary cost-benefit analyses that underlie wars as a "continuation of politics by other means" no longer apply' (Holsti, 1996). War in the non-Western world is seen here as distinct from war waged by Western powers; in the former case, war no longer serves a legitimate political purpose, it is not a means to an end, rather it is an end in itself (see also Shaw, 2003).

According to Antonio Cassese, former president of the international war crimes tribunal at The Hague, for the people of non-Western states war is apparently 'less a noble clash of soldiers than the slaughter of civilians with machetes or firing squads, the mass rape of women in special camps, the cowardly execution of non-combatants' (1998: 5). As a human rights campaigners' handbook, *Crimes of War: What the Public Should Know*, asserts in its introduction:

Wars [involving non-Western states] today increasingly are fought not between armies where officers are bound by notions of honour but by fighters ... who are not soldiers in the conventional sense of the word. The goal of these conflicts is often ethnic cleansing ... not the victory of one army over another. (Gutman and Rieff, 1999: 10)

No longer connected with rational political interests, it appears that conflict has a dynamic of its own. Sussex University professor Martin Shaw makes the point that for non-Western societies 'genocide may be discerned, therefore, in relatively limited mass killing' (Shaw, 2003). He argues that 'the concept of "genocidal massacre" should be proposed to cover smaller incidents, which are often a prelude to a larger-scale genocide' (Shaw, 2003). The use of the emotive term 'genocide' to describe these conflicts establishes them as qualitatively different from the slaughter of wars in which Western states are involved. Unlike war, which appears relatively more civilised in comparison, genocide is regarded as either inherently atavistic and irrational or as morally evil.

This re-representation of non-Western conflict as driven by atavistic desires of ethnic identity, economic crime and human rights abuse, rather than rational political causes, has been held to illustrate the incapacity of non-Western states and peoples and the need for international intervention. Mary Kaldor developed Holsti's themes with the concept of 'new wars', which has become the ideological template for current international security regimes (Kaldor, 1998). The concept of new wars takes the politics out of armed conflict in two ways. Firstly, the conflict or crisis in the non-Western state is held to be the product of a lack of domestic governance capacity which is exacerbated by rapacious or criminal elites which have no political legitimacy. Therefore the United Nations' Cold War approach of neutrality and respect for peace agreements drawn up by the parties to the conflict no longer stands; instead, international actors are held to be necessary to create and safeguard a just peace.

Secondly, and more importantly, politics is taken out of conflict by portraying the intervention (military or otherwise) of Western powers as above politics. There is alleged to be no self-interest at work in external intervention, rather it is equated with the neutrality of policing, merely enforcing international or 'cosmopolitan' norms and laws. Rather than war, there are crimes and human rights abuses (conflict in the non-Western world) or there is capacity-building policing and law enforcement (armed conflict undertaken by Western powers) (see further, Chandler, 2002a). Neither non-Western state 'failure' nor the international response to this are conceived in traditional terms of political interests. This discursive dichotomy, between the failed state and the post-national or post-political intervention, in one move delegitimises the political process of the state intervened in while at the same time setting up the intervening powers as being beyond or above political interests.

Rather than adopting the former UN position of being the Cold War neutral observers to a legitimate conflict of interests, or the nineteenth-century imperial position of assuming governing authority, today's international interveners assume capacity-building roles as the supporters and creators of state institutions in a situation where there are now alleged to be few legitimate domestic political interests which should be taken into account. The 'export of democracy' depends on an assumption that greater external regulatory power is disinterested, is purely facilitating the self-determination of those to be 'freed'. In the words of President Bush: 'The rulers of outlaw regimes can know that we still believe as Abraham Lincoln did: "Those who deny freedom to others deserve it not for themselves; and, under the rule of a just God, cannot long retain it"' (Bush, 2005). Without the assumption of disinterested capacity-building the power of 'liberation' would be merely a licence for tyranny which can 'deny freedom', rather than grant it.

The relationship between external intervening powers (increasingly seen as legitimate) and domestic political actors (now increasingly portrayed as pursuing illegitimate interests) has been transformed through a succession of innovative international policy shifts since the end of the Cold War. At the heart of this transformation has been the United Nations itself, which has extended its remit and reinterpreted the formal restrictions of the UN Charter while increasingly giving free reign to self-selected 'coalitions of the willing' to set their own conditions on when and how interventions should take place and be formally brought to an end (Holsti, 1996: 190–1; for an excellent survey see Chesterman, 2002). This transformation in international practice has been shaped by the demands of the US and its allies for a more interventionist remit from the UN, with UN Security Council resolutions depending on the willingness of major powers to take action as a precondition for UN resolutions in this sphere rather than following as a consequence of them. The dangers of extending UN mandates and redefining the parameters of Chapter VII interventions without securing member state consensus has resulted in the fraying of the international legal order and the undermining of the Security Council's role in legitimising acts of military intervention.

The UN's role has been transformed from the narrow diplomatic task of 'preventing war' to the interventionist state-building task of 'constructing peace'. Over the last 15 years, a process of international administrative oversight and intervention, which developed in a relatively arbitrary and ad hoc way, has been increasingly institutionalised. At the end of 2004, the Report of the UN Secretary-General's High-Level Panel on Threats, Challenges and Change, *A More Secure World: Our Shared Responsibility*, advised the establishment of a Peace-building Commission to oversee international support for failing and post-conflict states (UN, 2004). According to the UN advisers and the Secretary-General, Kofi Annan, a select committee of the 'great and the good' from around the world, acting under UN auspices, should have the requisite skills to help coordinate a panoply of international intervention, from early warning, through preventative action and on to post-conflict transitional administrations, where states are 'under stress or recovering from conflict' (UN, 2004: 83). While individual states and ad hoc coalitions have been happy unilaterally to lead diplomatic and military interventions, they have been less willing to shoulder the political responsibilities of post-conflict state-building, often leaving the UN to carry on the long-term work of democracy exporting and to bear the blame for the failure of intervention to live up to its justificatory promises.

THE 'ETHICAL TURN' IN INTERNATIONAL THINKING

The rejection of the domestic political sphere as a vital constitutive sphere, in which social and political bonds are constituted and strengthened, and the re-representation of this sphere as essentially one of division and conflict, has received relatively little critical evaluation from academic commentators involved in international relations and international security studies. In fact, since the end of the Cold War, new approaches to theorising security have stressed that domestic political processes are part of the problem rather than part of the solution to conflict and political and social division (see, for example, Booth, 1991; Krausse and Williams, 1997; Booth, 2005). Many of these critical approaches draw on post-positivist theorising and follow Foucault's widely cited inversion of Clausewitz, seeing 'politics as a continuation of war by other means' (Foucault, 2003). The politically constituted realms of states, in this reading, are the result of war and domestic social conflict, with the domination by victorious elites being enforced and reproduced by political processes of representation rather than military force. For these theorists, states inevitably engage in war and internal conflict as they are based on domination and relations of exclusion and exclusivity (see, for example, Campbell, 1998b; Keane, 2002).

For critical, post-positivist and normative theorists of international relations and international security, the political sphere is the problem to be addressed, not the sphere where solutions are to be found. Rather than starting from politics, from social forces and the clash of interests in society, many theorists start from ethics and norms and then seek to derive (non-exclusionary) political frameworks from this basis (see for example, Archibugi and Held, 1995; Falk, 1995; Linklater, 1998). The approach of privileging ethics above the political process, central to the 'ethical turn' in international theorising, fits closely with international state-building practices which privilege bureaucracy, law and administration above the political and may in part explain why there is little critical focus on these developments in many academic circles. In this regard, Kenneth Minogue highlights the despotic dangers of 'political moralism', which sees autonomy and independence – i.e. the political sphere – as a barrier to ethically derived notions of justice, and argues that this approach to politics is especially strong in discussions of international relations (see, for example, Minogue, 1995: 104–5). Where realist theorists often highlighted the autonomy of the political and the limits to bureaucratic attempts to impose law and administration over clashes of power and interest, today's intellectual fashion is to focus on the indeterminacy and socially constructed nature of power and interest, emphasising the importance of norms and law. For realist critiques of the privileging of law and administration above the political see, for example, the classic texts by E. H. Carr (2001) and Hans Morgenthau (1993, especially Chapter 3) (discussed further in Chandler, 2004a).

For realist theorists, such as Carr, the extension of international law to address international issues where there was no political consensus merely 'debased and discredited' international law by bringing power relations into formal relations of legal equality (2001: 188). As Milan University international relations professor Alessandro Colombo notes, the growth of international law has institutionalised the inequalities of power:

the just party always wins. Instead of the previous formal equality among states, the tribunal-war dictates a clear asymmetry between the sanctioner and the sanctioned. The party who acts in the name of law, democracy or, in extreme cases, mankind, cannot be put in the same conditions as the party who is brought to trial. (2004: 121)

The advocacy of new international norms and of 'cosmopolitan' law has gone hand-in-hand with the redefinition of the rights and constitution of the non-Western state (see further, Chandler, 2000; 2004b). The internationalisation of non-Western state institutions has taken place on the basis of empowering the bearers of human rights, which are held to be internationally constituted, rather than the domestically constituted bearers of civil or democratic rights.

Human rights are at the centre of new 'human security' doctrines where the focus is no longer on the autonomy of states but upon the internationally protected rights of individuals wherever they might be in the world. This is construed to be a moral or an ethical duty placed upon the powerful to take responsibility for empowering and giving content to the rights of those elsewhere (ICISS, 2001a). The 2004 Barcelona Report of the Study Group on Europe's Security

Capabilities, *A Human Security Doctrine for Europe*, argues, for example, that:

In the new global context, the European Union's security policy should be built on human security and not only on state security ... A human security approach for the European Union means that it should contribute to the protection of every individual human being and not focus only on the defence of the Union's borders, as was the security approach of nation states. (SGESC, 2004: 9)

Here the double move of depoliticisation central to the export of democracy under the rubric of good governance can be seen clearly. This double move depends on finding an Other on whose behalf the West can be said to be acting (see further, Chapter 4). On the one hand, there is the creation of a new externally constituted rights subject, the object of the export of democracy, universally judged to be 'freedom-loving' or democratic. In Bush's words: 'it is the policy of the United States to seek and support the growth of democratic movements and institutions in every nation and culture, with the ultimate goal of ending tyranny in our world' (Bush, 2005). This is the same rights-subject as that advocated by earlier proponents of Other-regarding internationalism under the Clinton administration. Mary Kaldor, for example, in her call that international interveners should base their policies on the 'bottom-up' demands of the same selected freedom-loving subjects, asserts that: 'it is always possible to identify local advocates of cosmopolitanism, people and places which refuse to accept the politics of war – islands of civility' (1998: 120). The grant of rights from external actors does not, of course, give the appointed or selected freedom-loving people the right to hold these external actors to account, or a right to assert their claims to political autonomy, as can be seen in the international protectorate and semi-protectorate regimes in Bosnia, Kosovo, Afghanistan and Iraq.

On the other hand, it is assumed that the EU (making the same claim to the projection of power as the US) has risen above the politics of state interests and that, as a post-national or post-political constellation, it is capable of representing and acting on behalf of the interests of 'every individual' regardless of which state they happen to be a citizen of. The EU asserts that it is not a political but a disinterested legal or administrative judgment that it makes in deciding which states need capacity-building in order to enhance the rights of their citizens. This is, in effect, a right of intervention which bypasses traditional international legal and political processes. The doctrine of human security imposes a demand for the internationalisation of the non-Western state which legitimises a range of policy interventions independently of the Security Council mechanisms of the UN; one which ultimately relies on the denial of power and interests. Western domination is denied through the representation of the exercise of power as a radical relation of empowerment and capacity-building.

Robert Cooper, policy adviser to the UK Prime Minister, Tony Blair, and the EU High Representative for CFSP, Javier Solana, has most successfully translated the projection of power into therapeutic ethics in his view of 'voluntary empire' where dominated states volunteer themselves for external intervention (2003: 70–2). He astutely notes that the 'voluntary empire' of state capacity-building encompasses nearly every international relationship between the West and the areas of the world subordinate to Western power. This voluntary relationship can be seen, for example, in the World Bank and IMF programmes of assistance, the post-conflict administrative regimes of Bosnia, Kosovo, East Timor and Afghanistan and in the tutelage relations of EU enlargement.

Where Cooper errs in his analysis is in inversing the dynamic behind these relations. Rather than Western states and international institutions exercising the drive to intervene and to regulate, it appears to be a demand emanating from the states being capacity-built. Cooper describes well the mechanisms of Empire in Denial but also seeks to promote its ideological framework where the active agents are those 'volunteering' for imperial rule. This is a conscious re-representation of the relationships of power involved. Cooper asserts that when it comes to EU accession, it does the candidate countries 'no harm to be able to take constitutional models and systems of regulation off the shelf', as if it was the accession states choosing their own forms of constitutional arrangements rather than having the EU *acquis* imposed with no room for derogation (2003: 72). The EU has only one way of relating to its eastern neighbours and that is incorporation on its terms; there is no smorgasbord of relationship or of policy options that candidate states can pick and choose.

The power of empire is denied in the discourse of neo-Wilsonian democracy promotion and state-building articulated by Western states and international institutions. Democracy promotion and state-building, rather than levelling the unequal playing-field of the global order, clearly reflect the institutionalisation of new hierarchies of power which operate under the therapeutic signs of empowerment and capacity-building.

POLITICS AS A BARRIER TO PEACE

Today's export of democracy occurs in a context of much diminished expectations for non-Western states in the wake of the perceived failure (for the most part) in the experiment in postcolonial independence (see Jackson, 1990; Holsti, 1996). The dominant consensus is that this failure lies largely with the political sphere in these failing states – positing the solution as one of good governance overseen by external enablers and capacity-builders. There is therefore a tendency for international interveners to separate the export of democracy and post-conflict state-building from the process of domestic politics in the state intervened in; a tendency to see state-building as a scientific, technical or administrative process which does not require a process of popular consensus-building to give the target population a stake in policy-making. Where the post-World War II external administrations of Germany and Japan engaged the local populations in a major project of social, economic and political reconstruction, and through doing so won a high level of popular legitimacy and support, international administrations, such as those in Bosnia, Kosovo and Iraq, have excluded all but token local input into the making and implementation of policy.

In the Balkans, the international administrations have not just operated above the sphere of representative politics but have also consistently criticised the programmes and personnel of the main political parties and argued that both the Bosnian and Kosovan electorate are not yet to be trusted with a meaningful vote. In the cause of exporting democracy, rather than deriving policy from local concerns and needs, the legislative process has been driven by technical and administrative 'experts' in Brussels and Washington. Policies have then been imposed through the international Office of the High Representative in Bosnia and the UN's head of mission in Kosovo. Locally accountable political leaders then must accede to these demands, under the threat of being dismissed on the grounds of 'obstruction'.

There has been a trend towards granting external administrative powers greater and greater remits of authority. This process is reflected in the Bosnian example, where close international oversight was intended to last for one year only, until the first state elections in September 1996. However, ten years on from Dayton, not one piece of substantial legislation has been devised, written and enacted by Bosnian politicians and civil servants without external guidance.

This is in marked contrast to Japan and West Germany where, in the first case, the external occupation lasted nearly seven years and, in the latter, there were four years of occupation and full control over industrial and security policy was returned ten years after the end of the war (see, for example, Dower, 1999; Williamson, 2001).

A decade on from the Dayton settlement of the Bosnian conflict, the lack of political autonomy for Bosnian representatives, and of political accountability for Bosnian citizens, is possibly the most remarkable feature of current state-building practices in this tiny and fragmented state. However, the lack of democracy in Bosnia has posed little barrier in the negotiations over the accession process towards European Union membership; in fact, the European Union has given its formal blessing to the maintenance of a highly restricted political sphere, with the establishment of the EU's Special Representative as the 'double-hatted' international High Representative in 2002. There would appear to be a clear international consensus that, for state-building and democracy promotion to be a success, rule by externally appointed bureaucrats is preferential to rule by Bosnian representatives accountable to Bosnian citizens (see further, Chapter 6).

It could be argued in 2005 that George W. Bush's second inaugural speech proclaiming the importance of the export of democracy and the ten years of state-building experience in Bosnia serve as potent symbols of the return of liberal faith in the science of law and administration, reminiscent of the interwar period of the last century. This is also evidenced in the return of the idea of conditional sovereignty, muted for Kosovo by the Independent International Commission (IICK, 2001), and the idea of 'sovereignty as responsibility', suggested by the International Commission on Intervention and State Sovereignty and given wide international governmental support (see ICISS, 2001a; Haass, 2003; UN, 2005b). The concept of unequal rather than reciprocal relations between sovereign states is reminiscent of the Versailles restrictions on the sovereignty of the new states established in Central and Eastern Europe.

In addition, there is clearly a renewed faith in the powers of international conferences and committees to establish the borders of states (the European Community Badinter Commission did this for the former Yugoslavia), to appoint external governors (as the Peace Implementation Council did for Bosnia and the United Nations for Kosovo), and to detail exhaustive recommendations of good governance as a condition for reciprocal relations in the international sphere. There is without doubt a growing consensus that international experts and bureaucrats can better govern a country than politicians accountable to the people who have to live with the consequences of their policy-making. At the same time there is a shift towards the legitimisation of international regulatory controls in the language of technocratic and administrative regulation rather than political interests.

There is another similarity to the era of Woodrow Wilson: the rejection of traditional ideas of empire. In our postcolonial era, there is little support for the return of direct forms of international regulation, for a new network of colonial protectorates bringing 'order' to the regions of the world threatened by failing states. Rather, new international administrative regimes are, in the terminology of Michael Ignatieff, most often run on the basis of 'Empire Lite' (Ignatieff, 2003). International administrators are loath to take any responsibility for, or to be held to account for, the policies they pursue or the outcome of their interventions into the political process.

At the same time, local actors are denied the political autonomy to reach their own compromise solutions and assume accountability themselves. Both Bosnia and Kosovo painfully highlight the contradictions of having regularly contested elections at state and provincial levels and, alongside this, the existence of a parallel administration headed by unaccountable international appointees with the power to draw up and impose legislation and sack elected officials. Yet these protectorate relations of external regulation in the cause of democracy promotion and state-building are merely the most transparent end of a continuum of new hierarchical relations transferring the mechanisms of good governance, under the international regulatory regimes of EU enlargement or the UN Millennium Development Goals (see, for example, UN, 2005a: Chapter 2; EC, 2006).

Under new international mechanisms of democracy promotion and state-building, the political process is squeezed from above and below. There is an increasingly diminished accountability for policy-making either domestically or internationally. In this sense, the borders between the domestic and international are being effectively erased. However, democracy promotion has done little to promote democracy. For example, the external regulation of the people of Bosnia and Kosovo as bearers of human rights – rather than as 'citizens' with rights of political equality – has done little to overcome the 'politics of exclusion'. But Bosnian and Kosovan political representatives who have been elected are not exceptional in being held to account more by international advisers, trainers and capacity-builders than by their voters, reducing political institutions to irrelevant talking shops. In this context, elections in the EU accession states and in other parts of the world no longer become a judgement on government policies; in fact, the inverse relationship is in play. Elections are openly seen as educational exercises where, in the process of exporting democracy, the voters submit themselves to the judgement of the international experts from institutions such as the EU, the Council of Europe and the Organisation for Security and Cooperation in Europe (OSCE) as to their political capacities as citizens.

A few international analysts have stood out against the view that the political process can be short-cut or replaced by bureaucratic and administrative edict. Amitai Etzioni and Francis Fukuyama have, for example, questioned what they see as 'over-ambitious societal engineering' (Etzioni, 2004: 15; Fukuyama, 2004: 123). However, for these authors, as for left-wing historian Eric Hobsbawm, the 'dangers of exporting democracy' have been held to be the over-optimistic aims of today's ideologically driven neo-Wilsonians (Hobsbawm, 2005). This critique, in fact, agrees on the essentials with the current practices of international state-building, suggesting that the process of spreading democracy is not straightforward, but differs in the importance attached to the ambitious aims involved.

Critics who argue that democracy and state-building necessarily imply autonomy – and believe that the export of democracy when translated into good governance regimes is contradictory – are much thinner on the ground. Gerald Knaus and others at the Brussels-based think-tank, the European Stability Initiative (EST), have attempted to initiate a debate on the 'Travails of the European Raj' in Bosnia, highlighting the limitations of the high-handed approach taken to post-conflict reconstruction (Knaus and Martin, 2003). William Bain has also challenged the 'New Paternalism' of the failed states discourse and highlighted the return of a more hierarchical world order with the institutionalisation of new forms of political inequality between states and between individuals (2003). Simon Chesterman's study of post-conflict international administrations points out that today's international rule over Bosnia and Kosovo provides even less local accountability than the last century's mandate system or that under the presently defunct UN Trusteeship Council (2004a: 45). Chesterman's in-depth comparative study also concludes that current international state-building practices are prone to a number of fundamental flaws which stem from the inequalities built into the relationship of political pedagogy and external regulation: the means are often inconsistent with the declared ends; the resources are often inadequate to achieve the ends sought; and finally, much policy-making is more declaratory than practical, being largely irrelevant to the tasks at hand (2004a: 238–49).

CONCLUSION

It is necessary to extend this discussion of the questions and contradictions raised by international state-building and democracy promotion in the specific post-imperial context of our times. In the case of Bosnia, for example, where a large amount of resources have been committed by the international community, it is undoubtedly true that external intervention has had a major impact on the political process on the ground. Without doubt, it is possible to have intercommunal peace and a high level of refugee return without democracy or the autonomy of the political sphere. Nevertheless, it should be noted that this is a best-case example; in Kosovo the internationally administered peace has not facilitated the return of ethnic-minority refugees, while Iraq under international administration failed even to achieve peace.

However, it is also becoming apparent that state-building requires more than the largesse – and coercive power – of external benefactors. Ten years after Dayton, the Bosnian state still lacks a secure basis in Bosnian society and commands little social or political legitimacy. While the international administration has been able to institute a large number of administrative and policy reforms to meet the externally decided needs of good governance, it has been unable to transform the social and economic conditions of the population or to establish Bosnian institutions of government – i.e. those institutions which are crucial to legitimising the Bosnian state and are capable of overcoming the divisions of the war. In this respect, the international experiment in state-building without democracy, or viewing democracy as an end instead of as a means, has revealed major shortcomings.

The irony is that the shortcomings of this approach are rarely seen as inherent limitations of the framework of exporting and imposing democracy. The international policy-makers engaged in democracy promotion and state-building, in fact, seem to see their limited success as evidence of the difficulties of bringing democracy to non-Western states, and thereby justifying their work. It is this disillusionment with democracy which suggests that we are not witnessing a return to the idealism of the interwar period. There appears to be little sense of belief that the international exporters of democracy will succeed in creating strong independent states which have a right to political and legal equality with the states that currently administer or advise them.

Rather than transforming the states that are the objects of democracy promotion and state-building, international policy is more of a distancing operation, designed to exercise influence without assuming direct formal responsibilities of power. This process already problematises the elected representatives and citizens of states receiving capacity-building support and establishes that the blame for any lack of progress will be seen as the responsibility of local actors rather than international overseers. Unlike the interwar period, it may be that the export of democracy says more about low expectations and a lack of US mission or desire to change the world, despite the interventionist state-building rhetoric which, from the start, has marked George W. Bush's second administration.

4

The Ethics of Empire in Denial

Until relatively recently, Western foreign policy as pursued by major states and international institutions was cohered by the project of furthering the national interest. National interests were conceived in terms of the geopolitical framework of the Cold War, in which development and financial aid was granted on the basis of the political allegiances of governing elites or on their ability to pay back loans from international financial institutions. In the 1990s, the policies of both national governments and international institutions underwent substantial changes. The pursuit of narrow views of national and financial interest was transformed by the development of what were seen as 'ethical' policy-making frameworks. Broader, people-centred, security and development concerns came to the fore which questioned established foreign policy approaches and the structural adjustment policies of the World Bank and the IMF. Emphasis was instead placed on promoting the democracy, human rights, and social and welfare needs of other populations.

This chapter argues that, since the end of the 1990s, we have witnessed a convergence of both national foreign policy and international financial institutional frameworks, a new shared agenda, which has taken the human-centred developments of 'ethical foreign policy' to a new level of engagement with non-Western states: one where interest-based frameworks of understanding the international sphere no longer appear to have any firm purchase. Whether the issue of concern is post-9/11 security threats or the pursuit of the poverty and development agenda, the policies forwarded tend to focus on mechanisms of capacity-building and social empowerment, targeted at non-Western states and societies. The needs of non-Western states and societies have assumed centre stage. Today the language of 'interests' has been superseded by that of 'Other-regarding' ethics which appears to have taken the politics of power and interests out of foreign policy.

FROM SCHMITT TO LÉVINAS: THE PRIMACY OF THE OTHER

In 2005 it was not the war on terror which occupied the international summits and meetings of the European Union, the UN, the

World Bank, the IMF, the G8 and the World Trade Organisation, but the global causes of poverty reduction, debt cancellation and international aid. The focus on the UN's Millennium Development Goals and the international campaign to 'Make Poverty History' has mobilised people, non-governmental organisations, governments and international institutions around an ethical foreign policy which has been much less divisive than that of humanitarian war and intervention. In Britain alone, 10 million people bought white wristbands, while across the globe it is estimated that 3 billion people watched the Live 8 concerts (Hertz, 2005). It would seem that the international agenda had been transformed in a way which would have been unlikely according to traditional views of foreign policy priorities.

In traditional political understandings of international relations, the formulation of foreign policy was based upon the self-interest of states and the international sphere was one in which these interests were articulated (see, for example, the key texts of post-World War II international relations theory, Waltz, 1979; Morgenthau, 1993; Bull, 1995). Conceptual frameworks for analysing foreign policy and international relations were based on clear conceptions of power politics, the interests of states, and calculations of geopolitical, strategic and economic interests. States were understood as the political subjects of international relations and to be acting on a rationalist understanding of their interests (Smith, 2001). The interests of states were therefore particularist and exclusivist ones, derived from their own societies, and potentially counterposed to those of other states in a 'friend/enemy' framework which Carl Schmitt understood to be the essence of politics (Schmitt, 1976: 35). For Schmitt, it was the fear of the Other, the potential threat posed by the Other, which generated political community and constituted and legitimised political authority. There could be no international politics, no inclusive national Self without the excluded foreign Other (see Mouffe, 2005).

Today the international sphere is no longer understood as constructed in the relationship of Self and Other. The Other has been transformed and is now increasingly represented as both the agent and object of foreign policy while the Self has been greatly diminished. 'Our interests' or 'national interests' are no longer central to the construction or the legitimisation of foreign policy practices. Where national interests appear in the speeches of Western leaders and in policy documents they are generally constructed as secondary, achieved as the by-product of meeting the security and development needs of the Other. There is no longer a context of 'friend/enemy': the Other – the object of foreign policy – is more likely to be defined on the basis of needs. Even where the language of threats is used the threat is not a traditional one but is framed in the context of unmet needs: the threat stemming from the weakness and incapacity of the Other (see, for example, Abrahamsen, 2005). Even more remarkably, the Other has increasingly assumed the role of the subject or agent of policy, with 'pro-poor' policy-making, African 'leadership' and 'country ownership' of World Bank and IMF poverty reduction strategies.

The Other has become central to frameworks of international policy-making at precisely the point when Western leadership faces the collapse of obstacles to the spread of democracy and the market with the end of the Cold War. Yet, since 1989, it would appear that the victory of the West has been increasingly talked-down. Rather than the possibilities that have opened up with 'The End of History' – the collapse of alternatives to Western hegemony – it seems that just at the point where the promissory notes are to be cashed the game has changed (Fukuyama, 1989). The ideological mainstays of the Cold War, the belief in the capacities for political and economic progress, have been increasingly undermined and disparaged. It is not just that democracy and development have been reinterpreted and ambitions lowered, to take into account the newly discovered constraints of global norms of good governance and the need for environmental and social sustainability – even the location of power and responsibility appears to have shifted. Rather than grasping the opportunities to reshape positively a new international order in the wake of Cold War division, Western states and international institutions would appear to be embarrassed by their power and influence.

Rather than asserting power in a confident fashion, the West's interaction with the non-Western world takes the form of a denial. It will be suggested below that Western denial of responsibility and accountability in relation to the non-Western world is resulting in the development of new mechanisms of intervention and regulation which separate policy-making power from political discussion and debate. Agency and responsibility are located increasingly in the Other – non-Western states and societies – while the power of Western states and international institutions is increasingly understated. In this context of denial and evasion, it would appear that Western states and international institutions have taken postmodern ethics to heart in their claims to be acting on the basis of their 'responsibilities to the Other' rather than being guided by self-interest (for example, Der Derian, 1995). The leading theorist of Other-regarding ethics in the twentieth century was Emmanuel Lévinas who argued that legitimacy should be derived from our 'fear *for* the Other': that the rights of a subject derived from ethical responsibilities to the Other (Lévinas, 1989: 82). For Lévinas, ethics preceded politics and – in the formulation of putting responsibilities to the Other prior to the freedom of the Self – he inverted Schmitt's conception of foreign policy-making and political identity. As David Campbell notes: 'Lévinas's thought is appealing for rethinking the question of responsibility ... because it maintains that there is no circumstance under which we could declare that it was not our concern' (Campbell, 1998b: 176). Putting responsibility before self-interest and ethics prior to politics fundamentally reworks traditional conceptions of foreign policy priorities.

For many commentators, this shift away from narrow self-interests of national security and financial interests and towards Other-regarding people-centred or human-centred concerns reflects the changed circumstances of our globalised and interconnected world since the end of the Cold War. If other parts of the world are unstable, poorly governed or in poverty, then they will pose a threat to the security of all states. After the events of 11 September 2001 it is held to be clear that no Western state can afford to ignore its responsibilities for what goes on beyond its borders (see, for example, SGESC, 2004: 9).

Western governments are held to be confronting new realities where there can be no division between acting morally (upon the moral duty to help others in need) and acting in an enlightened (as opposed to Cold War era, unenlightened) self-interest. There is a happy coincidence of ethics and political interests because now the political interests of Western actors and the needs of non-Western actors coincide. Any critique of Western foreign policy has to take on the ethical and political claim that Western states and international institutions are acting in the interests of those who need help the most, those facing political and economic exclusion. Rather than being justified on the basis of the political interests of Western actors, foreign policy today is increasingly legitimated on the basis of the needs of non-Western actors and is increasingly seen as led by these needs as articulated by non-Western representatives and advocates.

This framework of Other-regarding ethics is driving a separation between policy-making power and political mechanisms of responsibility and accountability. The process of denial – of rejecting Western authority and influence – is creating new forms of managing international relations in which the formal framework belies the content of power relations. Discourses and practices of Other-regarding ethics separate power from political subjects in three ways: firstly, they cast external policy-makers (Western states and international institutions) as powerless and disinterested actors; secondly, they dissolve concerns of interstate relations (foreign policy) into domestic policy processes through the focus on the institutional capacity of the non-Western state; and, thirdly, they transform the political sphere of non-Western states through recasting policy in 'needs-based' terms which necessitate a technical consensus, objectifying the Other as the political subject but one without agency. Today's Other-regarding ethical foreign policy takes three distinct forms:

1) *Needs not interests* – the needs of Others are the focus rather than the interests of the Western policy actor. Foreign policy increasingly reinterprets the projection of power and influence not in the form of concrete political interests but as ambitious general ethical aspirations. This policy agenda is seen as deriving from the needs of Others not from the direct interests of the Western actor. These general needs are likely to be so large, ambitious and interconnected that the focus on them impels global cooperation and new forms of international partnership. These Other-regarding aims and aspirations focus on themes such as 'making poverty history', dropping Third World debt, women's rights, human rights, health and educational rights or overcoming social and economic inequality.

   Unlike the ethical foreign policy of the 1990s which focused on specific and select cases of abuse or exclusion, the focus today tends to be less specific. The more abstract and grandiose the policy aspiration, the less open it is to opposition, either from non-Western states or other international actors. This framework appears as an inversion of traditional foreign policy – subordination to the needs of Others removes the traditional basis of self-interest and absolves the Western actor of direct accountability for outcomes as the policy process is also subordinate to the demands of international and global cooperation. This double subordination – to both other international actors and the demands of those in need – displaces the politics of interests with increasingly technical concerns of implementing shared agendas legitimised on the basis of needs.

2) *Domestic policy not foreign policy* – the removal of interest-based conflict and the projection of power as empowerment or capacity-building are increasingly removing the overt element of externality from Western relations with non-Western states. Western governments and international institutions no longer appear to be purely external actors, relating to non-Western states on the basis of intergovernmental agreements. The focus on working alongside and within, rather than against, non-Western governments is highlighted in the shift in discussion towards ways of strengthening state sovereignty rather than undermining it (see, for example, Keohane, 2003; Krasner, 2004; Chesterman, Ignatieff and Thakur, 2005a; Ghani, Lockhart and Carnahan, 2005).

On the basis of a shared partnership agenda or shared responsibility to meet the needs of the citizens of non-Western states, the division between the domestic and the international is increasingly blurred or obscured. This blurring takes its sharpest form in the concrete policy prescriptions that the internal/external partnership pursues which largely focus on non-Western state institutional capacity and the techniques of good governance, particularly in areas such as democracy, civil society and the rule of law. External conditionality is rapidly declining except with relation to matters of domestic state governance, while a quarter of all bilateral aid to Africa is now channelled directly into state capacity-building (CFA, 2005: 136).

3) *The participatory imperative.* As the needs of the Other increasingly become central to the legitimisation of foreign policy practices, the concern is with the political inclusion, voice and participation of the Other. The legitimisation of Western power is sought in the empowerment of excluded sections of non-Western societies, the foremost of these being 'the poor'. International policy forums require the engagement of the Other and international policy frameworks require the Other to be involved in the policy process, in fact, they cast the Other in a leading role. It now appears that needs-based international policy-making is actually made by and for Others. This dynamic of evasion takes a form of practices which increase the regulatory reach of external policy-makers and international institutions, extending from the institutions of the non-Western state into non-Western societies, as needs-based constituencies are created and given voice. The responsibility and accountability of Western powers and international institutions are increasingly sidelined by the focus on the Other.

In effect, Other-regarding ethical foreign policy frameworks of the 2000s have ensured that politics (understood as the clash of coherent interests) has been largely sucked out of foreign policy-making. As Western governments and international institutions wield increasingly greater authority over and inside the institutions of non-Western states the question of the legitimacy and accountability of this power has been increasingly evaded. In fact, the more that interests have been displaced by Other-regarding ethics the more it appears that interstate, or inter-national, relations have been relegated to the margins of international policy-making.

Western states and international institutions appear less as external or coercive forces and more as facilitators, empowerers and capacity-builders. In the context of the ethical frameworks of today, the key tools of intervention and regulation are much less likely to be ones of military intervention or coercive external conditionality. This form of ethical foreign policy has obfuscated the projection of Western power – making the projection of power appear as an act of empowerment rather than of domination – and, in the process, has transformed the appearance of the international sphere from one of power, coercion and contestation into one where it appears that non-Western states have ownership of policies which are externally imposed and where it is the poorest and most excluded sections of non-Western societies which are the agents of policy.

MORE NEEDS, LESS INTERESTS AND LESS ACCOUNTABILITY

With the end of the Cold War, questions were posed over the legitimisation of Western hegemonic power in the international sphere. Security interests, so dominant in the Cold War – in a clearly expressed struggle between two different superpower-led blocs with different ideological aims – waned as a justification for interventionist and regulatory frameworks through which the exercise of Western power could be articulated (see, for example, Laïdi, 1998). Problems of the articulation of a positive self-interest, as opposed to the expression of self-interest as a struggle for Cold War survival, were difficult to address for Western political elites. Western governments and leading political parties had increasingly little connection with their own societies and were undergoing their own struggle to reconceive their political purpose and coherence in the wake of the crumbling political framework of Left and Right. In this context, a positive political programme which could allow Western elites to take political responsibility for their international dominance proved illusive.

In the Cold War period, national interests in the West were fairly easily articulated against the security threat of the communist Other (Campbell, 1998a; Laïdi, 1998). A diverse range of values and aspirations were tied into this dichotomy of 'us' and 'them' and the underlying problems of articulating a positive collective vision (expressed clearly in the anti-Vietnam war protests and 'Culture Wars' from the late 1960s onwards) were ameliorated as long as the Cold War framework held (see Coker, 2001). With the end of the Cold War, it was much more difficult to substantiate both the basis of the common interests expressed in national foreign policy-making and the basis upon which any distinction could be made between an 'us' and a 'them'.

In the absence of the geopolitical divide of the Cold War, the foreign policy interests of Western political elites increasingly appeared as narrow ones of self-interest: the narrow political concerns of supporting political allies in other countries or the promotion of the interests of big banks and corporations in protecting their loans and investments. The everyday concerns and interests of foreign policy-makers appeared to be very distant from those of the public. Nevertheless, the international sphere became increasingly central to the self-identity of Western governments. It was in relation to the international that political elites sought to address the question of mission and coherence which was increasingly problematic in the domestic sphere. In the 1990s, concerns of human rights and practices of humanitarian intervention, particularly in the Balkans, made international policy-making central to the process of defining the values of US and British governments. In the words of Michael Ignatieff:

when policy was driven by moral motives, it was often driven by narcissism. We intervened not only to save others, but to save ourselves, or rather an image of ourselves as defenders of universal decencies. We wanted to show that the West 'meant' something. (1998: 95)

It was the distance which the international sphere provided that enabled values and higher aims to be more easily articulated (see Morgenthau, 1993: 49). Governments could declare their commitments to ethical causes which appeared to remove the accusation of petty self-interestedness and restore a sense of larger purpose (see Chandler, 2003). At the same time, the distance involved meant that there was less accountability if ethical foreign policy interventions failed to achieve their aims. As Ignatieff described, the attraction of ethical foreign policy was that there was always the get out clause, the moral exculpation, of 'we tried but they failed' (1998: 99).

The experience of using foreign policy to achieve largely self-serving domestic ends – of outlining a larger purpose and mission to government – was a mixed one. The distance and mediations of the international sphere were not adequate to enable governments entirely to avoid responsibility for the consequences of their interventions. In fact, the attempt to argue that 'we tried but they failed' was met with demands that we should not 'allow' them to fail and that the ethical imperative of meeting the needs of Others should not be restricted by outdated views of international law and should extend beyond impartial aid provision or neutral peacekeeping and even beyond a limited commitment to the 'risk-free' use of armed forces which prevented the deployment of ground forces (see, for example, Kaldor, 1998; Ignatieff, 2000; Wheeler, 2000). The clear power imbalance between Western powers and non-Western states made it difficult to avoid 'mission creep' – the extension of overt forms of regulatory control. Yet the more international mandates and remits were extended, the more the problems of matching ethical aspirations to results in practice were exposed. The 1990s experience of Somalia, Bosnia, and then of Kosovo, demonstrated the problems of taking direct responsibility for the outcomes of international intervention (a lesson that was reinforced with the debacle of the Coalition Provisional Administration in Iraq).

The ethical discourse of the 1990s was still clearly a discourse of 'us' and 'them' and suggested that only a select group of interventionist Western states were ethical enough to safeguard the interests of others (see also, Shaw, 1994: 180–1; Held, 1995: 232; Kaldor, 1998). The political responsibility was firmly placed on the shoulders of the intervening powers who inevitably failed to live up to the expectations generated by the rejection of traditional interests for Other-orientated ethical values. The defensive shift away from attempts to articulate interests merely resulted in strengthening the critique that it was the narrow self-interests of Western powers which prevented greater consistency in the practice of ethical foreign policy. In the 1990s, ethical foreign policy practices, particularly humanitarian intervention, came under sustained criticism for not being ethical enough. Not enough concern was held to be expressed with regard to intervening and providing support to fragile societies prior to collapse and civil conflict and neither was there felt to be adequate concern paid to post-conflict reconstruction and peace-building. These concerns were broadly articulated in the Brahimi report on UN peacekeeping reform in 2000 (UN, 2000) and in the ICISS *Responsibility to Protect* report, at the end of 2001, which called for greater attention to the 'responsibility to prevent' and the 'responsibility to rebuild' (ICISS, 2001a).

Since the late 1990s, the ethical grounding of 'liberal imperialism' has been challenged from within (Cooper, 2002). It has been Western states and international institutions that have made the running in shifting away from the antagonistic and divisive ethics of the 'interventionist' 1990s. In the 1990s, selected concerns of human rights and selective practices of humanitarian intervention seemed to conflict with Western self-interest and highlight these self-interests as a limiting factor. Other-regarding ethics in the following decade have recast the relations of Self and Other. The promises and aspirations on the part of the Western states, donors and international institutions have become much more ambitious than the selective ethical goals of the 1990s. In the following decade, the ethical claims multiplied exponentially, to 'saving Africa', 'eradicating poverty', 'combating HIV/AIDS', and 'promoting education/health/women's equality/youth rights everywhere'. In this extension of the object of need – in fact, in the universalising of this object – there is the appearance, at least, of a genuinely global agenda based on the needs of 'common humanity'. Central to this has been the merging of the self-interested concerns of security and the Other-regarding concerns of development and poverty reduction. This has led to the expansion of the ethical focus to the needs of a generalised Other.

The merging of development and security can be seen in the origination and the mainstreaming of the concept of 'human security' in the 1990s. This first emerged with the holistic paradigm of human development articulated in the early 1990s within the UN Development Programme (UNDP) by Mahbub ul Haq, originator of the Human Development Reports, first issued in 1990, and given intellectual foundation by Nobel Laureate Amartya Sen (see, for example, Sen, 1999). The UNDP's *Human Development Report 1994* was the first major international document to articulate the emerging consensus on the merging of security and development: the shift away from security perceived as the protection of Self (national) interest to the needs (economic, health, environmental, security, etc.) of the Other (UNDP, 1994: 22–5). In the late 1990s, the human security approach was increasingly mainstreamed by national governments and international institutions. In 2001, Sen chaired the International Commission on Human Security established by the UN. The 2003 commission report, *Human Security Now*, asserted that human security was not merely about meeting the security needs of the Other rather than the Self, but about empowering the Other (UN, 2003: 2). With the merging of security and development in the discourse of human security, the relations of power and interest are erased as the 'freedom' and 'empowerment' of the Other takes centre stage. As Gordon Brown, the UK government's Chancellor of the Exchequer, has argued: 'A century ago people talked of "What we could do to Africa". Last century, it was "What can we do for Africa?" Now in 2006, we must ask what the developing world, empowered, can do for itself' (Brown, 2006). The March 2005 report of the UN Secretary-General, *In Larger Freedom*, argues that 'the notion of larger freedom' at the centre of the report, 'encapsulates the idea that development, security and human rights go hand in hand' (UN, 2005a: 5).

It is 'fear *for* the Other' as much as 'fear *of* the Other' which is alledged to drive the foreign policy of ethics rather than interests. The common aspect is that of fear, but this should not blind us to the fundamental difference between foreign policies driven by a rational state subject to meet politically and ideologically cohered ends and foreign policy in which the policy-maker has disappeared as a rational subjective actor and merely reacts to the threats of the Other or acts only as facilitator and empowerer with no articulated and clear agenda or mission of its own. The less clearly articulated any foreign policy aims are the more needs and threats blur into an amorphous mass of Otherness.

This explains the prevalent approach where all problems are related to each other: poverty leads to human rights vulnerability and instability; insecurity from war or terrorism undermines economic development; and good governance, which safeguards human rights, helps prevent conflict and overcome obstacles to development (UN, 2005a: 5–6). Everyone is exposed to these risks and therefore all actors (state or non-state) share the same interest in addressing them. Acting in enlightened self-interest therefore means acknowledging the needs of Others. Global cooperation means that 'every country's policies take into account not only the needs of its own citizens but also the needs of others' (UN, 2005a: 6).

The sidelining of the United Nations when it comes to legitimising military intervention, for example, over Kosovo and Iraq, should not obscure the leading role of the UN as central institution of choice for the Other-regarding ethics of disinterested cooperation. The UN Millennium Development Goals have become the central mechanism of engaging leading Western states and international financial institutions in a new needs-based ethics of international regulation and the establishment of a new architecture for Western/non-Western engagement. There are eight broad goals, adopted at the UN's Millennium Summit in September 2000: eradicating extreme poverty and hunger; achieving universal primary education; promoting gender equality and empowering women; reducing child mortality; improving maternal health; combating HIV/AIDS, malaria and other diseases; ensuring environmental sustainability; and developing a global partnership for development (elucidated fully in UNMP, 2005a).

The guidelines for partnership were established with the first major shift away from external coercion and towards externally guided empowerment, the late 1990s development of the Highly Indebted Poor Country (HIPC) initiative and its extension to the replacement of structural adjustment programmes with poverty reduction strategies and their later integration into the broader regulatory frameworks of the Millennium Development Goals. The linking of development, security and good governance has emphasised the ends of development and security through the process of reforms of governance linked with greater amounts of external aid. This pact has been termed the 'Monterrey Consensus', elaborated in 2002 at the International Conference on Financing for Development, held in Monterrey, Mexico. In exchange for developing countries putting in place mechanisms to strengthen good governance and establish national development strategies, developed countries pledged to provide greater levels of support in terms of development assistance, trade reform and debt relief (UN, 2005a: 12).

The key concept in the foreign policy framework of Other-regarding ethics is partnership. Gone is the language of intervention and external conditionality. For the UN, at the heart of the Monterrey Consensus are 'the principles of mutual responsibility and mutual accountability' – all states are to be judged on their commitment and performance, not just non-Western states (UN, 2005a: 22). The conception of Western states or international institutions having distinct political interests is seen as one that no longer holds true today, beyond the idea that their interests are in technocratic and administrative concerns which are shared with those of non-Western states.

The greater, and more universal, the needs of the Other, the less focus there has been upon the Western Self. Rather than coercively highlighting particular examples, ethical projections of Western power have shifted to highlighting much more general problems, such as 'failed' and 'failing' states, poverty and exclusion. The Other has become generalised, less as a Schmittian threat, more as a generalised Lévinasian need. A need which is so great that no one country alone can take the responsibility of acting upon this ethical imperative. With the extension of 'needs' both the interests of Western powers and their particular or individual responsibility or accountability have been eroded.

FROM EXTERNAL RELATIONS TO PARTNERS IN GOVERNANCE

The ethical goals expressed in the mantra of development, security and human rights are writ large and express the ethical imperative of responsibility to Others while lacking a concrete high-profile focus which could entail a risk of more awkward questions being posed of Western governments. It seems that there is a division of responsibility; while the declaration of these ambitious goals is the task of government leaders, often made at intergovernmental forums, the translation of these abstract goals into policy is taken out of the political sphere of international relations. At the country-to-country level there has been a marked shift in emphasis away from foreign policy-making, or the articulation of clear external interests, to partnership assistance in the form of technical and administrative advice and expertise in state-building: strengthening, empowering and capacity-building non-Western state institutions.

It is the need to transform externally the governance of non-Western states which is the central theme which emerges from the global needs-based agenda. As UK Prime Minister Tony Blair's Commission for Africa report, *Our Common Interest*, states:

Africa's history over the last fifty years has been blighted by two areas of weakness. These have been capacity – the ability to design and deliver policies; and accountability – how well a state answers to its people. Improvements in both are first and foremost the responsibility of African countries and people. But action by rich nations is essential too ... Without progress in governance, all other reforms will have limited impact. (CFA, 2005: 14)

The UN 2005 Sachs report on the implementation of the UN Millennium Development Goals similarly argued that poor governance in non-Western states and the lack of state capacity were the key reasons for ongoing problems in meeting the MDGs and suggested greater attention to capacity-building state institutions in countries which are poor but reasonably well governed (most states, excepting those such as Belarus, Myanmar, North Korea and Zimbabwe) (UNMP, 2005b: 43). External capacity-building would therefore build on the aid given to countries which qualify for assistance under the US Millennium Challenge Account, have been involved in the HIPC process, are engaged in the New Partnership for Africa's Development (NEPAD) African Peer Review Mechanism (APRM) or have World Bank and IMF approval under the PRSP process. As the UN notes:

However well crafted on paper, investment strategies to achieve the Millennium Development Goals will not work in practice unless supported by States with transparent, accountable systems of governance, grounded in the rule of law, encompassing civil and political as well as economic and social rights, and underpinned by accountable and efficient public administration. Many of the poorest countries will need major capacity-building investments to put in place and maintain the necessary infrastructure and to train and employ qualified personnel. But without good governance, strong institutions and a clear commitment to rooting out corruption and mismanagement wherever it is found, broader progress will prove elusive. (UN, 2005a: 13)

Partnerships, with the goal of good governance and the capacity-building of non-Western states, are the framework through which the pursuit of ethical aspirations assumes the form of consensual mechanisms of the empowerment of Others. In this framework it is assumed that there are no political 'interests' involved, in the case of either Western states, donors and institutions or non-Western states. The Commission for Africa calls for 'a new kind of partnership', one that is no longer based on conflicting interests but technocratic management: 'In the past, contractual and conditional approaches were tried, and failed. What we are suggesting is a new kind of development, based on mutual respect and solidarity, and rooted in a sound analysis of what actually works' (CFA, 2005: 17).

In this regard it is often held that: 'Donors must change their behaviour and support the national priorities of African governments rather than allowing their own procedures and special enthusiasms to undermine the building of a country's own capacity' (CFA, 2005: 14). New approaches to good governance are held to stand 'in marked contrast to the approach of the 1980s and much of the 1990s, when aid was often ... aimed primarily at advancing the interests of the donor'

(CFA, 2005: 94). Aid was often 'tied', coming with a requirement to buy goods or services from the donor country, which often led to aid being expended on unsuitable or high cost outlays (CFA, 2005: 92). As UK Secretary of State for International Development Hilary Benn stated in 2005, the key concern of the UK government was to 'make a clean break from past practice which sought to enforce particular policy choices' (Benn, 2005: 1). The UK Department for International Development (DFID) has particularly emphasised the importance of intervention to 'support policy leadership by developing countries without imposing our own views' (DFID, 2005: iii):

In recent years the UK has been moving away from traditional approaches to conditionality. We believe that it is inappropriate and has proven to be ineffective for donors to impose policies on developing countries. Instead, we believe that successful aid relationships must be based on mutual commitment and dialogue, transparency and accountability. (DFID, 2005: 4)

The Monterrey summit and subsequent UN documents have been very quick to highlight that 'each developing country has primary responsibility for its own development' (for example, UN, 2005a: 12). 'Country ownership' has been central to post-1990s calls for ethical people-centred policy interventions. As the Commission for Africa report claims in its introduction:

Our starting point was the recognition that Africa must drive its own development. Rich nations should support that, because it is in our common interest to make the world a more prosperous and secure place ... But what is clear is that if Africa does not create the right conditions for development, then any amount of outside support will fail. (CFA, 2005: 1)

The idea of African 'ownership' through international 'partnership' has been the motivating factor behind regional as well as national initiatives. In this regard, the New Partnership for African Development, established in 2001, has been widely welcomed by Western governments as 'the most significant thing has come out of Africa ... because it is an African made, African owned and African driven process' (Benn, 2003: 7). The US aid and development policies operate on a similar basis of promoting external engagement as a product of developing country-led partnership. Partnership is the key principle of the MCA, established in 2004, and is heralded as one of the lessons learned from development aid over the past 50 years.

Operate as Partners: Working closely with the MCC [Millennium Challenge Corporation], countries that receive MCA assistance will be responsible for identifying the greatest barriers to their own development, ensuring civil society participation, and developing an MCA program. MCA participation will require a high-level commitment from the host government. Each MCA country will enter into a public Compact with the MCC that includes a multi-year plan for achieving development objectives and identifies the responsibilities of each partner in achieving those objectives. (MCA, 2005)

In the past, the relationship of external donors and non-Western states was a contractual one between two or more 'partners'. Contractual relations at the level of state governments made the lending and grant conditions the subject of international relations, i.e. they were officially negotiated between independent contracting subjects. This clarity and separation of international and domestic accountability has become increasingly blurred. Graham Harrison has used the term 'post-conditionality' to describe this blurring of the 'outside' and the 'inside' (2001):

post-conditionality [is] one aspect of the politics of adjustment, a more encompassing framework which is based on the ongoing power of the IFIs by virtue of the 'permanent crisis' of indebtedness ... post-conditionality is ... a useful characterization of a set of significant developments within donor-state relations, based on ... forms of donor intervention which are not merely based on the threat of sanction which is at the heart of the conditionality mechanism. (Harrison, 2001: 658)

Overt and clearly stated contractual relations between non-Western states and Western states and international institutions, such as those under the World Bank and IMF structural adjustment programmes, open the relationship to political accountability, bringing responsibility to bear on both the non-Western government and the bi-lateral or international donor. The Commission for Africa argues that:

We do not advocate a partnership where there is a narrow set of specific contracts between African countries and outside bodies. That risks becoming adversarial and unpredictable and does not show the trust and mutual respect which is vital for a deep partnership to work. Similarly a partnership based on heavy conditionality set by outsiders will fail. It too is destined to lose the solidarity which should bind a partnership together. The binding forces must be solidarity and mutual respect. (CFA, 2005: 89)

Here, the informal mechanisms of post-conditionality are argued for on the grounds of trust and respect for the Other, but the Commission's report also suggests other grounds for avoiding the formal contractual relationship – the fact that 'excessive conditionality together with demands for constant reporting risk making African governments feel more accountable to foreign donors than to their own people' (CFA, 2005: 92). If non-Western governments felt that they were more accountable to external actors and were highly conscious of their limited capacity to further the interests of their societies against these external pressures, this was because the mechanisms of external pressure were clear. Under more informal mechanisms, where external pressures operate within the policy-making processes of the non-Western state, rather than at the level of sovereignty – where governments have to publicly confront external actors – political clarification of the role of external influence is prevented.

External intervention is exercised in ways which blur traditional understandings of external and internal interests. Donor engagement no longer confronts non-Western states solely as an external imposition but as internal capacity-building, through a much closer and more intimate engagement with governing institutions, especially Ministries of Finance. Harrison acutely observes that the orthodox internal-external distinctions are less useful and that the 'national-international boundary has been rendered so much more porous' (2001: 661). The extension of the 'non-political' technocratic ethics of the World Bank to the fields of good governance and state capacity-building has meant the depoliticising of, and external regulatory intervention in, areas once considered to be the preserve of domestic regimes. The shift from government to governance, from policy-making as an internal process to an internationalised process, has gone along with externally driven democratisation initiatives (see further, Chapter 3). For example, the World Bank's 2000 strategy document *Reforming Public Institutions and Strengthening Governance* argues that, in Africa, managerial reform of governance could include, if necessary: 'Amending the constitution to redefine the role of the state, introduce new governance arrangements, change the machinery of government or alter the balance of power among the executive and parliament' (cited in Marquette, 2004: 420).

External regimes of governance have become internalised through state capacity-building in conjunction with debt reduction or increases in external aid in exchange for a more direct role for external actors in domestic policy processes. For example, in July 2005, the Paris Club of rich Western countries announced the biggest single debt relief in Africa's history with a plan to exchange Nigeria's foreign debt for the international regulation of its government's spending. Central to this was the establishment of a key policy coordination role for Nigeria's Millennium Development Committee. The committee, chaired by the President, Olusegun Obasanjo, internationalised the domestic policy-making process in Nigeria by including representatives of the World Bank and IMF along with representatives from international NGOs Action Aid and Oxfam (Elliott and Wintour, 2005). In the case of international development, capacity-building has often been focused on the Ministry of Finance. In Uganda and Tanzania, for example, the Ministry of Finance has received a lion's share of external funding for administrative reform programmes which have focused both on 'soft' capacities, i.e. the administrative and technical skills training of personnel, and 'hard' capacities, i.e. information systems and technologies. This external support has enabled the Finance Ministry to become the most powerful sector of government, in terms of capacity and influence (the Ministries of the Interior in contrast lack computerised systems and access to reliable information) (Harrison, 2001: 664–6). It is the sectors of government which have been capacity-built which are then the main conduits for external influence, leading the negotiations with the international financial institutions and being the authorising authorities for all project and programme funding regardless of the policy sector involved.

The process of capacity-building goes beyond the restructuring of government ministries to direct regulatory control over the policy-making process itself:

In fact, rather than conceptualising donor power as a strong external force on the state, it would be more useful to conceive of donors as part of the state itself. This is not just because so much of the budgeting process is contingent on the receipt of donor finance, but also because of the way programmes and even specific policies are designed and executed ... [D]onor sub-groups meet [with government officials] every fortnight or every month ... there is a group for each major industry which receives donor funding ... the purposes of which are to discuss policy progress, monitor the disbursement of funds, and consider further funding options. These meetings have become a routine part of the way the government works. (Harrison, 2001: 669)

In this context, it is difficult to conceive of the institutions of many non-Western states as having a 'domestic' existence. The civil service is trained and assisted by external experts and produces reports not just for government ministers but also for external donors and international institutions and foreign states. The government ministries develop policy in close cooperation with external bodies and often with the policy aim of influencing these authorities to continue or to extend their assistance. The institutions and mechanisms of governance of non-Western states are often no longer in any sense separable from the international mechanisms of governance which they are engaged with.

As Harrison notes, the focus on good governance and non-Western state capacity as the key to development and security 'lays culpability for the general failure of adjustment on the states themselves, not on SAP [Structural Adjustment Programmes], or the nature of global economic change' (2001: 660). As Western governments and international institutions then have little responsibility for political decision-making or accountability for outcomes, the everyday management of foreign policy and foreign development aid becomes a task for bureaucrats and administrative experts; and, if they fail, this does not reflect on the Western states and institutions involved. As Michael Ignatieff argues in his more recent work, with Simon Chesterman and Ramesh Thakur:

States cannot be made to work from the outside. International assistance may be necessary, but it is never sufficient to establish institutions that are legitimate and sustainable ... international action should be seen first and foremost as facilitating local processes, providing resources and creating the space for local actors. (Chesterman, Ignatieff and Thakur, 2005c: 384)

For these authors the 'key insight is that states cannot be made to work from the outside' and they stress that 'for international actors, this is a humbling conclusion' which puts the emphasis on the local actors who must 'seize responsibility – "ownership" in the present jargon' (Chesterman, Ignatieff and Thakur, 2005b: 9). The emphasis is on non-Western states to bear the accountability in the case of their failure to live up to the ambitious ethical claims made by Western states and international institutions.

Far from Western powers and institutions projecting a confident transformative project, the assertion of external power is held to be merely one of facilitating, empowering and capacity-building non-Western states. The projection of Western power takes the form of a non-political discourse where political interests are held to be subservient to the technical expertise of administration. Most importantly, the desire to deny Western influence and agency means that non-Western state institutions are increasingly colonised by external policy actors as international institutions seek to informalise their role in policy-making. This creates artificial state institutions which have a much more attenuated relationship with their own societies but also little influence with regard to policy negotiations with external actors. The close liaison between international institutions and international NGOs and leading government ministries has been driven by the informalisation of the regulatory process and the desire to avoid an open intergovernmental discussion of economic policy. It is this desire for evasion which would appear to be driving the shift from international to domestic discussion and the focus on state capacity, rather than any shift in the content of the policies or any desire to open up policy-making to wider consultation and involvement.

Despite the rhetoric of 'country ownership' there has been little change in the basic policy approach of international institutions or, of course, in the power relations involved. All national PRSPs must first be screened by joint-staff assessments from the staff of the World Bank and IMF. The approval of PRSPs is the fundamental condition for securing credit extensions, grants and debt relief, from other donors as well as new credits under the IMF's Poverty Reduction and Growth Facility (PRGF) – the successor to the Enhanced Structural Adjustment Facility – and the World Bank's Poverty Reduction Support Credits. (Rowden and Irama, 2004: 7–12). It would appear that the state capacity-building impetus stems from the need to present the process as one of partnership or poor state 'leadership' and 'country ownership' rather than Western imposition.

The shift from the projection of Western influence as a coercive external relation to a relationship of domestic partnership removes the emphasis on external accountability for policy and its outcomes. This has made state-building the central sphere of intervention for Western assertions of ethical purpose or mission and in the course of this process, both the foreign policy-making of Western states and the political sphere of non-Western states have been increasingly reduced to narrow technocratic and administrative concerns. The governance sphere of non-Western states is both the target for Western Other-regarding interventions and the excuse for ethical rhetoric not being matched by reality.

THE PARTICIPATORY IMPERATIVE

Power legitimated on the basis of the needs of the Other has resulted in new mechanisms and practices of legitimisation. Many of these have sprung from the participatory imperative, the externally imposed need not just to claim country ownership but also to demonstrate that the policies which are 'owned' are derived from the participation and consultation of those in need. Country-ownership, it appears, is not enough to distance policy-making in the West from the responsibilities of power. At the same time as non-Western states are becoming increasingly infiltrated by external agencies and core areas of governance internationalised, the ethical discourse of Western regulation stresses the 'opening up of new spaces for participation' and the increasing accountability and transparency of non-Western state policy-making. While good governance is increasingly being redefined as pro-poor accountability and efficiency, politics is increasingly displaced in non-Western states by externally framed spending plans which insist on 'needs-based' and 'goal-orientated' policy-making. Ironically, the more artificial the partnership between the international institutions and the non-Western state the more the process of denial is extended, pushing the dynamic of capacity-building and empowerment into societies themselves.

In the past, the demand for public consultation and participation in policy-making was proclaimed by social movements that sought to challenge the interests of powerful elites and to forward popular interests. Today, it is Western states and international financial institutions that are leading the demand for the extension of participation in the political process, for transparency and for consultation. It is important to recognise that the participatory framework which is being institutionalised under external guidance has little connection with forms of political participation being generated from within non-Western states themselves. The shift towards participatory regimes of needs assessment, policy consultation and monitoring of implementation comes from external institutions seeking to legitimise their technocratic agendas, ethically informed by the focus on those socially and economically excluded. As the UN Sachs report outlines, the integration of poverty reduction with the Millennium Development Goals necessitates the mapping out of needs according to locality and gender, followed by needs assessments which then have to be worked up into a framework of policy deliverables; the process from start to finish depending on an accountable and efficient public administration which involves participation, 'especially by poor people' (UNMP, 2005b: 36).

The Other-regarding ethics of Empire in Denial insist that today's regulatory 'package is not to be applied in a top-down fashion', but instead should be 'designed locally with strong participation' and even emphasises 'the importance of culture in shaping development goals and instruments' (CFA, 2005: 95). Rather than an external influence on the affairs of non-Western governments, pro-poor intervention is couched in the language of empowerment, against the 'interests' of both Western 'experts' and non-Western governing elites and favouring the traditionally excluded voices of women and youth (CFA, 2005: 141). International NGOs, such as Oxfam, Save the Children and Concern International, have been heavily supported by bilateral donors, such as the United States Agency for International Development (USAID) and DFID, in their capacity-building work. Participatory poverty assessments and poverty and social impact analyses (PSIAs) are often held to inform policy practices and put the needs of 'the poor' to the forefront. As Jeremy Gould and Julia Ojanen note:

The legitimacy of post-SAP policies is being sought through the establishment of direct channels of communication between the policy elite and 'the poor' – a sort of 'fast-track' democracy based on localized forms of 'participatory' and 'consultative' interaction. (2003: 15)

One way in which the external agenda of international institutions and major donors is facilitated through the mechanisms of empowerment is in the sidelining of the discussion of political interests. Like Baudrillard's 'Silent Majority' (1983), 'the poor' who are the object of the participatory imperative lack any collective social voice. They are a fictional political subject with 'nothing to do with any real population, body or specific social aggregate' (Baudrillard, 1983: 5). In fact, the poor – the basis of pro-poor policies – are specifically politically constructed so as to lack any political voice at all. Alastair Fraser argues that the framework of participatory poverty assessments, which highlight the needs of the most marginal sections of society, creates a participatory framework which ascribes identities on the basis of need rather than capacity (as elderly, children, poor, female, disabled, etc.). It is these ascribed identities which are legitimised over identities based on political organisation or political interests as represented by political parties or organisations.

Narrow political interests are seen to be illegitimate, as they are based on self-interest rather than on the good of society as a whole. As World Bank former chief economist Joseph Stiglitz argues: 'Openness, transparency, and democratic processes provide an important check on the operation of special interest groups and the extent of corruption' (cited in Marquette, 2004: 420). In the ethical discourse of the needs of the Other, traditional sectional political interests are understood to be corrupt and self-serving and to privilege private group interests over the needs of the community as a whole. Anti-corruption and transparency are tools which reinforce the technical vision of needs-based consensus, putting pressure on parochial or traditional ties of affinity as much as those of an overtly political nature. The abstract and non-political concept of the poor is called upon to legitimise the new frameworks of external regulation. In this way, participatory frameworks tend to privilege professional pro-poor advocacy groups, trained by international NGOs and able to express themselves in the technical form required of World Bank forums (Fraser, 2005: 329–34).

The participatory framework, focused on consensus around technical pro-poor approaches ensures that little disagreement is possible. As David Craig and Doug Porter note:

PRSPs provide a unique framing of poverty apparently amenable to diverse, often conflicting interests – in their preparation, ministries of finance sit together with ministries of local government, education or social welfare, and bilateral donors and IFIs commune with representatives of local and international NGOs, engineering contactors and private entrepreneurs. But the PRSP aims to be far more than a forum for exchange about priorities; rather, in practice, PRSPs must be administered according to globally prescribed budget management and accountability arrangements through which available resources are, and are seen to be, converted into measurable changes in agreed indicators of need. PRSP re-framing of poverty, via the combination of poverty assessments, macro-planning and budgeting with debt relief, plurally-funded poverty alleviation approaches and decentralized governance is now a fact of life in the bulk of poor countries. (2002: 10)

However, as Gould and Ojanen state, 'there is a risk of inflating the significance of the PPA' (2003: 71). As noted above, the separation between the policy-making process and the domestic political process makes the focus on participation a misleading one. In fact, the 'actual impact on policy substance is negligible'; the artificial mechanisms of participation seem to have been created less to regulate and control the policy process than to legitimise it (Gould and Ojanen, 2003: 76). What has changed under the framework of Other-regarding ethics is not the relationship of power between the non-Western state and international institutions but the accountability for policy-making. The focus on capacity-building has, in fact, meant a significant narrowing of the agenda of international relations. The problems of poverty and conflict are no longer seen as international problems, or even as questions which call for policy discussions around specific external relations, for example, the regulatory regimes of the international financial institutions. The focus has narrowed to the sphere of domestic governance questions and in particular the budgetary controls and expenditures in the fields of health and education (see Rowden and Irama, 2004).

The context and the top-down nature of the participatory imperatives would have to be ignored for these schemes to be made out to be more than decorative measures. As discussed above, the framework is premised on the prior acceptance of a range of policies and reforms deemed necessary for debt sustainability and the acceptance that the debt relief will be channelled into pro-poor frameworks. The fact that these frameworks are then held to be decided by participatory mechanisms of decision-making seeks to obscure the relations of policy-making power. PRSPs are held to enhance country ownership of economic and adjustment and reform programmes but as Craig and Porter note, they are a means of ensuring the depoliticisation of the policy process, taking poverty reduction outside the formal relations of government, through ring-fencing resources to particular needs in accordance with negotiated agreements (2002).

CONCLUSION

Many commentators focus on the power relations behind the new 'consensual' approaches (for example, Abrahamsen, 2004; Harrison, 2004; Fraser, 2005; Pender, 2005). However, the question that this chapter has sought to address is not whether power relations exist but, rather, why the exercise of power is expressed in these specific practices; why the mechanisms of regulation take the form they do. In doing this it has engaged with the Other-regarding ethics which appear to be increasingly influential in shaping Western foreign policy. It has suggested that Western governments and international institutions find it difficult to justify and legitimise their power of regulation over non-Western states, especially where the power relations are so clearly unequal, as with Africa.

It is in response to the current crisis of confidence in Western authority and purpose that there has been a rethinking of Western development policies and a shift towards much more informal relations of regulation which have enabled greater levels of interference in non-Western states but also have enabled Western policy-makers to shift the burden of responsibility for policy outcomes.

The ethics of the Other have enabled the past problems to be rewritten as ones of non-Western state-governing capacity at the same time as denying accountability for present policy strictures. Paradoxically, the attempt to deny power and accountability has driven the extension of external mechanisms of regulation. The reason for this is that needs-based, as opposed to interest-based, legitimacy has depended on the engagement with and, essentially, the creation of the Lévinasian Other in order to legitimise the Western Self. In order for the Other to be given the task of 'policy leadership' it needs to be artificially given shape and externally capacity-built. This process, as considered above, cannot be easily contained. The capacity-building dynamic necessarily extends from the non-Western state to non-Western societies as the Other-regarding ethical imperative of intervention demands legitimacy. This dynamic is key to understanding the particular form that Western regulation and the projection of Western power often assumes today.

5
Denial of the EU's Eastern Empire

According to the April 2005 report of the International Commission on the Balkans, *The Balkans in Europe's Future*:

If the EU does not devise a bold strategy for accession that could encompass all Balkan countries as new members within the next decade, then it will become mired instead as a neo-colonial power in places like Kosovo, Bosnia and even Macedonia. Such an anachronism would be hard to manage and would be in contradiction with the very nature of the European Union. The real choice the EU is facing in the Balkans is: Enlargement or Empire. (ICB, 2005: 11)

This quote sharply sums up the dilemma facing Western Europe, or the EU, with the end of the Cold War – how to relate to and manage its new eastern empire. The response of the EU has been to engage in external regulation and relationship management interventions but at the same time to deny that it is exercising its authority over the region. It is entirely appropriate for the international commission to pose the EU's policy choices as state-building or empire and it is this dilemma which has driven the enlargement process. This denial of empire has taken the form of state-building and the extension of the enlargement process to South Eastern Europe and the Balkans.

Where the international commission is slightly out of step with reality is in the assertion that the question of 'Enlargement or Empire' was one being posed in 2005. In fact, it was essentially resolved in 1999 when, with the end of the Kosovo war in April, the European Union headed an ambitious international experiment in state-building in the SEE region. State-building has enabled the EU to project its power in the therapeutic framework of capacity-building and empowering its eastern neighbours rather than posing the questions of political responsibility which are raised with empire. Instead of posing the question of Europe's imperial mission, state-building shifts the focus to the governing regime of the potential candidates.

State-building involves no less expenditure of resources than empire, in fact, if anything, state-building is more invasive and regulatory. Empire in Denial is not hesitant to intervene but to assume political responsibility. The state-building process of EU enlargement has been able to be highly regulatory precisely on the basis that the regulatory mechanisms invest political responsibility in the candidate countries while denying the EU's domination. In enlargement, domination and denial come together in a particularly forceful way. The EU's experiments in evading the political responsibilities of power have been described as implying no less than the 'reforming and reinventing [of] the state in South Eastern Europe' (ESI, 2001a: 18). As the European Stability Initiative observed:

A new consensus is emerging among both regional and international actors that the most fundamental obstacle to the advance of democracy and security in South Eastern Europe is the lack of effective and accountable state institutions. Strengthening domestic institutions is increasingly viewed as the key priority across the diverse sectors of international assistance, as relevant to human rights and social inclusion as it is to economic development and democratisation. (ESI, 2001a: 18)

This chapter considers the state-building practices of the EU in SEE in more detail, particularly as they have operated since 1999 through the mechanisms of the Stabilisation and Association process and the Stability Pact for South Eastern Europe. It seeks to highlight how the EU has denied its power in the very processes of exercising it, through: presenting its diktat in the language of 'partnership' and country 'ownership'; internationalising the mechanisms of its domination through engaging a multitude of external states and international organisations; internationalising or Europeanising the candidate state's core institutions of governance; and through engaging with and attempting to create a policy-advocating 'civil society'.

These features demonstrate a remarkably close affinity to the state-building processes exercised by Empire in Denial in Africa and elsewhere, through the development and poverty reduction agenda, and suggest that it is the process of denial which is key to understanding these mechanisms rather than the needs or problems of SEE states themselves. This chapter concludes by considering some of the limitations to this process, to be drawn out further in Chapters 7 and 8.

STATE-BUILDING

Although some ideas for the extension of external involvement in the region had developed prior to the Kosovo war, 'the NATO intervention undoubtedly acted as a catalyst in strengthening international political will for co-ordinated and preventive action in the region' (SPSEE, 2006a). The EU's Regional Approach of 1997 was replaced with a more ambitious one in April and May 1999: the Stabilisation and Association process. This process went beyond the offer of 'contractual relations' (Trade and Cooperation Agreements) to motivating reform through the prospect of potential membership once the relevant conditions had been met. The prospect of future EU membership was explicitly offered to Albania, Bosnia, Croatia, Macedonia and the FRY (Federal Republic of Yugoslavia, at the time of writing, the state of Serbia and Montenegro) at the Feira European Council in June 2000. The SAp involved preferential trade concessions, the CARDS programme and a new contractual relationship of reform assistance, the Stabilisation and Association Agreement (SAA).

In July 1999, the Stability Pact for SEE was launched which also sought to shape governance in return for the promise of integration into Euro-Atlantic structures. Founded at the EU's initiative, in the Stability Pact's founding document more than 40 partner countries and organisations undertook to assist in the capacity-building of the SEE states. The states and organisations involved in the Stability Pact make an impressive list, demonstrating the international collaborative nature of the state-building project which was to take a more generalised form in the 2000s. The members included the G8 members, EU member states, the European Commission, the countries of the region and their neighbours, international organisations, such as the UN, OSCE, Council of Europe, the United Nations High Commissioner for Refugees (UNHCR), NATO, OECD and international financial institutions, including the World Bank, IMF, the European Bank for Reconstruction and Development (EBRD), European Investment Bank and the Council of Europe Development Bank.

Unlike the EU, the Stability Pact was not a formal international organisation. Following the earlier creation of ad hoc international bodies to coordinate international activity in the region – for example, the Contact Group (of France, Germany, Britain, Italy, Russia and the US), responsible for coordinating policy on the Balkans, and the ad hoc coalition of 55 states and international institutions which formed the Peace Implementation Council (until 1995, known as the International Conference on the Former Yugoslavia), which took on formal responsibility for regulating the international administration of Bosnia. The Stability Pact had no formal constitution and no independent financial resources, relying on the Special Coordinator and a 30-member team funded by the European Union and headquartered in Brussels.

Under the auspices of the Stability Pact there has been an international division of labour, through which different areas of policy-making have been guided by different international bodies. The leading role in infrastructure development, economic restructuring and in general private sector development has been taken by the World Bank, European Investment Bank, EBRD and the IMF, with facilitating support from the European Commission. Initiatives in post-conflict reconciliation, refugee return, good governance, democratisation and institution-building have been led by the European Commission, bilateral EU member state programmes and other international organisations (for example, the Council of Europe and the OSCE). States in the SEE region have also received support under the European Community Humanitarian Office aid programme, macro-financial assistance to stabilise national budgets and, since 2001 in Macedonia, support from the Community's Rapid Reaction Mechanism.

The international institutions, involved in stabilising and integrating the SEE states within European structures, viewed the question of governance as one of the three central issues (along with security and economic reform) which needed to be addressed for a successful state-building outcome. Within the sphere of SEE state governance, it was the key issues of institution-building and of civil society development which attracted the focus of international regulatory bodies. Both institution-building and civil society development were fairly new areas for international policy initiatives at the time and both reflected the existing power the EU had over the region which enabled external institutions to take an active interest in questions which were previously seen to be ones of domestic political responsibility.

It is important to note from the start the artificial and somewhat forced nature of the justifications for the EU's state-building project. The problems identified in the governance sphere were not with the formal mechanisms of democratic government or the electoral accountability of government representatives but were concerns that went beyond procedural questions of 'free and fair elections' to the administrative practices and policy choices of governments and the attitude, culture and participation-levels of their citizens. Regarding institution-building, the European Commission asserted that:

The lack of effective and accountable state institutions hampers the ability of each country to co-operate with its neighbours and to move towards the goal of closer integration with the EU. Without a solid institutional framework for the exercise of public power, free and fair elections will not lead to representative or accountable government. Without strong institutions to implement the rule of law, there is little prospect that states will either provide effective protection of human and minority rights or tackle international crime and corruption. (EC, 2001a: 8–9)

Where, only a few years previously, free and fair elections where seen to be the main indicator of representative and accountable government, institution-building was now held to be the key to democratic development. According to the Commission, strengthening state institutions was vital for 'assuring the region's future, being as relevant to human rights and social inclusion as it is to economic development and democratisation' (EC, 2001a: 9). While SEE states met the traditional democratic criteria, necessary for the incorporation of new members, such as Spain and Portugal, into Europe-wide mechanisms in the past, they were now held to fail in meeting the new, more exacting, standards which are being laid down for membership of European bodies at present (see Storey, 1995: 131–51).

Regarding the second aspect of governance, civil society, the Commission was even more forthright in its condemnation of the aspiring members involved in the Stabilisation and Association process:

none of the countries can yet claim to have the level of vibrant and critical media and civil society that is necessary to safeguard democratic advances. For example, public and media access to information, public participation in policy debate and accountability of government and its agencies are aspects of civil society which are still largely undeveloped in all five of the countries. (EC, 2001b: 10–11)

In this case, the aspirant member states from the SEE region could apparently not even make a 'claim' that they could safeguard 'democracy' in their states without external assistance in the form of civil society capacity-building. In fact, the Commission was clearly concerned by society in the region as much as by government, arguing that the aim of its new programmatic development was necessarily broad in order 'to entrench a culture ... which makes forward momentum towards the EU irreversible' (EC, 2002: 8).

The Commission argued that its focus on building the capacity of state institutions and civil society development reflected not only the importance of this question and the clear needs it had identified, 'but also the comparative advantage of the European Community in providing *real added value* in this area' (EC, 2001a: 9; emphasis added). It would appear that the SEE states were fortunate in that their wealthy neighbours to the West had not only identified their central problems but also happened to have the solutions to them already at hand.

THE UNEQUAL 'PARTNERSHIP'

Accession

The EU has operated a series of concentric circles of membership with regard to the states of SEE. In the first circle are the accession states Bulgaria and Romania: accession negotiations were concluded in December 2004 and a Treaty of Accession signed in April 2005 with a view to the two states joining as full members in January 2007. In both these states the EU has provided aid to support the governance framework through the Phare initiative. Approximately one-third of this funding was given to support institution-building, one-third for strengthening the regulatory infrastructure needed to ensure compliance with the *acquis*, and the remaining third to support policies of social and economic cohesion (EC, 2001c: 9). The financial support provided by the EU was an important resource for both these states; Bulgaria, for example, received around €300 million a year in Community grant-financed, preaccession assistance, equivalent to over 2 per cent of its GDP (EC, 2001d: 12).

The accession process effectively transfers large areas of government policy-making into the hands of EU officialdom as strict measures are laid down for adopting the EU *acquis* covering 29 Chapters amounting to almost 90,000 pages of EU regulations which must be adopted and implemented for membership. The 29 Chapters of the EU *acquis* concern: movement of goods; movement of persons; provision of services; movement of capital; company law; competition policy; agriculture; fisheries; transport; taxation; economic and monetary union; statistics; social policy and employment; energy; industrial policy; small and medium-sized enterprises; science and research; education and training; telecommunications and information technologies; culture and audio-visual; regional policy and coordination of structural instruments; environment; consumers and health protection; justice and home affairs; customs union; external relations; common foreign and security policy; financial control; and financial and budgetary provisions.

Both governments followed a prescribed framework establishing the National Programme for the Adoption of the *acquis* which detailed policy progress in each area as well as addressing additional accession criteria. There can be little doubt over the far-reaching nature of EU mechanisms intended to reshape the governance framework of these candidate countries. In order to facilitate this process, the governments of Bulgaria and Romania are funded by the CARDS programme, which assists:

in their efforts to adopt the *acquis* and strengthen the institutions necessary for implementing and enforcing the *acquis*. This also helps the candidate countries develop the mechanisms and institutions that will be needed to implement Structural Funds after accession and is supported by a limited number of measures (investment or grant schemes) with a regional or thematic focus. (EC, 2001c: 9–10)

The funding priorities are those that fit with the mechanisms of the EU, reshaping the domestic policy processes to follow external institutional requirements for EU relations both now and in the long-term future. In the direct field of governance reform, the framework for the reform of the public administration, civil service, parliamentary and executive procedures, the judiciary, and policing is drawn up by the EU and the specific content is guided through 'twinning' mechanisms, whereby external civil servants and policy-makers are drafted in by the EU (see below). This process has had little input from the elected political representatives or the citizens of these two states. In fact, in the October 2005 annual monitoring report on their progress, the European Commission complained that the *acquis* have not yet been fully translated into either Bulgarian or Romanian because of difficulties in recruiting and training the necessary staff to translate and revise the required 6,000 pages a month (EC, 2005a: 10).

The stabilisation and association process

Launched in May 1999, to cover Albania, Bosnia-Herzegovina, Croatia, Macedonia and Serbia-Montenegro, SAp is the cornerstone of EU policy towards SEE state-building through 'anchoring the region permanently to the development of the EU itself' (EC, 2001a: 3).

This 'anchoring' is seen as crucial to the encouragement of reforms in the governance sphere, relating to the rule of law and democratic and stable institutions. The legitimacy of the EU's relationship of regulation is based on two grounds, the promise of aid and of EU membership at some point in the future. The policy of aid in return for the EU's regulatory control over the reform process is underpinned by the CARDS assistance programme providing €4.65 billion over 2000–06. The legitimacy of this buying of external influence is bolstered by the promise of EU integration, i.e. 'on a credible prospect of membership once the relevant conditions have been met' (EC, 2001a: 3).

The November 2000 Zagreb Summit endorsed the SAp objectives and conditions, namely the prospect of accession on the basis of the Treaty on European Union and the 1993 Copenhagen criteria, the CARDS assistance programme and the countries' undertaking to abide by the EU's conditionality and to participate fully in the SAp process. Ahead of the EU-Western Balkan Thessaloniki summit in June 2003 the General Affairs and External Relations Council adopted the Thessaloniki agenda for moving towards European integration, strengthening the SAp by introducing new instruments to support reform and integration efforts, including European Partnerships, and this time including Kosovo, as governed under the auspices of UN Security Council Resolution 1244, within its remit (see, for example, EC, 2005b).

The European Union General Affairs Council argues that, for the SEE states, the process of formulating the SAp contract is 'both pedagogical and political' (EU, 2001). The 'pedagogical' aspect of the process highlights the relationship of subordination involved. As the EU reports 'the "Consultative Task Force/High Level Steering Group" approach has proved an effective means of focusing authorities' minds on essential reforms and of engaging with them *in a sustained way to secure implementation*' (EU, 2001: IIIc; emphasis added).

The SAp is closely linked with the EU-led Stability Pact, which comprises of a Regional Table and three Working Tables. The focus of this chapter is Working Table I, which concerns democratisation and human rights. These Working Tables are held to treat the SEE states as equal partners:

A special feature is that at Regional and Working Tables, representatives of the South Eastern European countries are, for the first time, on an equal footing with those of international organisations and financial institutions in advising on the future of their region and in jointly setting priorities concerning the content of all three working areas. (SPSEE, 2002a)

However this 'equal footing' does not extend to the key policy-making body, the High Level Steering Group (HLSG). The HLSG is jointly chaired by the European Commission and the World Bank and includes the finance ministers of the G8 countries, the country holding the EU presidency and the Netherlands, together with representatives of international financial institutions and organisations and the Special Coordinator of the Stability Pact.

The European Commission stresses that there is 'a close *partnership* with SAp countries' (EC, 2001a: 7). This partnership is held to start by involving countries closely in the programming, including discussions on current CARDS strategies. Countries are also involved in on-going dialogue on developing annual action plans. The European Commission strongly emphasises the importance of country 'ownership':

This partnership helps promote each country's sense of *ownership* over Community assistance that is crucial if it is to have the desired impact on the ground. This national commitment is all the more important for future CARDS support, such as institution building, which require the countries to undertake reforms if the assistance is to be effective. (EC, 2001a: 7)

Country ownership is clearly central to both the EU SAp and the Stability Pact processes. However, it is clear that the promotion of ownership is being pushed by the EU itself and does not involve any real equality of input over policy guidelines. While the formal regulatory mechanisms stress partnership and country ownership, at the informal level real ownership is exercised by the European Commission. This leaves little room for ownership for SEE states excluded from the international coordinating mechanisms, essentially under the control of the Commission itself:

First, the Commission co-chairs and is guided by the High Level Steering Group for South East Europe that provides overall guidance on donor co-ordination. Second, the Commission maintains a Joint Office with the World Bank to help co-ordinate and develop support to the region. Third, the Commission plays an active and leading role with the countries and international community in the three tables of the Stability Pact for South East Europe. (EC, 2001a: 8)

The elements of international strategy negotiated with the SEE states are developed in the context of broader international coordination with international institutions responsive to the demands of non-SEE states. As the Commission states, the CARDS strategies are determined through other regulatory mechanisms, not partnership with SEE states:

[T]he CARDS strategies will be part of a *coherent international community response* to help the region meet its substantial development and SAp challenges. The mechanisms for this *co-ordination* effort – on overall CARDS strategies, on annual programming and on implementation of specific programmes and projects – are already in place. (EC, 2001a: 8)

Once the SAAs are signed the relationship of regulation becomes fully institutionalised (the SAAs are legally binding international agreements) (EC, 2002: 4). The first SAA agreement was signed with Macedonia in April 2001 and entered into force in 2004 and the second, with Croatia, in October 2001, which entered into force in 2005. Albania signed up to the formal process of negotiating the SAA in 2003 and Serbia and Montenegro and Bosnia-Herzegovina in November 2005. The agreements are then 'the principal means to begin to prepare themselves for the demands that the perspective of accession to the EU naturally entails' (EC, 2001a: 3). These demands are determined by the EU and considered to be so onerous that the SEE states will need the additional encouragement of conditionality:

The Stabilisation and Association Agreements, then, are posited on respect for the conditionality of the Stabilisation and Association process agreed by the Council. But they also bring with them a dynamic means of operationalising that conditionality and give the EU the leverage necessary to get the countries to adopt genuine reforms with a view to achieving the immediate objectives of the agreements. The mechanisms of the Agreements themselves will enable the EU to prioritise reforms, shape them according to EU models, to address and solve problems, and to monitor implementation. (EU, 2001: III)

The EU attains the necessary 'leverage' over SEE states through conditionality at three levels – the SAp, programme and project levels. At the SAp level, lack of progress in the reforms advocated by the EU in the economic, political and social spheres can lead to CARDS assistance being frozen or 'granted through other means' (EC, 2001b: 24). If the EU chooses it can invoke 'programme conditionality', threatening to close certain aid programmes if the country concerned fails to satisfy the external administrators with regard to 'specific reform targets or adoption of sectoral policies' (EC, 2001b: 25). 'Project level conditionality' can apply to ensure that the candidate state meets 'specific conditions' judged to be related to the project's success.

The SAp is a contractual relationship. But a contract made between two unequal parties, with only one party being the judge of whether the conditions of the contract are met and in a position to coerce the other. From the EU perspective, the political strategy towards the region 'relies on a realistic expectation that the contract it enters into with individual countries will be fulfilled satisfactorily' (EC, 2001a: 3). The contracts commit the SEE states to a relationship of subordination to EU mechanisms. They establish formal mechanisms and agreed benchmarks which enable the EU to work with each country towards meeting the required standards and focus attention on key areas of governance concerns – human and minority rights, stable democratic institutions, standards of political behaviour and independence of the media (EC, 2001a: 3).

CARDS programmes of assistance, the major external aid associated with the SAp, focus on clearly defined EU priorities. The first priority institution-building area in terms of overall CARDS support is:

Familiarisation of the *acquis communautaire* as countries start to move their legislation – especially on areas covered under the SAA – more into line with the approaches used inside the EU. This will focus on core *acquis* issues relating to the internal market. (EC, 2001b: 37)

This is followed by civil service reform to develop 'administrative procedures in conformity with EU standards', fiscal and financial management reforms, trade and customs regulation and reform of the legal and administrative framework of justice and home affairs (EC, 2001b: 38). The SAp and the priorities within it reproduce the framework that has already been adopted by the EU in its dealings with the accession states, as illustrated above.

The Commission's desire to impose a pre-established agenda of state-building governance reform, which seems to assume that there is a 'one size fits all' method of strengthening SEE government institutions, its desire to enforce its leverage over the SEE region through a number of mechanisms of conditionality, and the stress upon EU managerial control and coordination of external directives, together leave little doubt that the SAp process is far from one of partnership. Yet, the partnership element has been central to keeping the EU's options open with regard to the membership process. As Christopher Bickerton notes, partnership does not just conceal the power inequalities involved in the process of integration, preventing candidate states from negotiating the transitional measures adopted by existing members. It also helps to mitigate tensions and uncertainties of existing member states about enlargement by creating a flexible framework in which the vicissitudes of internal EU institutional wrangling can be played out as problems with the pace of capacity-building and ownership in the applicant states (Bickerton, 2005a; see also Grabbe, 2003).

In many ways, the relationship of inequality between elected representatives in the region and the external regulatory bodies, such as the EU, is highlighted in the international regulation of Bosnia and Kosovo. Bosnia and Kosovo, rather than standing out as exceptions because of the restrictions on local sovereignty and self-government – thereby institutionalising a relationship of inequality and external domination – in fact, indicate with greater clarity the problems of governance and civil society in the context of an unequal partnership. In both Bosnia (under the administrative regulation of the international Office of the High Representative) and Kosovo (where the highest civilian power is the United Nations Special Representative) there are elected governments at local, regional and state levels. In both cases the international administration is held to be part of a contractual process moving towards ownership, self-government and integration into European structures (see, for example, Chandler, 2005a; van Meurs and Weiss, 2005).

THE DYNAMIC OF EXTERNAL REGULATION

There is ambiguity and uncertainty in the framework of integrating the SEE region which stems directly from the fact that this is not a process involving equal partners. The speed and nature of the association process lies largely out of the hands of SEE states themselves. Although offering the 'carrot' of EU membership the contractual relationships established between the EU and SEE states are flexible and ambiguous ones, liable to shift and change (see Zielonka, 1998). The EU is an Empire in Denial because it has difficulty legitimising its power through a coherent expression of its aims in SEE. The member states themselves are not convinced of their ability to justify their power openly to their own publics and are therefore ambivalent about taking on the responsibilities of its exercise. As the International Commission on the Balkans expresses the fears:

If Europe's neo-colonial rule becomes further entrenched, it will encourage economic discontent; it will become a political embarrassment for the European project; and, above all, European electorates would see it as an immense and unnecessary financial and moral burden. (ICB, 2005: 11)

Empire in Denial seeks to absolve the neocolonial power of the political consequences of the perceived threat of failure in the East. EU enlargement is talked up as an immense achievement in the spread of democracy and peace without the overt use of imperial power, but underneath the rhetoric there is an unease that the 'EU's lack of vision', the political elites' lack of connection with their own societies, will undermine the project (Leonard, 2005: 10). The attitudes of European voters and their disconnection from the elite are painfully felt as the problem holding back the open exercise of power – i.e. that they would be unwilling to bear the financial and moral burden of empire in the East. In fact, this inverses the dynamic of denial. It is the lack of self-confidence of the European elites which leads them to see their power over SEE as a burden rather than an opportunity and makes them reluctant to take responsibility openly for their power in the new enlarged Europe. Instead, the rhetoric is one of distancing, of capacity-building and the talking up of the independence and accountability of the 'partner' states being prepared for accession. In this way any successes can be proudly taken credit for and any failures seen to be the result of the candidate states themselves.

The question of dependency of the SEE partners upon the policy imperatives of their external 'tutors' is particularly important when the broader context of European enlargement is considered. The Stability Pact and Stabilisation and Association process were not launched merely with the idea of integrating SEE states but also as a mechanism of directly regulating the region to address perceived sources of instability. This was most clearly articulated in the Stability Pact, initially launched against the background of Slobodan Milosevic's continuing hold on power in Belgrade, intended to send an important signal to the opposition that Europe was willing to aid Serbia on the condition of his removal from power (ESI, 2001a: 5). This perspective led to the admittance of Montenegro as an 'early beneficiary' to the Stability Pact, focusing attention on resistance to the Belgrade regime. The concern of the EU has not been so much with the benefits to SEE states of membership of European institutions, or with their rapid accession, but rather with experimenting with mechanisms of regulation and control over the region.

Despite the EU's quite different aims, the Stabilisation and Association process is promoted to the states of the region as an essential prerequisite for EU membership. This contradiction between the processes of regulation and their means of justification has led to increasing numbers of 'hoops' for the candidate countries to jump through and shifting and ambiguous discussions of the level of 'standards' necessary for compliance and for completing the different stages of the membership accession process. All of which suggests that for EU policy-makers the greater concern has been with the process of 'tutoring' rather than with the end product of membership, which formally legitimates the process in SEE states. This was highlighted in November 2001 when the EU announced that of the twelve candidate countries for enlargement in 2004, the SEE states of Bulgaria and Romania would be the only two whose membership would be postponed.

This concern with regulation rather than with opening up institutions based on genuine partnership means that attempts to compare the SP and SAp with earlier institution-building between equals – in the OECD, Council of Europe, NATO, the European Coal and Steel Community and today's European Union – are more likely to confuse than clarify our understanding of the processes involved. This process of institutionalised ambiguity creates few problems for the EU, which has not committed itself to a firm time-scale for integration. In fact, the EU mechanisms explicitly allow for the process of tutoring to take place independently of movements towards membership, i.e. the explicit recognition that measures for 'stabilisation' may be decoupled from moves towards 'association' (EC, 2002: 9). This is where the regional approach seems to fit in.

The SAp programme appears at first sight to be potentially contradictory in that it attempts to develop three methods of regulating the SEE region: firstly, through providing the promise of future membership of the EU; secondly, through encouraging a regional focus, encouraging SEE countries to develop bilateral and regional relationships between themselves as the basis for greater economic and political stability in the region; and, thirdly, through stressing the individual conditions in each state – a 'flexible' approach, which 'allows each country to move ahead at its own pace' (EC, 2001a: 3). The regional and individual approaches allow the policy agenda of SEE states to be set independently of the progress towards membership. The Zagreb Summit placed considerable emphasis on this aspect and the EU began a process of establishing a network of close contractual relationships (conventions on regional cooperation) between the signatories, mirroring the bilateral relationship with the EU through the SAAs.

As the desire to maintain a process of regulatory control ('stabilisation') is divorced from the goal of EU integration, the regulatory process has increasingly come to be seen as lacking legitimacy in the SEE region. Economic and social sacrifices, which might make sense in the context of certainty about EU integration, have less appeal when it seems that policy is externally imposed with little promise of improvement. As Ariel Cohen, a leading specialist on the US Foreign Policy Council, noted regarding Bulgaria: 'The defeat of the Union of Democratic Forces (SDS) and of former President Petar Stoyanov at the elections last year was considered a step back in Washington ... I respect the political and economic reforms achieved by Bulgaria. But the Bulgarian electorate had a different view' (Karaboev, 2002).

Elections, which put pressure on elites in the region and expose their lack of policy-making autonomy, are seen as potential barriers to the EU programme, encouraging governments to renege on commitments to privatise or close down loss-making state-owned companies. As Phelim AcAleer, the Bucharest correspondent for the *Financial Times*, noted the Romanian government was torn between implementing its populist election programme, which took the Social Democrats to power in 2000, which promised measures to alleviate poverty, and imposing EU-required cut-backs in government subsidies:

They have done a little bit this year, and they need to do a lot more next year. And after that, then we are looking at elections, and then we are looking at sweeteners rather than pain. And the EU was quite clear that there needs to be pain before there's gain, so next year's quite crucial. (Tomiuc, 2001)

While SEE governments are increasingly dependent on external policy-making, the EU is under little pressure to deliver on its side of the partnership. In fact, the governance and civil society sphere of reforms increasingly portray the problems of squaring the external orientation of policy with domestic concerns as one of the SEE states' own making. The top-down regulation of SEE region is based on the assumption that the international community, particularly the EU, is in a better position to guide political development in SEE than the political parties and elected representatives. This has led to a 'vicious circle' of external regulation as external institutions seek to ensure that their agendas are kept to.

'High intensity' institution-building

The European Union approach is moving beyond 'low-intensity programmes', where assistance is provided from a distance, such as donating equipment to government departments or sponsoring study trips abroad for civil servants. Learning from the more direct forms of regulation and internationalisation of domestic mechanisms of governance and administration in Bosnia, Brussels policy-makers advised that governance reforms were more likely to be successful when directly administered by international advisers:

The weaker the surrounding institutional environment and the domestic agents, the greater the intensity which is required of international assistance to make an impact ... High intensity programmes are those where the aid provider becomes sufficiently engaged with the domestic institutions to identify the specific obstacles to reform, and to develop solutions adapted to the local circumstances ... Working jointly with the responsible domestic institutions ... [t]winning involves the secondment of experts from EU member states to work in the equivalent institutions in the candidate country for periods of a year or more, to help with the technical development and institutional reform required for the implementation of the *acquis*. (ESI, 2001a: 25)

Not only are the policy goals for SEE governments established externally, they are also being implemented with little domestic input into discussion and debate. In fact European Commission programmes, such as those funded by the CARDS programme, tend to bypass mechanisms of democratic accountability entirely. For example, the European Commission's bilateral assistance increasingly involves the direct regulation of SEE state governance mechanisms:

The ambitious goals in this area require the development of new instruments under CARDS. To this end, the traditional instruments of technical assistance and supporting equipment supplies will be complemented by the use of twinning, whereby member state civil servants shall be seconded to work directly with their counterpart officials in national SAp administrations. In addition, a General Support Facility shall be financed at the regional level that, modelled on the Taiex instrument, will provide seminars and supporting technical advice to all five of the countries on the institutional strengthening issues arising from the SAp in general, with a particular focus on the approximation of legislation and policies towards the EU *acquis*, such as the internal market. (EC, 2001a: 9)

Rather than discussion of EU legislation being under the control of SEE state civil servants and elected representatives, the process of policy-making is becoming directly taken over by seconded EU civil servants, drafting and advising on the necessary legislation. This process reduces the policy preparation process in SEE states to that of the quasi-protectorates of Bosnia and Kosovo where international institutions have taken over the role of preparing policy for the elected representatives to assent to.

Just as in the quasi-protectorates, where elected representatives are guided through the prescribed policy process by international advisers, the Stability Pact seeks to guide parliamentarians directly. The international advisers argue that 'it is necessary to encourage activities of parliaments to introduce and implement necessary legislation with a view to creating strong democratic institutions' (SPSEE, 2002b). This Parliamentary Task Force is led by the Strasbourg-based International Institute for Democracy which assists the parliamentary Troika of the Council of Europe, European Parliament and OSCE Parliamentary Assembly and other NGOs in guiding the parliamentary process in the 'young democracies' of SEE.

In this context of increasing direct external regulation, it appears that when the EU calls for greater transparency and accountability for SEE governments, what is meant is greater accountability to the international community rather than to their citizens. For example, the policy-making process may have been opened up to review by the legal and constitutional 'experts' of the Council of Europe, but this process of revision and rewriting, in fact, takes the policy process further away from elected representatives and their constituents (CoE, 2000: §27).

It is clear that administrative capacity-building under EU auspices, which focuses on policy outcomes through externally managing the policy process, has the unintended outcome of undermining institutional capacities. For Bulgaria and Romania under the accession process, a central part of Phare assistance actually funds EU member states, whose expertise is bought in to assist in drawing up and overseeing administrative procedure through the long-term secondment of civil servants and accompanying short-term expert missions and training. The process of 'twinning' now covers all 29 policy areas pursuant to the *acquis* (EC, 2001c: 13). It is not surprising that, in the context of growing external regulation of the administrative process, the Romanian government announced a 30 per cent reduction in numbers of civil servants (as of September 2001, staff numbers were reduced by 22 per cent) (EC, 2001c: 18). According to the European Commission this has reduced already low levels of administrative capacity and left several important ministries understaffed.

Governance by task force

While formally declaring the need to strengthen the rule of law and state institutional capacity, the European Union also stresses the dangers of the SEE state being too strong in relation to regional groups, local councils, ethnic minorities and civil society. In order to restore the balance the international community supports the institutions and organisations, which are held to represent the public interest against the particular interests of the elites – often held to have 'captured' state power in order to pursue their personal interests rather than those of society. These alternative voices are then represented through internationally sponsored policy forums, think tanks and task forces which use their international influence to shape government policy independently of elected parties, which rely on domestic support alone.

In a number of SEE states, such as Bulgaria and Albania, internationally sponsored think tanks and policy centres have played a major role in policy initiatives (see van Meurs, 2003). The Stability Pact, under Working Table I, has established a number of task forces, which develop and implement policy without being dependent upon state-based democratic processes. For example, the Human Rights and Minorities Task Force 'has drawn up a comprehensive programme for the promotion of multiethnic coexistence and for the protection of minorities' (SPSEE, 2002a: 6). In areas of minority rights, the external drawing up and imposition of policy can increase fears and concerns (see, for example, Donev, 2003). However, the Stability Pact assumes that the external establishment of campaigns around minority rights questions are beneficial and has also established Human Rights Centres and urges that 'legislation reviews, awareness campaigns, and promotion of the status of [the] Roma population are important activities' (SPSEE, 2002a: 6).

The Stability Pact has gone further in this direction through its Good Governance Task Force, focusing on the development of local governments and the establishment of ombudsman institutions and the reform of public administration. This Task Force uses the framework of the Enhanced Szeged Process, a mechanism originally established to support opposition forces in the FRY during the Milosevic regime, during which time over 40 partnerships were concluded with cities and local authorities governed by opposition parties in Serbia. In

March 2001, the process of direct intervention in domestic politics to support favoured political groupings was extended beyond the FRY to Macedonia, Bosnia and Albania (SPSEE, 2002a: 6-7).

The Good Governance Task Force has prioritised 'reinforcing local and regional self-government as a basis for the establishment of sound democratic institutions in the region and promoting trans-frontier co-operation between local and regional authorities' (SPSEE, 2002c). In order to support decentralisation reforms, the Stability Pact provides policy advice and legislative expertise to develop effective local democratic institutions at municipal and regional levels. However, the policies pushing for decentralisation for the region respond to the concerns and assumptions of international institutions rather than domestic demands. The Council of Europe sponsors the Good Governance Task Force, which develops Council of Europe policy for the SEE states, in cooperation with other organisations. The problem is that the policy being developed by the Stability Pact, in this area, stems from the concerns projected by external bodies, rather than regionally based institutions. Although the participation, for example, of the EU Commission, OSCE, UNDP, USAID, World Bank, OECD, Open Society Institute, Assembly of European Regions, Eurocities and the Local Government Information Network, may well be useful, the dominance of non-regional bodies inevitably creates pressures on SEE states to accept policies which have little domestic purchase.

A trenchant assessment of the Stability Pact in this area, for the Centre for European Policy Studies, argues that 'the huge proliferation' of task forces and policy working groups, amounting to around 200 ad hoc policy forums 'should be reversed' (Emerson and Whyte: 2001). The problem with these internationally sponsored policy mechanisms is not merely the huge bureaucracy created and overlapping mandates. The development of new institutional networks of policy-making, independent of the SEE state and reliant on external funding, produces a number of potential unintended outcomes which result from separating the policy process from mechanisms of local accountability and consensus-building. As noted above, this may result in policy-making that runs the risk of failing to recognise local problems or to adapt to local circumstances. The more serious risk is that of the fragmentation of domestic political processes. If regional and local assemblies or ethnic and national minority groups are encouraged to seek external means of support, this may cause friction or lead to a breakdown in relationships with central state institutions.

Civil society?

The European Commission emphasises that civil society, particularly independent media and NGOs are vital to the governance process:

[T]here is also a need for a more active civil society, requiring not only greater openness and accountability on the part of the government but also access to funding to empower the general population, media and non-governmental organisations to generate this activity. (EC, 2001a: 10)

Empire in Denial seeks to enlist civil society as local advocates for its regulatory power and as supporters for its focus on the reform of candidate state institutions:

In all states of the region, there is a need for a constant effort to nurture and strengthen the policy consensus behind reforms, stressing the benefits, fostering realistic expectations and, wherever reforms involve short-term costs, explaining the rationale ... Where the public consensus collapses, a political opportunity will be created for anti-reform parties, including intolerant nationalists, to challenge the Europeanisation project. (ESI, 2001a: 26)

Civil society advocates are perceived to be crucial to the legitimacy of Western institutions' denial of their power. Civil society is turned to in the attempt to substantiate the argument that external regulation is led by the demands of those with the correct understanding of the 'genuine' needs and interests of their societies. Empire argues that elected representatives do not necessarily have the best interests of their own societies at heart as political elites represent sectional interests and that therefore listening to the voices of the 'excluded', as articulated by their civil society interlocutors, is essential to successful reform. The drive to regulate is alleged not to come from Brussels but from civil society supported and facilitated by the EU's administrators.

It is this artificial and dishonest drive to empower civil society that results in a highly bureaucratised process of funding civil society projects and initiatives. The bureaucratic distancing of the EU from its civil society funding results in what has been termed the 'projectisation' of policy initiatives, where they become ends in themselves, isolated from society (Stubbs and Papic, 1998: 44). The limitations of this approach are unintentionally highlighted in the Report of the Special Delegation of Council of Europe Advisers to the Stability Pact (CoE, 2000). The report urges a 'significant', 'vigorous' and 'committed' awareness-raising campaign supported by Stability Pact resources ('political, intellectual and financial') to stress the values and principles of multi-ethnic and multi-cultural society and democratic citizenship. It advises that in each country this campaign should be run by a local campaign committee and should follow a common Stability Pact structure laid down by a '"Regional and European Panel" of well-respected personalities of high moral standing and authority, to be appointed by the Stability Pact structure' (CoE, 2000: §22). The Brussels bureaucrats stress that the panel should represent different sectors of society, including the arts and sports, and that the committee of 'high moral standing' should give a strong public message of support and be involved in participating and advocating for the campaign.

The implicit assumption that EU policies will win more support if put into the mouths of others is clear across the range of civil society-building programmes, which have now been externally prioritised. The Stability Pact has actively intervened to strengthen civil society in SEE states. In October 2000, Working Table I adopted a Charter on NGO–government partnership in the region. This Charter commits SEE states to promoting the development of NGOs and civic initiatives, adopt respective legislation, and promote state–NGO partnerships on a sustained and systematic basis (SPSEE, 2002a: 8).

The external funding for civil society organisations, encouraging NGOs to participate in the policy-making process, to publicise information more widely and to advocate on behalf of the interests of those who may be excluded by mainstream political parties, has so far attracted a high level of international funding. In SEE states like Bosnia, where the focus on civil society has been prioritised over a number of years, nearly 80 per cent of the budget of NGOs is provided by external funding (Sali-Terzić, 2001: 156). However, despite the financial input, recent surveys suggest that civil society-building has met with limited success (see, for example, Donev, 2003; Ruli, 2003). As one report on civil society-building in Bosnia notes, 'non-governmental organizations have frequently emerged according to donor's interests, rather than those of the citizens affected', creating a situation where 'numerous non-governmental organizations have burgeoned, without a flourishing civil society' (Sali-Terzić, 2001: 143). As another commentator describes:

The politics of support to civil society are in many ways inadequate ... it 'covers' a very minor elite within the population. Consequently, this 'elite' is professionalized, it separates itself from the 'grassroots' problems and social reality. Hundreds of round tables and workshops are 'produced', attended by the same 100-200 civil society 'partisans'. As a result, one receives a fictitious view of the great efforts of local partisans and international organizations, which results in a 'virtual civil society'. (Papic, 2001: 15)

The funding of civic associations, which support the policies forwarded by international donors, has put NGOs in a similarly isolated position as the political elites which are equally dependent on external support. Although these NGOs have influence in government circles in SEE states, a major report suggests: 'it is a question whether these [NGOs] represent anyone else in addition to those who work in them. Being dependent on donors' priorities, they are withdrawing from contacts with those whom they are to represent' (Sali-Terzić, 2001: 153). The report concludes that the burgeoning sphere of NGO civil society is serving the interests of the external funders but failing in any long-term aims of social change:

In conclusion, the development of the NGO sector in the manner in which it has been taking place in Bosnia and the issue of legitimacy and credibility of those organisations (with some exceptions) may become a very serious issue. NGOs are often too far from their 'bases', failing to reflect their interests and needs and responding to the needs of donors instead. On the other hand, international donors, or the international community in Bosnia, is using NGOs which are financially or otherwise dependent on them, to demonstrate that they are doing what the Bosnian citizens, seemingly represented by NGOs, would like to see them doing. (Sali-Terzić, 2001: 154)

The European Commission states that the expected results from its governance support programme are the 'enhanced level of civil society activity (including NGO) and greater public participation in the efforts for democratic stabilisation' (EC, 2001a: 36). It would appear, however, that its programmes for enhancing the role of NGOs in the policy process can have unintended results of marginalising public participation further by isolating policy-making from a broader constituency and legitimising policy made by international administrators with only limited elite consultation.

LIMITATIONS OF EXTERNAL GOVERNANCE MECHANISMS

The phantom state

A major limitation of external regulation in the governance sphere, identified in this chapter, is that of institutionalising the fragility of the SEE state and dependency on external mechanisms of regulation and conflict management. This problem arises because of the imbalance of power between the EU and states in the region, which has led to external regulation and reform of the governance sphere being shaped by EU concerns more than the needs of the people of the region.

The fact that international funding under Phare and CARDS and other assistance programmes is determined by EU requirements, decided in Brussels, does not appear to be a problem to many policy-makers. However, the experience of EU state-building suggests that externally imposing reform programmes does not always result in desired outcomes. The European Commission recognises the 'impressive' advances made towards democratic stability in the SEE region, including democratic changes in Croatia and Serbia, the diminishment of state manipulation of the media, moves towards facilitating the return of refugees and internally displaced people, and new laws, especially concerning media freedom, election law and minority rights (EC, 2001a: 9). However, the Commission argues that for SEE as a whole 'the process of democratic stabilisation is far from complete and the treatment of minorities lies at the heart of the problem' (EC, 2001a: 9). As the European Commission extends the list of prerequisites for EU membership, the priorities of the Commission become increasingly divorced from everyday experience.

As SEE governments, on the whole, satisfy EU requirements, the focus of governance and civil society development is increasingly on questions which would be problematic for the more economically advanced EU members, let alone the poorest. For example, the Commission argues that SEE governments need to do more to facilitate refugee return, to safeguard democratic freedoms and respect for cultural, religious and linguistic diversity, and to end exclusionary practices which effect the integration of Roma and other ethnic minorities. Countries such as Romania, with an average income of $100 per month, one of the poorest in Europe, have pushed resources into improving the care of institutionalised children and improving the position of Roma. However, because these policy priorities cannot be addressed at the level of special policy initiatives and do not reflect the general level of social and economic development of the region, the European Commission initiatives tend to be highly artificial. More problematically, they are pushed through with little regard for domestic perceptions of policy priorities. The majority of Romanians do not regard the Roma as discriminated against and surveys show less than 10 per cent share the European Commission's view that action needs to be taken in this area (see Mungiu-Pippidi, 2003: 263–5). Even when these externally driven directives are followed by the government, there is little chance that they will transform broader social conditions or the attitude of the population and therefore the international institutions are unlikely to be satisfied.

The artificial nature of policies imposed through external administrators, developed through the myriad of think tanks, focus groups and task forces and advocated by civil society NGOs is apparent in every SEE state. Often these externally reliant policy forums have little awareness of the social and economic limitations to their 'ideal' solutions and those involved in policy processes have little relationship to broader social concerns. One insightful policy report, which studied judicial reform in Bosnia, highlighted how, even in key areas of governance, reform can fail to have any impact. In this case, a new judicial service law was externally imposed, which among other reforms increased judicial salaries. The ministers responsible for the relevant budgets only learnt of this decision in the press and did not have the means to pay. Because the policy reforms were imposed without consultation or the agreement of local bodies, the consequence was merely that judicial salaries have fallen further into arrears (ESI, 2001b: 6). Policies that look good on paper can easily be artificial if they bypass domestic political processes.

The governance and civil society programmes developed by the Brussels bureaucracy appear to give little room for the consensus-building and socially legitimating role of the political sphere. There seems to be a view that questions of governance and social regulation can be best resolved through the top-down regulation of EU administrators, coupled with the public awareness campaigning of externally funded NGOs. It would appear that the SAp and the SP place more faith in stability coming through EU conditionality and international regulation than through the strengthening of domestic state institutions through democratic processes.

Where there is a divergence between EU priorities and domestic concerns, the process of reform can result in isolating ruling elites and potentially destabilising the political sphere. If political institutions become isolated from society, policy does not meet the needs or interests of citizens and governing parties can lose legitimacy. This is highlighted in the institutional surveys which note the disconnection between political party election programmes, responding to the concerns of the electorate, and government policy which is dictated by external conditionality. As Genc Ruli notes with regard to Albania:

While the numerous reforms of democratisation and institution-building have created, and even improved the democratic shell of Albania's institutions, they failed to protect our fragile democracy ... The distancing of the leading elite from the voters is now the most dangerous phenomenon. The elite's reform agenda is no longer the public agenda ... While the electoral programs of political parties contain promises that take into account the electorate's immediate necessities, government programs are drafted entirely around donor's conditionality and recommendations. This 'bigamy' of the leading elite detaches it even more from the population. (Ruli, 2003: 152)

Regulation of the political sphere without representation by the elected leaders means that there is little domestic accountability or stake in the political process. This process is well summed up by Genc Ruli as 'democracy without citizens' or 'democracy without politics' (Ruli, 2003). Across the new EU accession states there has been a clear consensus that the political process of policy-making has been removed from the domestic sphere. As Anna Gryzmala-Busse and Abby Innes note, the lack of Eastern European input into the accession process has 'eradicated both detailed and ideological debates over many areas of public policy' (2003: 64).

Kristi Raik observes, in her work on Estonia, that the public are alienated from the mass of rules and regulations imposed from outside and employ a tool of 'double-think', making compliance only ever tokenistic, in much the same way as they reacted to the laws and regulations which were imposed from Moscow (Raik, 2004). In fact, some SEE oppositionists have voiced complaints that regulatory rule from the EU is even more undemocratic than that imposed by the Soviets, as at least the Soviets allowed states to deviate from their system as long as they paid lip-service to the Soviet ideal, for example, allowing private agriculture in Hungary or a prominent role for the Catholic church in Poland.

The problems of 'high-intensity' institution-building and the external imposition of policies is clearest in states such as Bosnia where the highest level of resources have been devoted to international assistance in the governance sphere. A detailed Brussels policy assessment concludes that attempts to short cut problems of domestic support for external policies by imposing legislation has marginalised the political process and calls for a 're-evaluation of the role of politics' (ESI, 2001b: 1). The authors highlight that good governance and capable state institutions can only emerge through making the policy process accountable to the citizens of the state: 'good solutions are those which emerge from a political process' (ESI, 2001b: 7).

CONCLUSION

It seems that rather than EU membership being considered as important for the development of SEE states, for the EU it is the relationship of tutelage that is the key factor, making the process of relationship management more important than the goal and in many cases an end in itself. The EU's initial concern was not enlargement per se in SEE but the ability to exercise its power without taking on the overt responsibilities of empire. State-building only developed as, in many ways, an ad hoc response to this problem through a process of experimentation. While the gains of institutionalising external regulation in this way appear clear to external policy-makers, they may not be so apparent in the SEE region itself. The focus on the process as an end in itself has also meant that much of the governance/civil society programme has been an artificial one.

The Stability Pact is seen as a 'two-way street' whereby SEE states 'must first implement appropriate reforms' in regard to economic and political processes and, in exchange, donors undertake to support the construction process through assistance and credits (SPSEE, 2002a: 13). This is portrayed to be a reasonable exchange or a contractual relationship of a partnership – however, in this process the domestic political process has been marginalised. In effect, the SEE states are expected to sacrifice domestic policy-making for the promise of financial aid and integration into European and Euro-Atlantic structures.

There are risks attached to this form of Empire in Denial which threaten to reveal the content of empire below the capacity-building forms of denial. Because the links between SEE states and their societies were already weak in the aftermath of the collapse of the state socialist systems of rule the mechanisms of denial appear fairly clearly. The state and society actors 'empowered' by the West appear alien and distant from their own societies and lack the legitimacy which comes from strong mechanisms of social connection. The stability of these mechanisms of regulation may be tenuous.

However, the mechanisms of SEE state-building, such as the SAp and the SP, were not designed in the main to make European domination more palatable to the candidate states and societies. There is little threat to empire emanating from the candidate states themselves; despite growing disillusionment and alienation there is little in the way of political alternatives. The key to understanding these mechanisms and the emphasis on partnership, ownership, good governance and civil society-building is the internal need for empire to deny itself. It is the fact that the EU cannot handle the political responsibilities of empire that has driven the state-building dynamic, not the problems of asserting power over SEE. This dynamic of denial will be further clarified in the next chapter where the EU's denial of its protectorate powers over Bosnia will be analysed in greater detail.

6
Denying the Bosnian Protectorate

The Bosnian protectorate has been denied by empire from the very moment of its establishment with the 1995 Dayton peace agreement. This denial has taken two main forms. The first strategy of denial was in establishing the domination of the US and the EU from the beginning as an exercise in state-building. Bosnia was to be an independent sovereign state where formal political responsibility rested with its elected government, not its international administration. Denial moved further in 1999 with the gradual handover of power to the EU and particularly with the EU's assumption of formal control of the state-building process in 2002. This second stage of denial has sought to distance the EU from the administrative powers exercised by its own Special Representative as head of the Office of the High Representative and the shift to the informal mechanisms of domination exercised through the Europeanisation of the Bosnian state's own institutional framework, particularly the Directorate of European Integration.

Empire in Denial has successfully shaped the international understanding of the post-Dayton decade. Many commentators suggest that the transition to Bosnian ownership has been held back by the Dayton framework, which created a weak central state and a country divided into two separate entities, the Republika Srpska (RS) and the Muslim-Croat Federation, with ten cantonal governments, as well as an autonomous region, Brcko. Yet, ten years on, the idea that the postwar transition has been frustrated by a surfeit of Bosnian governing institutions, protected by their Dayton status, could not be further from the truth. Rather, the international powers of administration, under the Office of the High Representative, have been vastly increased, demonstrating that the Bosnian institutions established by Dayton are administrative shells. There has been a transition away from Dayton, but this has been from the ad hoc regulatory controls of the self-selected 'coalition of the willing', the Peace Implementation Council, towards an expanded framework of European Union regulation, covering all aspects of the post-Dayton process. Dayton has created an 'informal trusteeship', with external institutions rewriting their mandates and powers. But despite the transformation in post-Dayton mechanisms, it is still too early to talk of any indications of a shift towards Bosnian ownership.

There is a consensus about Dayton – that is repeated so often it is virtually a mantra of international officials – that the 1995 peace agreement was a treaty 'designed to end a war, not to build a state' (for example, Denitch, 1996; Ashdown, 2004). Commentators regularly argue that Dayton was negotiated by the nationalist parties, whose leaders caused the war in the first place, and that it therefore secured the power of these ethnically based political parties (for example, Kaldor, 1997: 28–30). Essentially, therefore the political process since Dayton has been seen as 'the continuation of war by other means', in an inversion of Clausewitz's doctrine (Ashdown, 2004). The domestic political process in Bosnia is seen as illegitimate and fundamentally flawed. It is alleged that the numerous annexes and small print of the Dayton agreement have tied the hands of the international community and created a complex set of political institutions which stymie the building of a strong centralised state and continue to enable ethnically based political parties to dominate the policy-making process. Dayton and, by implication, the Bosnian voters and their representatives, in this reading, bear the responsibility for the weakness and lack of legitimacy of central state institutions and the failure of the state-building aspirations of Bosnia's international benefactors.

This chapter seeks to establish that this consensus is based on a myth and that the Dayton agreement has, in fact, created an informal trusteeship which has made opaque the relations of authority and accountability. The framework created at Dayton has been an extremely successful experiment in mechanisms of Empire in Denial. This framework was an extremely flexible one, which enabled international actors, unaccountable to the people of Bosnia, to shape and reshape the agenda of postwar transition. The Bosnian experience, the ambiguity of the Dayton framework and the confusing 'dual regime' of elected governments and external overseers, is highly relevant to current discussions of the strategies and mechanisms of state-building. There are increasingly vocal calls among academics and policy-advisers for the extension of similar forms of external management where, it is asserted, state-building 'cannot be adequately addressed within the confines of conventional sovereignty' (Krasner, 2004: 1). For example, Robert Keohane suggests that 'regaining sovereignty need not be [the] long-term objective' for external state-builders (Keohane, 2002; 2003), Stephen Krasner argues for experiments in 'shared sovereignty' (Krasner, 2005), James Fearon and David Laitin have called for the establishment of 'neo-trusteeships' (Fearon and Laitin, 2004) and the International Commission on the Balkans report, led by former Italian Prime Minister Giuliano Amato, has suggested new forms of 'guided sovereignty' for Yugoslav successor states such as Kosovo (ICB, 2005).

The study of Bosnia's experience of informal trusteeship or shared sovereignty – where international legal sovereignty exists without the rights of traditional or 'unconditional' sovereignty (see Krasner, 1999), demonstrates some of the limitations of this approach to international state-building. Without the traditional rights of sovereignty there has been little need to politically engage Bosnian citizens in the post-conflict process of transition. The main transition which has taken place has been from the ad hoc policy ownership of self-selected members of the PIC to direct regulatory control under the aegis of the European Union. This transition has taken place through informal and unaccountable mechanisms of external regulation, and has been imposed from above without any debate or genuine involvement of the people or elected representatives of Bosnia.

The relations of informal trusteeship have resulted in a situation where there is little accountability for the policy results of external rule. Formally, Bosnia is an independent state and not an international protectorate. The ambiguity between the formal international legal status of Bosnia and its de facto status, under international administration, has resulted in a discourse which pins the blame for the lack of post-conflict transition on Bosnian institutions, established under the Dayton settlement, and Bosnian voters and representatives. Focusing on the informal relations of power and political influence allows a different picture to be drawn, which questions the common assumption that Bosnian political institutions have too much power and influence and the conclusion that international administrative authority needs to be further strengthened. In fact, it is suggested here that the flexibility of external mechanisms of regulation has been a central factor in 'sucking out' the capacity of Bosnia's political institutions and undermining the legitimacy of the Bosnian state (see further, Ignatieff, 2003: 98–101; Fukuyama, 2004: 139ff).

The following section briefly considers the growing shift towards informal trusteeship mechanisms of regulation in both state-building policy discussions and in international practice. There then follows an analysis of the origins of the Dayton agreement, after which the post-Dayton developments are briefly analysed in two stages. The first period is from 1995 to 1999, during which time the powers of the PIC High Representative were extended, but with little clear policy direction or end point for the ad hoc international administration. The second period, from 2000 to 2005, saw a gradual transformation of external regulative mechanisms under the leadership of the European Union, which laid a comprehensive framework for European ownership of the post-Dayton process. Throughout both these periods, Bosnian input or ownership of the policy-making process has been little more than rhetorical. Dayton has provided the framework in which the external process of managing the post-Dayton peace has been transformed beyond recognition, while the population of Bosnia and their elected representatives have been marginalised from the political process and the elected bodies bypassed by the creation of new ad hoc mechanisms of direct and indirect EU interference.

INFORMAL TRUSTEESHIP

As considered in the chapters above, the instruments of governance of the non-Western state have been increasingly internationalised while leaving formal state sovereignty intact. This is highlighted in the 2005 report by the International Commission on the Balkans (ICB), which recommended that the EU jointly shares the management of the Balkan states to facilitate the state-building and member state-building process, rather than pursuing traditional external state-supporting policies and assistance which were held to be inadequate to meet the needs of EU integration (ICB, 2005). With regard to these more invasive measures of state-building, where the EU increasingly takes on the task of implementing as well as developing the policy framework, Bosnia is becoming a template rather than an exception. The Commission therefore recommends a similar process of direct regulation or informal trusteeship for Kosovo with a suggested transition from the current UN-protectorate status (formal trusteeship) to 'independence without full sovereignty' – independence which, while reserving to the EU the core regulatory powers of the United Nations Mission in Kosovo (UNMIK) administration, frees the international state-builders from their formal accountability. The next stage for Kosovo would then be that of 'guided sovereignty', where EU leverage, as a formal 'partner', would be directed through the accession negotiations, with the final stage being that of 'shared sovereignty', when Kosovo claims EU membership (ICB, 2005: 18–23).

The ICB report argues that states without full sovereignty are the solution to the failure of the Balkan's own state-building projects. Rather than state-building, the EU will be doing member state-building in the region – creating states which never have to confront the destabilising difficulties of 'unconditional sovereignty' (Keohane, 2002: 756). The Commission argues that the EU is forced into this role by circumstances and 'has become a reluctant state-builder', having no choice other than state integration if it is to avoid 'allowing a black hole to emerge on the European periphery' (ICB, 2005: 30, 38). US international relations theorist Robert Keohane argues that the EU has been the leading experimental force in developing new approaches to post-conflict state management, demonstrating 'that regaining sovereignty need not be one's long-term objective' (2002: 756). For Keohane, the EU can help the US avoid direct accountability for the outcomes of regime change – by blurring the location of sovereign power – suspending sovereignty while maintaining the fiction of state independence:

The European experience suggests that the Afghans should not necessarily seek a sovereign Afghanistan to fight over among themselves. Instead, Afghans and their friends should try to design institutions for Afghanistan that would enable external authorities to maintain order. (2002: 757)

Stephen Krasner suggests that informal trusteeship, which he terms 'shared sovereignty', avoids the problems of short-termism implicit in transitional administrations, which promise the return to full sovereignty, as well as the accusations of colonialism, which would follow the development of formal trusteeships. As considered above (Chapter 2), international legal sovereignty allows post-conflict states to enter into partnerships which informally violate their sovereign rights (Krasner, 2004: 24).

The following sections of this chapter demonstrate that the Dayton agreement provides an important example of shared sovereignty in practice – an indeterminate extension of external regulation and the denial of political autonomy by voluntary agreement. However, the obfuscation of the relations of power and authority involved in this process of informal trusteeship has meant that nearly all commentators have tended to focus on the formal institutional arrangements of the Dayton settlement rather than the informal processes involved. There has, therefore, been little weight given to the importance of Bosnia, as a leading example of state-building approaches which have moved beyond attempts to restore traditional sovereignty. Once this is recognised, it is then possible to consider the pros and cons of this approach based on practical experience. In this regard, it will be suggested that the restricted nature of Bosnia's political autonomy and informal hollowing out of central state capacities for decision-making have undoubtedly undermined the possibilities for bridging Bosnia's divisions by enhancing the political authority and broader social legitimacy of state institutions.

THE ORIGINS OF DAYTON

Post-Dayton Bosnia is fundamentally distinct from the formal protectorates of Kosovo and East Timor, which involved the direct oversight of the United Nations under UN Security Council resolutions 1244 and 1272. Bosnia is an independent sovereign state and member of the United Nations. As William Bain correctly notes, Dayton did not establish a formal protectorate relationship, instead Dayton is 'legitimated by the principle of consent' (2003: 150). Rather than an external imposition, Dayton formally appears to be a treaty made by the local powers – Bosnia and its neighbours, Croatia and the rump former FRY. It is not by UN Security Council resolution but by the coercive fiction of 'local consent' that international actors were invited to oversee Dayton and to install the temporary post-conflict administrative mechanism of the OHR. This was an office only 'consistent with relevant United Nations Security Council resolutions', not formally run by or directly accountable to the UN (Chesterman, 2004a: 76).

The parties on the ground who consented to the agreement and had formal ownership of it were coerced into signing it and had little say over the content of the 'agreement'. Dayton was in essence a US-managed process and the agreement was initialled on 21 November 1995 at the Dayton air force base in Ohio (Holbrooke, 1998). The European powers resented being sidelined by the US and lobbied Washington for UN involvement in overseeing the implementation of the peace agreement. The US refused and the Europeans responded with the idea of establishing a Peace Implementation Council. This could, firstly, help to provide some sense of international legitimacy in the absence of UN involvement and, secondly, and more importantly from the European perspective, ensure that Washington included the Europeans and others in the policy process.

The PIC was a legal figment, designed to cohere the international management of the Dayton process, but *without* the restrictive ties of international law. Dame Pauline Neville Jones, former Political Director of the UK Foreign and Commonwealth Office and leader of the British delegation to the Dayton peace conference, was instrumental in the establishment of the PIC. As she later described it: 'Everybody knew that this was a phoney. Everyone also knew that we had to find something' (Jones, 2004). On 8–9 December the first PIC conference was held at Lancaster House in London; prior to this, 'all the agencies had been drilled' and 'everyone knew their lines' and a detailed transitional programme for Bosnia was established (Jones, 2004; see also PIC, 1995). On 14 December the Dayton peace agreement was formally signed in Paris.

The Dayton process was based on the arbitrary and ad hoc use of international power to establish a unique regime of post-conflict external regulation, one without previous historical precedent. The lack of international legal accountability explains the ad hoc and flexible nature of the powers of the High Representative. Prior to the negotiations in Dayton, the US envisaged control of both military and civilian implementation in postwar Bosnia and planned a very powerful role for the High Representative. During Dayton, the European governments made high-level *démarches* insisting that the civilian role was emphasised and requesting that the High Representative be a European. The US partly conceded, but, in so doing, sought to reduce the significance of the High Representative (Bildt, 1998: Chapter 9). Once agreement was reached, it was understood that the High Representative would always be a European, although one chief deputy was likely to be German and one American (Cousens and Cater, 2001: 46).

The Europeans had to fight their corner for more influence for the High Representative by stealth. The definition of the role and authority of the High Representative was intentionally left ambiguous. The Europeans wanted to have more influence but could not openly state this in the formalising of the Dayton annexes in the run up to the PIC conference, otherwise the US would have opposed this. As Dame Pauline Neville Jones relates, the key victory for the Europeans was to manage to insert a role of 'coordination and facilitation' for the High Representative (GFA, 1995: Annex 10). Once the job was secured, the Europeans subsequently undertook a lot of 'underpinning', i.e. allocating tasks to strengthen the position. This they were able to do gradually as long as the US was happy that there would be no interference with the NATO security operations. For this reason, the US prevented the European-led High Representative from developing any meaningful mechanism to coordinate relations between the civilian and military roles. However, as the security aspects of Dayton implementation became less important, the US was willing to let the Europeans bear more of the burden and the High Representative's civilian role become more central.

The Dayton process was an ambiguous, ad hoc and unaccountable one from the outset. At the time of its establishment, the Peace Implementation Council tasked with overseeing the implementation of Dayton had no international legal standing. According to Dame Pauline Neville Jones, the PIC 'was working in a legal vacuum' (Jones, 2004). It was only after the event, on 15 December, that the PIC was recognised, in United Nations Security Council Resolution 1031, which cast retrospective legitimacy on the proceedings.

The Dayton peace agreement was unlike any other peace treaty of modern times, not merely because it was imposed by powers formally external to the conflict, but because of the far reaching powers given to international actors, which extended well beyond military matters to cover the most basic aspects of government and state. The majority of annexes to the Dayton agreement were not related to the ending of hostilities, traditionally the role of a peace agreement, but rather to the political project of state-building in Bosnia, of 'reconstructing a society' (Bildt, 1996a).

Reconstructing Bosnian society was undertaken in the same interventionist spirit as Dayton itself. Carl Bildt, the first international High Representative for the new state, described the Dayton agreement as 'by far the most ambitious peace agreement in modern history' (1996b). It was ambitious because, under the guise of a negotiated peace settlement, external powers represented themselves as capacity-builders in seeking to build a state for others – a state which was not a product of popular consensus or popular involvement and one which, unsurprisingly, was seen by many Bosnians as an external imposition. The marginalisation of the people of Bosnia from their own political system by external powers was summed up in Bildt's observations on the new constitution (Annex 4 of the Dayton framework agreement): 'No-one thought it wise to submit the constitution to any sort of parliamentary or other similar proceeding. It was to be a constitution by international decree' (Bildt, 1998: 139).

Although often presented as a peace agreement rather than a framework for the reconstruction of Bosnia, the civilian annexes comprised five-sixths of the Dayton accords and involved a wide range of activities in which international actors, coordinated by the OHR, were mandated temporarily to play key coordinating roles (Gow, 1998: 169). For this reason, the state-level elections, to be held within nine months of the signing ceremony, were initially held to be crucial for restoring ownership over the new state to its citizens. Under the formal Dayton agreement there was to be a year of internationally supervised transition, during which there would be elections and the establishment of the political institutions of the new state, which were to be elected and directly accountable to the people (see Chandler, 1999: 43–51).

1995–99: STRENGTHENING THE HIGH REPRESENTATIVE

The planned year of internationally supervised transition to self-governing democracy was due to end with the election of state and entity bodies in September 1996, symbolising 'the democratic birth of the country' (PIC, 1996a: §27). Although these bodies were elected under internationally supervised and ratified elections, the transitional international administration was prolonged for a further two-year 'consolidation period' and then, in December 1997, extended indefinitely. The extension of the time limits for international withdrawal and the creation of new mandates for international agencies, coordinated by the Peace Implementation Council, was initially justified by the ambiguous wording of the Dayton agreement itself but later by increasingly subjective interpretations of the mandate by the High Representative, including innovative reference to the 'spirit of Dayton'.

The Dayton agreement provides little guidance for understanding the extension of international mandates or the mechanisms of international administration over the new state. This is because the agreement was ostensibly a treaty between the regional parties and not formally a treaty between the international agencies and the government of Bosnia. The Dayton agreement was rigid where it concerned the limits to Bosnian self-rule but extremely flexible in relation to the powers which international actors could exercise over this nominally independent state. As Paul Szasz notes, the Dayton agreement was 'merely a part of total arrangements to bring peace to Bosnia' (1996: 304). It is worth quoting at length the international constitutional lawyer closely involved in the development of Dayton:

Explicitly mentioned or merely implied by those texts are a host of other agreements or arrangements, which are to be concluded ... by or within the numerous international organisations assigned various roles by these texts, and which may take the form of bilateral or multilateral executive agreements, resolutions of the [United Nations] Security Council or decisions of NATO, the OSCE ... and other organisations ... [E]vidently the parties to the GFA [General Framework Agreement] and the ancillary agreements could not bind these external actors ... nor, of course, are these external actors precluded from taking steps not foreseen in these texts. (Szasz, 1996: 304)

This flexibility has been exemplified by the extension of the powers of the OHR. The High Representative has explained this process as one which has no fixed limits: 'if you read Dayton very carefully ... Annex 10 even gives me the possibility to interpret my own authorities and powers' (Westendorp, 1997). The pattern of ad hoc and arbitrary extensions of international regulatory authority was initially set by the PIC itself as it rewrote its own powers and those of the High Representative at successive Peace Implementation Council meetings. The most important of these were the initial strategic six-monthly review conferences: at Florence, in June 1996; Paris, in November 1996; Sintra, in May 1997; Bonn, in December 1997; and Luxembourg, in June 1998.

The PIC Florence Review conference, in June 1996, gave a mandate to the PIC Steering Board to discuss the extension of international involvement for a two-year 'stabilisation period' (PIC, 1996a: §24, §27). In the run-up to the September 1996 elections, the PIC increasingly sought to downplay their importance and top international officials, such as Flavio Cotti, OSCE Chairman-in-Office, stressed that the elections were merely a step in the right direction: 'We have opted to hold the elections above all because they should be viewed as a small, but still the first, step towards the path of reconciliation' (OHRB, 1996a). Clear electoral victory for the main three nationalist parties, at state, entity and cantonal levels, was then used to justify a rethink on the 'conclusion of the year-long mandates of the implementation agencies', suggesting that the peace process would not be 'consolidated' until further state, entity and cantonal elections in September 1998 (OHR, 1996: §27, §90).

The Paris Ministerial Meeting of the PIC Steering Board, in November 1996, decided to extend the year of transition, which was due to end the following month, for a further two years. During this new consolidation period, the High Representative was mandated to draw up two successive twelve-month 'action plans'. These OHR action plans were to be approved by the PIC, in consultation with the principal international institutions involved in implementing the peace agreement, and their implementation would then be reviewed at mid-term (PIC, 1996b: §4). The new extended role of the High Representative was accompanied by reinforced powers to make recommendations to the state and entity authorities, and in the case of dispute, to give his interpretation and make his recommendations public (PIC, 1996b: §6). This period of preparation for consolidation was rounded off at the 4–5 December 1996 PIC conference in London, which approved an action plan for the coming year containing detailed policy recommendations (OHRB, 1996b).

The first action plan mid-term review took place at the Sintra meeting of the PIC Steering Board, in May 1997. Here a new package of measures to ensure cooperation with the High Representative was announced, including the capacity to pursue deadlines announced by the PIC and enact measures in the case of non-compliance (PIC, 1997a: §92). These measures included visa restrictions on travel abroad for 'obstructive' Bosnian representatives as well as economic sanctions targeted at a local level and the capacity to curtail or suspend any media network or programmes which contravened 'either the spirit or letter' of the Dayton agreement (PIC, 1997a: §35, §36, §70).

The extension of the international institutional mechanisms of regulation meant that the Bosnian state bodies had little influence over either policy development or its implementation. At state level, Bosnian representatives had only a limited opportunity to discuss policy proposals drawn up by the Office of the High Representative in coordination with other international bodies such as the World Bank and IMF. At the most, the Bosnia institutions could make very minor alterations to OHR pre-prepared packages or attempt to delay their implementation.

Having been relegated to the status of 'an extended working group', capable only of discussing policies drawn up and implemented by international institutions, it was little wonder that the Bosnian state bodies were increasingly sidelined by the OHR. Even limited discussion and debate in Bosnian government assemblies was viewed by the High Representative as unnecessary and evidence that: 'Democratisation has a long way to go before one can safely say it has truly taken root in a country with no political experience of its benefits' (OHRB, 1997c). The cut and thrust of democratic consensus-building, at the level of the tripartite Presidency, Council of Ministers and Parliamentary Assembly, was often seen as an unnecessary delay to vital policy implementation. These discussions created further work for the High Representative, as affirmation of international policy in these bodies nearly always required 'prompting by, or support from, my Office' (OHR, 1997: §18). Compared to the swift signature of the chief administrator's pen, the joint institutions were judged to be 'painfully cumbersome and ineffective' (OHRB, 1997c).

The 'cumbersome' need to acquire the assent of elected Bosnian representatives was removed when the Bonn PIC summit, in December 1997, gave the High Representative the power to directly impose legislation, giving international officials both executive and legislative control over the formally independent state. The OHR was now mandated to enact 'interim measures' against the wishes of elected state, entity, cantonal and municipal elected bodies. These decrees were to remain in place until formally assented to by the respective level of government. The 'Bonn powers' also enabled the High Representative to dismiss elected representatives and government officials held to be obstructing the OHR's task of implementing the Dayton agreement (PIC, 1997b: XI).

It should also be highlighted that the extended mandates laid down at Bonn were qualitatively different from earlier extensions to the OHR's powers: the new mandates granted by the PIC, to itself, for the purpose of overseeing Bosnia were also made indefinite (PIC, 1997b: XI). International withdrawal and the ceding of sovereignty and policy-making powers to Bosnian institutions was now to be dependent on an ill-defined set of 'benchmarks' to be determined by the PIC at a time of its own choosing (see PIC, 1998a: §108).

Since December 1997, successive High Representatives have grasped the opportunities unaccountable power has provided, claiming that it is up to them to decide their own remit (for example, Rodriguez, 1998). These arbitrary powers have been regularly used to impose legislative measures against the will of elected bodies and to sack hundreds of Bosnian public officials, from members of the Presidency and entity prime ministers down to municipal civil servants (see OHR, 2005).

By 1999, the PIC and the OHR had accumulated an array of powers unimagined in 1995 when the Dayton agreement was signed. Yet, despite the new mandates and the indefinite extension of the power to impose legislation and to dismiss non-compliant officials, the international state-builders appeared to be running out of ideas. The international bureaucracy increasingly appeared to be running the country with little purpose or legitimacy.

The initial experiment in the state-building mechanisms of Empire in Denial had failed to allow Western actors to evade political responsibility because the capacity-building international administration developed its own powers in an ad hoc and unplanned way, reacting to every problem by the further extension of its formal remit. The bureaucracy, in effect, pushed to extend its formal powers to match its informal relationship of power. This failure of the state-building mechanisms to distance the West from political responsibility exposed the lack of any international direction in the running of the Bosnian state and the artificial nature of the state capacity-building practices (see Chandler, 1999). It was the failure of the initial state-building approach to Bosnia which informed the overhaul of the approach to state-building in the region after 1999, as outlined in the previous chapter.

The war over Kosovo, and the more interventionist approach of the European Union to the region which followed, finally provided the international administrators with a framework through which they could revamp their regulatory role (Kemp and van Meurs, 2003: 63–4). The transformation of the role of the administrative overseers was not to come from any new attempt to involve or engage with the people of Bosnia, but from new practices which sought to operate through the institutions of the Bosnian state rather than against them and attempted gradually to conceal the direct and coercive exercise of external power.

2000–05: THE TRANSITION TO EU OWNERSHIP

Prior to 2000, the EU had been closely involved in the work of the Office of the High Representative, for example, at its June 1998 Council meeting declaring the establishment of an EU/Bosnia Task Force, with the aim of increasing cooperation and assisting in policy-making in the crucial areas of judicial reform, education, media, good governance and economic reform (PIC, 1998b: VI). However, despite an increasingly direct EU input into policy-making, the EU played a subordinate and supporting role within the PIC Dayton framework rather than dictating its own terms. The PIC Declaration from the December 1998 Madrid meeting, for example, stated that Dayton implementation was the priority and that it was Bosnia's 'performance in implementing its Dayton obligations' that would dictate 'the pace of integration into European structures' (PIC, 1998b: VI). The close involvement of the European Union in Bosnian politics was formally limited to the 'civilian implementation of the Dayton agreement'.

From 2000 onwards this relationship was to be reversed. The flexibility of the Dayton framework was to be fully revealed as the mechanisms of regulation shifted informally from the PIC to the EU and, without the need for any formal consultation of the people of Bosnia, Dayton gradually was to become subordinate to the requirements for eventual EU membership. Even more remarkable, the 'temporary' powers of international policy imposition under the OHR were to be transferred to the EU itself, operating on its own behalf. In effect, the EU would be mandated to negotiate with itself in determining every aspect of policy-making in Bosnia.

In March 2000 the European Union announced a Road Map as a first step for Bosnia in the SAp. This document established 18 key conditions which Bosnia had to fulfil in order to start the preparation of a Feasibility Study which would then form the basis of negotiations for a Stabilisation and Association Agreement. These conditions covered far reaching policy reforms concerning elections, the civil service, state institutions, border services, the judiciary, trade regulations, foreign direct investment, property laws and public broadcasting (EURM, 2000).

This shift in perspective, away from international regulation under the increasingly strained legitimacy of the High Representative's interpretation of the Dayton agreement, towards regulation legitimised by the requirements necessary for the EU accession process was confirmed by the Peace Implementation Council at the May 2000 meeting in Brussels (PIC, 2000). As Carl Bildt noted at the meeting, in his capacity as the Special Envoy of the UN Secretary-General to the Balkans: 'the discussion has moved away from the exit strategies of the international community from Bosnia towards, instead, the entry strategies of Bosnia into the international community in general and Europe in particular' (Bildt, 2000).

From May 2000, the main objectives of European Union assistance have not been couched in terms of supporting Dayton but in the much more inclusive terminology of support for Bosnia within the framework of the SAp (EC, 2003a). More importantly, the framework used by the PIC and the OHR has increasingly been shaped by the EU Road Map and subsequent EU strategies of engagement rather than by Dayton itself. In fact, too strong an attachment to the Dayton settlement, through the defence of entity rights and 'vital interests' protections for Bosnia's constituent peoples, have been interpreted as a barrier to legislative progress towards EU integration (EC, 2003c: B.1.1).

At the Zagreb summit of EU and regional top officials, in November 2000, the Bosnian leaders fully committed themselves to meeting the Road Map conditions and the Zagreb Declaration has subsequently been used by the Office of the High Representative to bring EU requirements under his mandate of regulation and coordination (ECZD, 2000). High Representative Wolfgang Petritsch admonished Bosnian state leaders in June 2001 and urged 'responsible politicians to straighten out their priorities and to increase their efforts to fulfil the conditions of the Road Map as soon as possible' arguing that 'integration with Europe is the only way to improve the life of citizens throughout the country and should be pursued with unrelenting determination for the benefit of all citizens' (Petritsch, 2001b).

Following the Zagreb Declaration, the EU established a CARDS programme and a programme of EU technical assistance for Bosnia. In 2001, the European Commission adopted a Country Strategy for Bosnia which covered the period 2002–06 and provided a framework for EU assistance. Since 2001, assistance of more than €240 million has been committed under the CARDS programme, supporting Bosnia's participation in the Stabilisation and Association process. The EU also increasingly deployed conditionality in the granting of macro-economic support in return for recommended economic and political reforms (EC, 2004a: §3.2).

The transfer of power to the EU more directly can be seen in the OHR's 2002 reform of the Council of Ministers with the post of Chairman of the Council no longer subject to eight-month rotation but held for the whole of the legislative period and becoming a central administrative role, involving responsibility for the work of the DEI – established under the same edict and charged with the task of preparing a strategy of European integration (OHR, 2002e).

The DEI has, in effect, become the key executive body of the Bosnian government, supported in its operational structuring and institutional linkages by funding directly from the European Commission. The DEI is the main partner to the European Commission in the SAp and has been tasked with 'special responsibilities', including negotiating and supervising the implementation of agreements made with the EU. Based on the centrality of the EU accession process, the Chairman of the Council of Ministers has been granted a high level of executive authority, becoming the de facto Bosnian Prime Minister; in fact,

Paddy Ashdown has referred to him in just this way (EC, 2003c: B.1.1.3; ICG, 2003). The Chairman has the task of coordinating strategies and policies among state institutions and between entity governments and of ensuring the harmonisation of Bosnian laws with the *acquis communautaire* of the EU. His office has the assistance of EU advisers to draft new laws compliant with the *acquis* and to conduct the compliance check of any legislation proposed by Bosnian legislators themselves.

The strengthening of executive power through the new institution of the DEI has been an integral part of the transition to more direct EU involvement, which has necessitated the 'rebranding' of the 'anomalous' Bonn powers of the High Representative. The EU has stated the problem in these terms:

They certainly raise justified questions about Bosnia's ability to sustain a SAA. Nevertheless, while the 'Bonn Powers' are certainly anomalous among EU partner states, their existence in Bosnia need not automatically exclude that country from moving towards SAA negotiations. To make this case, Bosnia needs to give evidence that the powers are generally declining in relevance and that their use occurs ever less within core SAA areas. (EC, 2003c: B.1.1.5)

Interestingly, the use of the Bonn powers to impose legislation by edict is not necessarily seen as problematic for Bosnia's closer integration into the EU. There is a clear danger of double standards in the EU turning a blind eye to the lack of democracy in Bosnia. For this reason, the November 2003 SAp progress report seeks to downplay the undermining of democratic processes involved in the use of High Representative edicts. The EU suggests that this is often merely a matter of imposing 'soft decisions', alleging that the OHR steps in merely to follow up policies already agreed in advance. Closer informal EU cooperation with the DEI and the Chairman of the CoM means that agreements can then be imposed on governments at entity level without this appearing to be a 'hard' exercise of coercive power. The EU, in fact, wishes to conflate external diktat with freely negotiated agreement in stating that: 'Current evidence suggests ... that the "push" of the Bonn Powers is gradually being replaced by the "pull" of European institutions' (EC, 2003c: B.1.1.5).

This process of alleging a basis of policy agreement which is then imposed through 'soft decisions' could be seen in the OHR's establishment of special reform commissions, involving appointed Bosnian nationals and chaired by international representatives. These commissions have helped provide a veneer of agreement without going through a formally accountable political process. They have been used for policy issues where the OHR faces clear popular opposition, for example, on indirect taxation, defence, intelligence services and on the reform of the Mostar city council administration. Three of the four commission's findings have then been imposed by edict (the exception is the Defence Reform Commission). In the case of the Mostar commission, the major administrative reforms were imposed despite a marked lack of any agreement by Bosnia participants (CRCM, 2003; OHR, 2004). The dishonesty of the process was highlighted by the use of agreement on minor issues to argue that the imposition of the major reforms was merely the use of 'soft' power, clarifying reforms on which there was largely agreement (Perry, 2004).

At the EU Thessalonica summit, in June 2003, additional instruments to enhance EU regulation in Bosnia were developed. These included a Joint Declaration on Political Dialogue aimed at reinforcing the convergence of positions on foreign policy questions to reach alignment with the EU Common Foreign and Security Policy (EC, 2003c: B.3.1). The most important EU initiative, however, was the development of a new European Partnership, established to 'enrich' and 'intensify' the SAp, setting out Bosnia's political, economic and other priorities (EC, 2004b). The Partnership priorities are divided into short-term, of one to two years, and medium-term, of three to four years, and include over 50 areas where policy reforms are required to meet EU demands for 'harmonisation', from the reorganisation of political institutions and public administration to privatisation and sensitive economic programmes to remove 'labour rigidities', 'implement bankruptcy legislation' and 'lower the ratio between government expenditure and GDP'. These restrictive economic policies are sensitive as they would mean reducing social welfare protection in a state where half the population is already, according to the EU, 'at or near the poverty line' (EC, 2003c: C).

The priorities of the Partnership are based on the EU's political and strategic priorities in the light of their assessments of the Bosnian government's Annual Reports. However, it should be noted that there is no relationship of accountability or Bosnian ownership involved in this priority-setting process. The Partnership policy guidelines only involve 'informal consultations' with Bosnian representatives (EC, 2003b: §2). The Bosnian government is then 'expected to respond to the European Integration Partnerships by preparing and implementing Action Plans, with a timetable and details of how they intend to address the Partnership's priorities' (EC, 2003b: §2). The EU provides security, funds the international assistance and runs the policy programmes for Bosnia. If this is a European partnership it is a highly unequal one (see Chapter 5).

The increased intensity of EU engagement with the Bosnian policy-making process has necessitated the reinforcement of the meetings of the EU/Bosnia Consultative Task Force, to assist in the Annual Reports and annual Action Plans. The EU has also established a Coordination Board for Economic Development and EU Integration in order to develop medium- to long-term economic strategy and direct the Bosnian Council of Ministers in the formulation of a Poverty Reduction Strategy Paper in negotiation with the World Bank (EC, 2003c: B.3.7.1). In order to ensure that the DEI can cope with the huge amount of directives flying from Brussels to Sarajevo, the EU will be seconding civil servants from EU member states to work as advisers as well as providing targeted technical assistance and institution-building support under CARDS (EC, 2003b: §2).

While the real transition to European Union ownership has been largely operating at the informal level this has also begun to be reflected in formal changes, such as the EU Police Mission replacing the UN Mission to Bosnia at the end of 2002 and the EU's assumption of the NATO Stabilisation Force (SFOR) military security role at the end of 2004 (EC, 2004a: §2.2). The ending of the UN International Police Task Force (IPTF) mandate is illustrative in this regard as it did not result in any greater ownership for the Bosnian authorities. Under the EU, in the first ever civilian crisis management deployment under the European CFSP (EUPM, 2004), the mandate of the mission is no less authoritative than that of the UN IPTF. It establishes 'a broad approach with activities addressing the whole range of Rule of Law aspects, including institution building programmes and police activities' and is designed not merely to support Dayton implementation but also to support the EU's institution-building under the CARDS regulations and the SAp more broadly (EUPM, 2002: §3). The Head of Mission reports to the EU's Special Representative who reports to the Secretary-General/High Representative for CFSP, thus ensuring a 'unified chain of command': a chain of command which does not involve any Bosnian input or accountability (EUPM, 2002: §7).

Lord Paddy Ashdown was named as the first European Union Special Representative in Bosnia in March 2002, taking up his duties when he assumed the position of the High Representative that May.

The creation of Ashdown's 'double-hatted' position as both EU and PIC representative marked a clear signal of transitional intent. As far as Paddy Ashdown understood his position, he was to be the last High Representative. By this he did not understand that ownership was to be given to Bosnian institutions but rather that his role would be taken over by new mechanisms of the European Union. In the event this handover process was delayed by a year or more and Ashdown was replaced by the former German Post and Telecommunications Minister, Christian Schwarz-Schilling, at the end of January 2006.

This move reflects other formal organisational changes. In 2002, the PIC was 'streamlined' providing a clearer European coordinating role. A Board of Principals was established as the main coordinating body, chaired by the EU Special Representative and meeting weekly in Sarajevo. In real terms it would seem that the Office of the High Representative is already more dependent on the EU than the PIC and in 2003 the EU provided over half of the OHR's operating budget, which in 2004 was €21.1 million. Contributions to the OHR budget broke down as follows: EU 53 per cent, USA 22 per cent, Japan 10 per cent, Russia 4 per cent, Canada 3 per cent, Organisation of the Islamic Conference 2.5 per cent, others 5.5 per cent (EC, 2004a: §5). The, so far, largely informal process of EU regulation is now a contractual one with Bosnia's formal signing of the Stabilisation and Association Agreement in October 2005.

The SAA is an international agreement that has precedence over any other laws of the country. After being signed, the agreement becomes enforceable when it has been ratified by the Bosnian government, European Parliament and the national parliaments of EU members. Following this Bosnia will be legally obligated to undertake certain activities within SAA areas within strict time limits. Through the overseeing and implementation of the Stabilisation and Association Agreement the EU Special Representative and the executive policy-making institution of the DEI will maintain full regulatory control over the post-Dayton process.

CONCLUSION

By the end of 2005 the EU was routinely involved in every level of Bosnian policy preparation and implementation and annual Bosnian government work plans were being drawn up to meet the comprehensive SAp requirements. There can be little doubt that there has been a transition from the ad hoc, unaccountable, and largely unfocused, rule of the Peace Implementation Council. Yet this transition has not been one towards Bosnian ownership. Even the EU recognises that 'Bosnia "ownership" of reform remains limited' with international initiative, input and pressure guiding the process of transition (EC, 2004a: §2.3). As far as the engagement of the people of Bosnia or their elected representatives is concerned, little has changed over the ten years since the Dayton agreement. The Bosnian public have been excluded from the transition process and while there is general support for EU membership there has been little public discussion of the costs and benefits involved.

Rather than state-building, it would appear that ten years of informal trusteeship or shared sovereignty under the framework established by the Dayton agreement, have done little either to build the capacity of the Bosnian state or to legitimate it in the eyes of the population. The powers and the authority of the state have been subsumed by external actors and this process has prevented any real policy-making power being devolved to elected bodies, which were initially to have taken over government responsibilities following a year's transitional period.

Today, Bosnia is administered less through the heavy-handed and publicly recognised powers of the international High Representative and more through the policy-making power of Brussels, implemented with the assistance of the EU-funded and advised Directorate of European Integration. The fact that the governing and policy frameworks are understood, by Western commentators, to be shaped more by local actors than external ones demonstrates the ideological power of Empire in Denial and the success of the state-building experiments. This success has been in large part down to the post-1999 EU enlargement mechanisms which have more effectively distanced empire from political responsibility than the initial heavy-handed and crude mechanisms of the Office of the High Representative. Once the mechanisms of external regulation are revealed, the hollowness and self-serving nature of the arguments of Empire in Denial – which assert that the external administrators have been constrained by Dayton or attempt to blame the farce that is Bosnian state-building on the people of Bosnia and their elected representatives – stand exposed.

7
Techniques of Evasion (1)
Anti-corruption Initiatives

Ten years after Dayton, problems of good governance, particularly those of tackling corruption and establishing the rule of law, are widely alleged to be the central questions facing Bosnia's international state-builders. The following two chapters focus on these spheres and consider the practices taken within them as techniques of evasion used by Empire in Denial. Anti-corruption and rule of law regulation both seek to impose the will of empire but do so within the depoliticised administrative and technical framework of good governance. These regulatory frameworks are evasive ones because rather than empire taking political responsibility for its regulatory policies it seeks to assert that its actions are merely facilitating the will of the governed, aimed at empowering and capacity-building both states and their citizens.

In putting anti-corruption at the core of its good governance initiatives, the international administration in Bosnia reflects an increasing international consensus that sees corruption as the central barrier to external state-building initiatives. This chapter considers the anti-corruption policies developed in the past decade and assesses how the anti-corruption agenda and its related policy practices, overseen by Bosnia's international administrators, have impacted on strengthening and building trust in Bosnia's public institutions.

Both the development of anti-corruption strategies and their use as a component part of international programmes for good governance are fairly recent developments. Corruption only became an issue of international concern with the development of international state-building practices in the 1990s. Yet, over the last decade, major world powers and international agencies, such as the IMF, World Bank, United Nations, OECD, the G8 group of industrialised nations and the European Union, have increasingly focused on the problem of corruption and the development of regulatory practices to combat it (Robinson, 1998: 1–2; Doig and Theobald, 2000; Szeftel, 2000). It is now a central assumption of the state-building discourse that anti-corruption strategies are a core component of good governance strategies and can be effective in increasing the accountability of state institutions and revitalising networks of trust in civil society (US, 1999; Theobald, 2000: 149).

The Stability Pact for South Eastern Europe proclaimed that it was making the fight against corruption a top priority upon its founding in 1999. This commitment has been formally endorsed at regular summits over the last seven years and, in February 2000, Stability Pact countries, including the EU member states, the countries of the SEE region, and the international donor community, established the Stability Pact Anti-Corruption Initiative (SPACI), designed to play a lead coordinating role in developing and expanding policy practices in this area as part of the state-building process in the region. The members of SPACI had no doubt that this major initiative was necessary because corruption was at the heart of practically all the problems facing the region:

The damage caused by corrupt practices in Southeast Europe is well known. Corruption has eroded the rule of law and the stability of democratic institutions, breaching fundamental rights and freedoms and undermining the trust and confidence of citizens in the fairness and impartiality of public administration. It has undermined the business climate, discouraged domestic and foreign investment, wasted economic resources and hampered economic growth, thus threatening the very objectives of peace, democracy and prosperity in Southeast Europe. (SPSEE, 2006b)

It seems that this catch-all capacity of corruption, to be blamed for every problematic aspect of SEE social, economic and political life, has made the issue central to the politics of Empire in Denial. It would appear that when it comes to the question of corruption, assumptions can be allowed to replace any serious research, and anecdotes or statistical correlations can be allowed to do the work of political analysis. There is unfortunately no space available here to undertake a broader critique of the methodological approaches which international institutions, engaged in state-building, have taken towards corruption, but it should be clear from a cursory examination that the focus on the issue has followed rather than led the transformation in international approaches to external regulatory control of the governing institutions of non-Western states.

The lack of proof or analysis needed to substantiate international institutional assertions that combating corruption must be the central focus of their policy-making and capacity-building role reflects the fact that the issue seems to be one of common sense, in much the same way as racial and cultural understandings of problems were in previous eras. Anti-corruption appeals to the administrative professionals engaged in Empire in Denial, as it legitimises increased regulatory intervention and at the same time portrays this regulative control as merely the imposition or upholding of technical standards or universal practices, undertaken to 'empower' the citizens or to uphold and strengthen democratic institutions. Not only do the practices of anti-corruption appear to be technocratic and non-political they also create the framework through which the political framework becomes 'corruptionised' – focused not on political differences but on procedures, etiquette and administrative standards. Policy failings in SEE states, or even shifts in EU policy with regard to enlargement (EC, 2005a) can then be put down to the 'corrupt' cultural or administrative failings of non-Western state governments and their citizens.

Over the last ten years a high international profile has been given to the development and implementation of an internationally coordinated anti-corruption strategy in Bosnia. This experience allows anti-corruption strategy, and the good governance agenda informing it, to be assessed and for some lessons to be drawn regarding the external management of capacity-building programmes designed to strengthen state institutions on this basis. The following sections consider the centrality of the issue of corruption and the practices of anti-corruption to the international administration of Bosnia, international community responses to the problem of corruption, especially in relation to public awareness and institution-building, and the questions arising from this experience.

'ONLY THE HIGHEST STANDARDS WILL DO'

In March 2005, the Croatian member of the Bosnian presidency, Dragan Covic, due to become chair of the presidency in June 2005, was dismissed from his post, without appeal, by the international High Representative Lord Paddy Ashdown. This was not for any opposition to the Dayton peace settlement nor for any obstruction to the EU integration process – in fact his performance in post was praised by Ashdown (Ashdown, 2005). Covic was just the most recent of a long line of highly ranked elected politicians to be forced out of office, or barred from running for high office, on the grounds of anti-corruption and the promotion of good administrative practices.

Ashdown's rule as High Representative was marked by the priority he gave to emphasising good governance and anti-corruption initiatives. After only a few days in office, in June 2002, he sacked Nikola Grabovac, Minister of Finance and Deputy Prime Minister of the Bosnian Federation (FBiH) on the grounds that Grabovac had failed to act according to the highest standards of ministerial responsibility in the wake of the AM Sped affair, where public money from the federal government was misappropriated by the director of the private company, even though there was no allegation that the lapse in financial controls reflected on Grabovac personally (Chandler, 2002b). In the same week, Ashdown forced the resignation of the RS Minister of Finance, Milenko Vracar. In April 2003, Mirko Sarovic, the President of the RS, was forced to resign to maintain Bosnia's 'standards of political responsibility', again, on the basis of allegations which were not proven in any court of law (Ashdown, 2003a). Mila Gadzic faced charges and was forced to resign from her position as Minister of Foreign Trade and Economic Relations in the state government in August 2003. In June 2004, Ashdown removed 59 elected and appointed RS officials at entity and municipal level on the basis of allegations of their failure to carry out their responsibilities (in relation to the Hague international criminal tribunal) and 60 municipal bank accounts were removed from the Serbian Democratic Party (*Srpska Demokratska Stranka*, SDS), and funds of up to 1 million KM transferred to state institutions. In December 2004, Ashdown prevented Milorad Dodik from running for the post of RS Prime Minister because criminal charges had been laid against him.

Lord Ashdown administered the Bosnian protectorate according to rules of good governance which are much tougher than those of many Western democracies, where there is no expectation that government ministers (or even US presidents) should resign on the basis of allegations which are yet to be proven in a court of law. In the Grabovac case, the issue was that of ministerial responsibility for 'the actions or inactions of his ministry', again, a question where there are no common guidelines for practice, nor any consensus on rules, even among members of the European Union. The Office of the High Representative claimed the dismissal was justified on the grounds of Bosnia's particular need for 'proper governance and transparency'. Ashdown stated in the wake of the Covic dismissal that Bosnia needed to be ruled according to even higher standards than those existing in established Western democracies, which 'have long histories, well founded stability and the established trust of their citizens', because its 'democracy is still very fragile, its peace not yet fully secured and its institutions in their infancy'. He continued:

The truth is, as we all know, that Bosnia's institutions still have to win the trust of their citizens. And one of the reasons for that distrust, as every citizen knows, is the dangerously close connection between criminality and politics, as well as the high levels of corruption in Bosnia's political structures and governmental institutions. None of this is to say that any individual is guilty of the indictments laid against them. It is merely to assert that, if Bosnia is to win the trust of its citizens, without which no secure form of Government or stable peace can be established, then, in choosing which standards are appropriate to Bosnia, only the highest will do. (Ashdown, 2005)

Corruption and bad governance practices, rather than the dominance of the international administration or residual interethnic mistrust, are alleged to be the key reason, why Bosnia's citizens feel little connection to institutions of the Bosnian state. For Lord Ashdown and the international administrative Office of the High Representative, the need to win the trust of Bosnian citizens and legitimate Bosnia's ruling institutions has necessitated an international focus on corruption and the prioritisation of anti-corruption measures.

One other consequence of the anti-corruption campaign and holding Bosnia's politicians to the highest standards of good governance is held to be a cleansing of the political system itself:

And there is another reason why holding to this principle, however difficult, is so important to Bosnia's future. Next year, after the 2006 elections, the winning political parties will have to consider whom they choose for high government positions. Perhaps the fact that politicians' immunity is now severely limited and that we have held to the principle of resignation in the case of criminal indictment will cause political parties to think twice about putting forward for high office individuals who have a questionable past or close connections with the criminal world. If so, then this would be the biggest step ever taken to cleaning up Bosnian politics and would open the way to new, younger and cleaner hands to take over the government of this country. (Ashdown, 2005)

This chapter questions whether the international administration's approach to anti-corruption and good governance over the past ten years has, in fact, contributed to building trust in Bosnia's public institutions or to the undermining the ethnic electoral segmentation of Bosnian society. It also seeks to question the international administration's allegations of a partnership between the main nationalist political parties, corruption and organised crime, which are repeated so often that they are simply assumed to be true by most commentators and international officials. It will be suggested that the tendency to see the political sphere as one of crime, corruption and sectional interests is a one-sided and problematic reading of the situation in Bosnia, one which marginalises the capacities of the political sphere to generate trust in state institutions and posits external rule as both necessary and legitimate.

CORRUPTION

From the late 1990s onwards, the discussion of corruption in Bosnia has been highlighted as a political question of good governance through the assertion of a link between the nationalist political leaderships and criminal elements involved in tax and customs evasion. The question of corruption in relation to good governance in Bosnia was first highlighted in July 1997 when UK Foreign Secretary Robin Cook accused nationalist politicians on all sides of a failure to tackle customs irregularities and the black market (Binyon, 1997). The problems of customs collection were explicitly linked to the political institutional framework as Cook suggested that this was a political manipulation designed to undermine 'the ordinary peoples of Bosnia's right to accountability' (OHRB, 1997a). Within a month the corruption issue was transformed as policy NGOs like the International Crisis Group called for the OHR to take action in this otherwise neglected area (OHRB, 1997b). In response to this pressure, the High Representative's Office proposed to establish an Anti-Fraud Unit. This was endorsed at the December 1997 Peace Implementation Council forum in Bonn and the Unit was established within the OHR Economics Department in April 1998.

A March 1998 survey on Bosnia by the anti-corruption NGO Transparency International reported that the creation of criminal centres of power and the political framework inherited from the communist regime had created an atmosphere where the 'style of government is essentially top-down, with "rule of party" rather than "rule of law", and an absence of accountability and transparency let alone a culture of consultation and consensus building' (Dlouhy, 1999). The 'rule of party' was held to undermine the new institutional structures established by Dayton and necessary for self-government. Corruption was blamed not only for the lack of democratisation but also for the international community's failure to attract foreign investment, necessary to free Bosnia from international assistance

(Wilkinson, 1998). The *New York Times* alleged in August 1999 that: 'As much as a billion dollars has disappeared from public funds or been stolen from international aid projects through fraud carried out by Muslim, Croat and Serbian leaders who keep Bosnia rigidly partitioned into three ethnic enclaves' (Hedges, 1999). According to Peter Singer, writing in the *World Policy Journal*, in Bosnia 'the true power brokers are an ultra-rich elite at the helm of combined political/economic/criminal networks' who dominated 'a veiled structure of domestic control which hinders international efforts at reform in all areas and at all levels'; he concluded that 'the result is that the rule of party comes before rule of law' (Singer, 2000).

In July 2000, the US Congress General Accounting Office (GAO) report into corruption in Bosnia concurred that the root cause of corruption was Bosnia's political leadership (Pardew, 2000). Harold Johnson, GAO's Associate Director, responsible for preparing the report, argued in Congress that there was little evidence that US strategy adequately addressed 'the underlying causes of corruption and lack of reform, namely the continued obstructionist behaviour of hard-line nationalist political leaders' (Johnson, 2000). Jacques Klein, the UN's Special Representative to Bosnia, viewed that: 'Dayton stopped the violence, but it did not end the war, and the war is still being fought bureaucratically through obfuscation, delay and avoidance by a group of leaders who do not want to lose power' (Hedges, 1999). He was supported by Richard Holbrooke, US ambassador to the UN and architect of the Dayton agreement, who spoke out on the eve of the November 2000 elections, accusing Bosnia's leading politicians of being 'crooks pretending to be nationalists' (*Reuters*, 2000).

However, where corruption claims have been investigated there has been relatively little evidence of the involvement of leading political parties. In fact, even more surprisingly, the OHR and other international bodies have at no point produced a comprehensive report documenting the extent of corruption and fraud in Bosnia and Herzegovina (CILE, 2000: 14). As Sam Gejdenson argued at the US House of Representatives International Relations Committee in September 1999, one of the problems with addressing the issue has been 'exaggerated guesstimates of corruption figures and misidentified reports' (Gejdenson, 1999). Gejdenson, the top Democrat on the Committee, argued that the problems had been 'grossly overstated' and that Bosnia was facing troubles no different from those of other emerging democracies in the region (Wolfson, 1999).

The US government's General Accounting Office's July 2000 report found no evidence to support the widely repeated *New York Times'* claim (Hedges, 1999) that American or international aid was 'being lost to large-scale fraud or corruption'. One of the main examples of losses was the US Embassy's loss of $900,000 in operating funds due to the failure of the bank holding these assets. Out of the total of $1,000 million spent on Bosnia since 1995 by the US government, this was a very small proportion, less than 0.1 per cent, and it was believed that the full amount could be recovered (Tully, 2000). Nevertheless the GAO report also suggested that 'crime and corruption were endemic at all levels of Bosnian society' (Marquis and Gall, 2000). This view was not based on hard evidence of endemic corruption but 'a near consensus of opinion among officials we interviewed' that endemic crime and corruption threatened Dayton implementation (Johnson, 2000). Similar subjective anecdotal evidence is produced regularly, along the lines of Transparency International interviews which operate on the basis of general 'perceptions' of corruption (Heywood, 1997).

The OSCE Citizen Outreach Campaign Anti-Corruption Opinion Poll in 2000 asked questions such as 'Do you believe that corruption exists in Bosnia and Herzegovina?', asked people to gauge the level of corruption from 'endemic' to 'insignificant' and asked 'Is corruption affecting the continuing development of Bosnia?' (OSCE, 2000a). Earlier subjective opinion poll evidence of corruption, such as that conducted in December 1999 by the US State Department, indicated that over 50 per cent of Bosnian citizens believed corruption was prevalent in government and business. However, this is, firstly, anecdotal, but secondly, consistent with similar polls in Central and Eastern Europe (OSCE, 2000b). There is a clear danger that citizens' disillusionment and alienation from the reform process, expressed in a generalised sense that 'the politicians are only in it for themselves and are corrupt', are being used by external institutions to pursue their own regulatory agendas. This chapter suggests that rather than addressing the problems of state capacity by giving citizens a greater stake in the processes of government, anti-corruption initiatives, undertaken for their own purposes by external bodies, can only feed existing levels of cynicism and alienation, further weakening state capacity.

The main evidence of political collusion seems to be the claim that 'Bosnian authorities may be using the foreign donations to make up for income the government has lost to crime'. According to the

GAO this could be 'hundreds of millions of dollars' (Marquis and Gall, 2000). The IMF estimates that the bulk of this is due to black-marketing of cigarettes, with an estimated $230 million lost annually (Mirosavljevic, 2000). More often figures for corruption are not even 'guesstimates' of the level of tax and customs evasion but established simply on the basis of the budget deficit made up by the international administration. The Dutch ambassador to the UN therefore puts the annual figure at $500 million (Mirosavljevic, 2000). Of course, tax or customs evasion is hardly unique to Bosnia. In Britain the estimated loss to the tax payer from cigarette smuggling alone is estimated at far more than in Bosnia, at £4 billion annually. However, no commentators have considered this to be corruption despite the vastly superior resources in the hands of the UK government to prevent such illegal black market activities (*BBC*, 2000). Nevertheless, even at this level the facts are not clear concerning a lack of local commitment on the issue. Allan Wilson, General Manager of the International Customs and Fiscal Aid Organisation Office in Banja Luka, stated that the international monitors were 'impressed with the achievements of the Sector for Customs Frauds of the [Srpska] Republic Customs Administration, obtained in spite of the shortage of personnel' (Mirosavljevic, 2000). While Bosnian Federal police in Tuzla Canton developed a compendium of case files running to 5,500 pages (CILE, 2000: 14).

From the available evidence, the political ties to corruption, assumed by the international community policy-makers developing large-scale anti-corruption initiatives, are yet to be conclusively established. In August 2004 the publication of the in-depth Transparency International *National Integrity Systems* study report on Bosnia-Herzegovina was heralded at a major Sarajevo press conference and endorsed by international representatives, such as the UK ambassador Ian Cliff, who emphasised the headline findings of a 'serious corruption challenge'. Unfortunately, few people appear to have read further into the report to question the methodology used, for example: that of implying levels of corruption from correlations with economic indicators such as unemployment levels or government economic subsidies; the use of conclusions from other agencies, such as USAID or the OHR, without supporting data; or the repetition of unfounded allegations made elsewhere. When pressed to come up with evidence of links between Bosnian government officials and crime or corruption the TI report is revealing:

Although a great number of criminal charges have been brought against public officeholders, only one judgement has been delivered so far ... The Basic Court in Banja Luka found Mr Nenad Suzic, the former RS minister of education, guilty of abusing his office. In particular, during his term as minister of education, Mr Suzic approved £5,000 for postgraduate studies in Great Britain for the daughter of a politician, at that time president of the municipal assembly of Prijedor. (TI, 2004: 23)

Even this one case is not yet settled and has been appealed. It would seem that although there are undoubtedly cases of political representatives acting corruptly, there is no evidence that Bosnia is, in this regard, any different from any other Western state, and certainly no evidence that the problem is in any way exceptional. Detailed investigative evidence is scarce, and disturbingly so, for a policy issue which is held to assume such central importance to the country's future. In September 1999 the FBiH government established a Commission of International Legal Experts to investigate international press allegations of political corruption, to consider the cause and extent of corruption, and to recommend measures to improve anti-corruption efforts. The Commission reported in February 2000, concluding that 'the nature of corruption in Bosnia is not ... systematic corruption organized by all three sets of "nationalist leaders"' (CILE, 2000: 21). The International Commission stated:

The types of corruption and organized crime afflicting Bosnia are similar to those that afflict other Central and East European states and states of the former Soviet Union, where they are endemic at the domestic level. They relate primarily to tax evasion, customs evasion, and misappropriation of domestic public funds. In Bosnia, they are augmented by the fact that a significant volume of illicit and contraband goods passes through the country on their way to Western Europe ... The Commission found no reliable, quantitative estimate of the total level of corruption in the Federation. It may be, however, that the level and type of corruption in Bosnia differs from their Central and Eastern European neighbours in a number of important ways. According to some NGO workers familiar with the problem in these countries, corruption in Bosnia is "bush league" by comparison, and neither as highly organized nor as sophisticated. (CILE, 2000: 21-2)

From the evidence alone it would appear that the most effective strategy for tackling the problems of budgetary deficits through tax and customs evasion would be through assisting Bosnian police, prosecutors and judges with the resources to investigate cases with the support of the United Nations Mission in Bosnia-Herzegovina (UNMIBH) International Police Task Force (now the European Union Police Mission) and the European Commission's Customs and Fiscal Assistance Office (CAFAO) programme. However, subsuming international anti-corruption strategy under the mechanisms of good governance has meant that the international focus of resources has not been centred on dealing with corruption as part of the drive against major crime. International institutions working in Bosnia have used anti-corruption initiatives primarily to introduce mechanisms of good governance. These governance mechanisms include: regulative measures to increase government transparency; initiatives to strengthen the workings of Bosnian government institutions; and public awareness campaigns to inform and encourage the public to see corruption as a major political issue. It is these aspects of systemic anti-corruption strategy, rather than international support for criminal case work, that this chapter seeks to examine in more depth.

INTERNATIONAL STRATEGY

The Luxembourg Peace Implementation Council Steering Board, meeting in June 1998, encouraged the OHR to coordinate the international community in implementing a comprehensive anti-corruption strategy. The Madrid PIC, meeting in December 1998, reiterated concerns regarding a comprehensive anti-corruption strategy:

The Council expresses deep concern about continuing corruption and evasion of public funds. It welcomes the High Representative's development of a comprehensive anti-corruption strategy which will ... provide the framework necessary to identify, develop and implement changes in the structure and procedures of government, to significantly reduce corrupt activities and to establish a public awareness program ... The High Representative will take the lead in coordinating International Community efforts aimed at eliminating opportunities for corruption, tax evasion and diversion of public revenue; ensuring transparency in all phases of governmental operations; strengthening the legal system and the judiciary; and implementing control mechanisms and appropriate penalties to ensure compliance. A key component of the strategy will be to develop a public awareness campaign to educate citizens about the deleterious effects of corruption on their lives and on society. (OHR, 1999a: 6)

In February 1999 the Anti-Fraud Unit launched its Comprehensive Anti-Corruption Strategy, defining corruption, using the World Bank definition, as 'the abuse of public office for private gain' (OHR, 1999a: 6). The OHR's Comprehensive Anti-Corruption Strategy was approved by the Peace Implementation Steering Council and closely involved the United Nations, European Commission, the World Bank, US Treasury, US Justice Department and USAID. In addition to the individual case approach, providing assistance to the investigation and prosecution of major criminal cases, there was to be a two-track approach to deal with systemic political corruption: one track dealing with public attitudes, the other attempting to marginalise the influence of nationalist parties.

The Comprehensive Anti-Corruption Strategy sought to address 'Bosnian mindsets' through education and public awareness campaigning. According to the OHR: 'An informed citizenry is crucial for the success of any anti-corruption program. If the public is apathetic towards corruption and accepts it as an inevitable presence, efforts to alleviate corruption will be futile' (OHR, 1999a: 11). The assumed connection between nationalist party dominance and corrupt practices was to be regulated by establishing mechanisms of external oversight to safeguard governing structures from party-political influence, ensuring transparent financial management with strict control and monitoring of public revenue, tax and customs regulation. The work of government itself was to be closely monitored by parliamentary commissions, audit institutions and transparency offices.

PUBLIC AWARENESS

The systemic anti-corruption strategy involves a high level of international involvement in public education and political awareness to facilitate greater public involvement in the political process. The public education campaign is premised on the assumption that the people of Bosnia are unaware of their real interests in this area or are unable or unwilling to express them and therefore are in need of education and capacity-building from their international administrators. Christopher Bennett and Gerald Knaus argue: 'Most Bosnians are aware how corrupt their leaders are and secretly support international efforts to restructure their country. But given their dependency on the current system, they are not yet ready to demand reforms, transparency and accountability' (Bennett and Knaus, 1999). According to the director of the US State Department's Office of Bosnia Implementation, David Dlouhy: 'democratic concepts of accountability to the public and transparency are not yet second nature to most Bosnians' (Dlouhy, 1999).

This need for increased awareness about the issue of corruption is seen to fit in with broader governance aims of developing a more participatory political environment, undermining the influence of the three main nationalist parties, and with replacing the political salience of ethnicity with themes which cut across ethnic lines. As James Pardew, Balkans special adviser to the US President Bill Clinton and a number of secretaries of state, stated:

Our strong preference would be that the Bosnians undertake the changes themselves because it is clearly in their long-term, collective self-interest to do so. To promote that kind of thinking, we set a high priority on promotion of independent media, support of open and transparent elections, and encouragement of pro-reform and pro-Dayton leaders and political candidates, regardless of ethnic background or party. (Pardew, 2000)

In fact, the segmented voting patterns of Bosnian voters and political corruption have become increasingly interlinked in the minds of Bosnia's international administrators, with electoral support for the leading nationalist parties seen as an indicator of public attitudes towards corruption. For this reason the international institutions involved in the Bosnian political process have heavily emphasised the question of political corruption in the run-up to a number of elections. The OHR has stated that: 'only when citizens recognize corruption and are aware of its effects, will they be able to make the correct choices at the ballot box' (OHR, 1999a: 38). It would appear that the anti-corruption strategy is a highly politicised one. According to Peter Singer, the anti-corruption issue is the strongest card the international community has in encouraging political opposition to the leading nationalist parties:

[T]he one issue that has consistently motivated Bosnian voters to turn against the ethnic-nationalist parties is graft – when it is fully exposed. Voting for reconciliation with 'the enemy' is one thing, but it is a lot easier to abandon party allegiances in order 'to get rid of those thieves'. Exposing, condemning, and removing corrupt officials from power is one of the few points of leverage against the nationalists that is popular with the typical Bosnian on the street. Anti-corruption is the best multiethnic issue of all. (Singer, 2000)

The OHR asserts that: 'The ultimate success of the battle against corruption will be determined by the political will of the citizens of Bosnia and Herzegovina and the expression of that will in the election of their leaders' (OHR, 1999a: 41). To this end, the OHR has made public awareness a central pillar of its anti-corruption strategy, stating: 'All segments of society, from children in primary school to the business community and government officials, must be made aware of both the nature and consequences of corruption' (OHR, 1999a: 11). Often public anti-corruption awareness campaigns are timed to coincide with elections, where critical campaign slogans such as 'Gdje idu nase pare?', 'Where is our money going?', seek to bolster the opposition and are promoted in special TV episodes, radio spots, jumbo poster campaigns and special comic books and animated video clips, which are all designed to 'inform citizens about how they can become involved in the fight against corruption, by insisting on their right to a responsible, accountable government' (OHR, 2000a).

Until 2002, the OSCE was directly responsible for organising elections in Bosnia and played a central role in encouraging non-nationalist parties through attempts to 'raise citizens' awareness of corruption, thus allowing voters to make an informed choice at the polls' (OSCE, 2000d). Like the OHR, the OSCE also ran major anti-corruption publicity campaigns in the run-up to elections. Rather than making any specific allegations of corruption against the major parties, the OSCE would instead urge voters to speak out against corruption 'in general' by voting for 'anti-corruption' candidates (OSCE, 2000c). The Civil Society Anti-Corruption Public Outreach Programmes organised by local internationally funded NGOs and OSCE Community Facilitators set up radio shows, public tribunes, roundtable discussions and public meetings and crudely argued for the public to support the opposition parties who were raising awareness about government corruption.

While all Bosnian parties condemned corruption, the international education and public awareness campaigns created tensions with Bosnian politicians. For example, it was in the context of publicising political corruption that the OHR Anti-Fraud Unit briefed the, later discredited, material to Chris Hedges from the *New York Times* (Dlouhy, 1999). The resulting catalogue of misrepresentations played a useful role in legitimising increasing international pressure on Bosnian institutions but brought angry responses of bias from the then Bosnian President Alija Izetbegovic (A. Izetbegovic, 1999; B. Izetbegovic, 1999). Despite the anti-corruption campaigning focus, funded and encouraged by international institutions at successive elections, up to the present time the main nationalist parties have continued to dominate the political scene and achieve much better showings than expected, while no genuine cross-ethnic political alternative has emerged. This would appear to indicate some limitations to the strategy of making political corruption and good governance central political issues at elections.

It seems that the anti-corruption campaigns have promoted political cynicism rather than a hope for political change, and have backfired on the international community in this respect. Voting returns indicate that, while the public awareness aspects of the international anti-corruption strategy have been successful in getting the message across, this has neither had a beneficial influence on levels of public political participation nor had any positive impact on levels of trust and cooperation either within or between ethnic groups. It seems that the conclusion Bosnian voters have drawn from the institutionalisation of anti-corruption into every walk of life has been that no politicians can be trusted. While the international community promoted the corruption issue partly as a way of undermining support for the nationalist parties, the impact has been a wider one, undermining the political process more broadly. If all politicians are corrupt then voters are less likely to see change and progress as possible through the ballot box.

Evidence indicates that far from anti-corruption being a vehicle for broadening support for multi-ethnic parties, the issue seems to be one that favours the nationalists. The less trust people have in the broader political process, the more likely it is that parochial and local links will come to the forefront. This is supported by literature on the importance of high levels of generalised trust for establishing intercommunal bonds rather than particularistic communal identities, 'bridging' social capital as opposed to 'bonding' social capital, in the terminology of Robert Putnam (Putnam, 2000: 134–47; see also Fukuyama, 1995). If elected representatives are just out to line their own pockets then they cannot be trusted to prioritise the interests of their voters. Concern over representation can only lead to a higher level of insecurity and atomisation. Political pessimism and insecurity are more likely to lead to support for nationalist parties or to non-participation than to support for parties which promise political change. It is little surprise that in the run-up to subsequent elections, the key concern of the OHR has been whether voters will vote at all. These concerns seem justified with turnout dropping to 45 per cent in the local elections of October 2004, with young and urban voters abstaining. The low level of participation has been widely held to have benefited the nationalist parties, with younger, urban, less politically aligned voters more likely to abstain and more politically connected elderly and rural voters more likely to vote (Dervisbegovic, 2004).

INSTITUTION-BUILDING

According to leading international politicians and policy-makers, the popular nationalist parties are putting the personal interests of the political elites above those of the Bosnian public: 'politicians play the nationalist card to mask their lack of commitment to develop state institutions. For them, public accountability and personal responsibility are notoriously absent' (CILE, 2000: 6). The former High Representative, Wolfgang Petritsch, argued that the political elites had the wrong approach to the political process: 'The government is there to work for the citizen, and not the other way around' (Petritsch, 2000). For Petritsch: 'the corruption of public institutions is one of the most serious and major obstacles' preventing Bosnia becoming integrated in European institutions (CILE, 2000: 26). Because the problem of corruption is seen to lie with Bosnian politicians themselves, they are caught in a no-win situation. They have been criticised for failing to do more than create committees and commissions that have not 'measurably' reduced crime and corruption (Johnson, 2000). Yet, when they do form anti-corruption teams headed by the entity prime ministers and involving key ministers such as the Minister of the Interior and Justice and members of the intelligence and security services and customs, they are accused of attempting to hamper anti-corruption initiatives or of seeking to whitewash the situation (Mirosavljevic, 2000).

The response from international policy advisers has been to call for more regulation of the actions and power of Bosnian politicians. One approach has been to call for the decentralised powers at entity, canton and municipal level to be weakened. For some commentators the problem is that there is too much government in Bosnia, with the division of responsibilities, between the state and entity governments, making it difficult to clearly allocate responsibility (Wilkinson, 1998; Martin, 1999). A similar complaint is expressed by advisers who argue that all levels of political authority need to be restricted: 'The basic difference between the two entities of Bosnia is the fact that there are three levels of corruption in the Federation (municipalities, cantons and the Federal authorities) there are "only" two in the

Republika Srpska (no cantons)' (Divjak, 2000). International analysts argue that: 'Without dismantling Bosnia's existing domestic power structures, there is no way out of the current quagmire' (Bennett and Knaus, 1999).

The only solution to corruption appears to be greater external regulation. Steve Hanke, John Hopkins professor and adviser on economic issues to the Bosnian government, suggests the solution lies in 'shrink[ing] the size of the government down to almost zero ... That is the only way to get rid of corruption. Have no aid, no government officials, minimum state' (Wood, 1999). Professor Hanke argues that the monetary system set up by the US and the IMF is 'the only non-corrupt institution in Bosnia ... because it is run by a foreigner' (Wood, 1999). Rather than strengthening Bosnian political institutions, the OHR has targeted them as the central problem, stating that there is no evidence of corruption regarding internationally administered funds, but that: 'Corruption and fraud, which are undoubtedly a serious problem in the country, primarily centre on the misuse of local public funds and budgets' (OHR, 1999a: 13). International policy, informed by good governance principles, starts from the assumption that elected government is an opportunity for corruption and inevitably leads to the conclusion that 'corruption-busting is therefore a task for the West' (Bennett and Knaus, 1999).

The Bosnian political institutions are increasingly restricted or bypassed by current international policy. They are restricted through external pressure on policy-making. As James Pardew states, the US government is working with the IMF, World Bank and EBRD to strengthen conditionality 'to apply as much leverage as possible to overcome resistance by the Bosnian leadership to implement the changes necessary to undercut corruption' (Pardew, 2000). They are bypassed by the creation of new regulatory mechanisms which include little Bosnian representation; for example, the Anti-Corruption and Transparency Group (ACTG) formed by the OHR, with the objective of strengthening international efforts. The membership comprises a dozen international organisations, as well as the US government's newly formed Anti-Corruption Task Force. The ACTG does not, however, include any participation by Bosnian officials or independent experts (CILE, 2000: 39). This trend to bypass or restrict the political institutions is supported by the ESI Bosnia Project which warns that transferring responsibility for governance and overseeing the operation of public institutions to Bosnian political leaders would be a mistake. Far from giving elected representatives increased authority the ESI suggests that more control should be given to Bosnian civil servants backed by the international community (ESI, 1999).

This consensus of international support for anti-corruption mechanisms of good governance to take precedence over representational mechanisms of government has led to the politicisation of the question of corruption and the practices of anti-corruption and the 'corruptionisation' of the political process. In other words, the political process is increasingly played out through the language of corruption and anti-corruption. Allegations of corrupt practices have been used to provide a blank cheque to legitimise political interference by international administrators and taken up as the language of political and personal faction-fighting between Bosnian parties themselves, attempting to use external regulatory power against their political opponents. Questions of political power and resource distribution which could have been justified in political terms of international administrative or of party-political interests have been corruptionised – i.e. taken out of the public political sphere. They have been turned into administrative and bureaucratic questions of administrative etiquette and good practice or of good governance, alleged to stand independently of – or over and above – political interests. Whether an issue remains one of political choice or is corruptionised is a matter of international administrative decision – a 'speech act' in the analogous framework of 'securitisation' developed by the Copenhagen school of security studies (Buzan, Wæver and de Wilde, 1997).

The focus on the politicisation of corruption and anti-corruption or the corruptionisation of political-administrative external regulation is a useful framework for analysing this issue in the Bosnian context. This framework of analysis places the focus on the 'speech act' – the decision to name an act as 'corrupt' – rather than taking a prejudged view that corruption is normatively bad or that the definition of corruption is in any way a given rather than a constructed one.

This politicisation of this process is clearly illustrated in the wake of the success of the nationalist parties in the November 2000 elections. The issue of political corruption was high on the agenda as international representatives discussed the options for dealing with what was considered to be a political impasse (see Chandler, 2001). As the Chairman of the US Senate Foreign Relations Committee, Senator Joseph Biden, stated in January 2001:

If there isn't some significant attempt to deal with the stranglehold the nationalists have on the country on the part of these leaders ... we'll start to wash our hands of it [because] you have a position where the three major parties have just decided to split up the country and split up the booty and the spoils. (*Reuters*, 2001)

Despite the expressed wishes of Bosnian voters, on the basis of opposing corruption the international administration was able to push through the creation of non-nationalist administrations at both entity and state levels. On the basis that international action was necessary to put the public interest above corrupt sectional national interests, there was a high level of international involvement in the make-up of the post-election government in the RS. The US ambassador to Bosnia, Thomas Miller, warned in December 2000 that Washington would no longer provide funds to the entity if the SDS was allowed to form a government or if SDS representatives were included in a coalition (*RFE/RL*, 2000). Luke Zahner, deputy spokesman for the OSCE, stated that if the RS government wanted international donor support, it must forego the election process and instead install a government of experts (*RFE/RL*, 2000). Under international pressure, the Prime Minister of the RS assembly, Mladen Ivanic, was appointed from the Party of Democratic Progress (*Partija Demokratskog Progresa*, PDP), which came second in the elections with 13 per cent of the vote. After consulting with High Representative Petritsch, Ivanic presented a new government of technocrats and professionals with little or no political involvement (Cvijanovic, 2001). Ivanic's government included only one openly declared SDS member, Goran Popovic, the Minister for Trade and Tourism. Under international threats to withdraw funding, Popovic was later replaced, which meant that the new RS government was led by an internationally vetted group of technocrats and excluded any representatives of the dominant political party (Kovac, 2001).

A similar level of interference ensured that a Western-backed coalition of parties took power in the FBiH. Immediately following the elections, ten leading Croatian Democratic Community (*Hrvatska Demokratska Zajednica*, HDZ) representatives were removed from the cantonal assemblies in the FBiH for breaches of OSCE election rules, and in March 2001 the High Representative dismissed the Croatian presidential representative, HDZ leader Ante Jelavic, and three other leading Croatian representatives. The basis for these dismissals was the allegation that Jelavic and others were 'not concerned about the well-being and position of the Croats' but were 'criminal elements'; the HDZ's desire for greater decision-making autonomy was alleged to have nothing to do with legitimate politics, but to be solely criminally motivated, 'to allow them to continue to pursue their personal interests and to further enrich themselves' (Petritsch, 2001a). Despite the fact that the HDZ received the support of the majority of Bosnian Croats, the UN Mission in Bosnia argued that the leadership of the party was only concerned with their own narrow personal interests (OHR, 2001c). This move was supported by leading Western states and the international community institutions (OHR, 2001b). James Lyon, the Balkans Director of the International Crisis Group, stated:

I would not like to mention names of individuals or companies, but corruption is in the essence of the HDZ. It exists in the name and in the interest of corruption ... the party leadership does not really care about the interests of the Croat people, but only about its own pockets. (OHR, 2001c)

High Representative Paddy Ashdown has used allegations of corruption to impose his will on the political process by dismissing politicians and disciplining political parties, controversially arguing that rather than seeking agreement with the self-interested major parties he will do what he thinks is right for the country as a whole 'in defence of the interests of all the people of Bosnia'. Rather than giving political representatives a major say in Bosnia's future he has argued that the constitutional political process should be seen as less important: 'We need to worry less about constitutions ... we need to spend less time talking to politicians, and more time talking to teachers, judges, businessmen and returnees' (cited in Chandler, 2002b).

Transparency International's 2004 *National Integrity Systems* report found that one of the main problems in the prosecution of corruption cases has been the politicisation of the process, stating that 'the proceedings have largely been hastily initiated, with the aim of appeasing the public or discrediting a political opponent' (TI, 2004: 23). The international administration's politicisation of corruption has done little to strengthen trust in public institutions or the rule of law according to the leading policy NGO in this area. Regarding Ashdown's dismissal of RS officials and the freezing of bank accounts in June 2004, the report argues:

The High Representative has demonstrated that he can bring charges against any individual in BiH without presenting sufficient (or any) evidence and that the entire process of 'democratic' elections comes close to being a farce. Dispossessing legal entities of their funds without a proper public investigation and a trial would be classified as theft in any Western democracy. Regardless of the profiles of the 59 individuals removed from office, many of whom are widely considered to be crooks, no trial has been set and they have had no opportunity to present their case. Besides, pressing criminal charges and presenting a clear case would have done more for the national integrity system of the country and would have painted a powerful image of the 59 individuals and their party. (TI, 2004: 24)

The undermining of domestic political and legal processes in the cause of anti-corruption and good governance is inherently self-defeating on its own terms. The creation of a modern state framework requires that Bosnian political institutions are strengthened rather than external administrative powers. In fact, the desire to restrict and regulate the Bosnian political elites can only weaken trust in political institutions.

CONCLUSION

The international community's systemic anti-corruption strategy has been useful in terms of legitimising international regulatory power and reposing this power in depoliticised administrative terms, but it has been less successful in its stated aim of strengthening Bosnian state institutions and it is unsurprising that to all intents and purposes it would seem that the goal of such policy practices is to marginalise the sphere of politics rather than address the problem of corruption. However, as suggested above, it would appear that the anti-corruption focus has little specifically to do with the context of Bosnia. The policies and frameworks pursued are those that have been developed, as strategies of Empire in Denial, by a range of international institutions, from the World Bank to the agencies of the United Nations, engaged in state-building. The process has gone further in Bosnia because there is much less resistance to the rule of international bureaucracy.

The process of imposing decisions that the international bureaucracy expresses in capacity-building terms as being in the public interest has strengthened external mechanisms of international governance but undermined domestic Bosnian institutions of government, weakening political institutions and discouraging public participation in the political sphere. If international administrators are deciding which parties represent the public interest and which policies they should be implementing then there is little room for political contestation or for public involvement. The current policies for promoting good governance in Bosnia, such as the international anti-corruption campaigns, beg the question of whether the international administrators see the sphere of internal Bosnian politics as necessary at all.

The narrow view of legitimate politics, apparently held by Bosnia's international overseers, reduces Bosnian political institutions to the role of administrators of international policy decrees. The regulatory policies of Empire in Denial are projected in the language of good governance agendas vis-à-vis leading nationalist political parties which are portrayed as corrupt precisely because they are engaged in representing and negotiating on behalf of the particular interests of their constituencies and therefore, by definition, conflicting with the public interest. However, there is nothing innately corrupt or problematic about politicians supporting the aims of a particular political constituency. The reflection of particular interests is the essence of representational politics; all political parties historically reflect particular social, sectional or regional interests. In a highly segmented society, such as Bosnia, it is inevitable that elected representatives will reflect this social division. The international community is, in fact, calling for a Bosnian political class that is apolitical, which does not reflect these particular concerns and therefore is disconnected from Bosnian society.

As commentators have noted in relation to other good governance initiatives, there is a clash between the demands of these programmes, such as anti-corruption campaigns, and the demands of politics because the public interest demands impartiality while 'the stock in trade of party politicians is partiality' (Williams, 2000). Politics would indeed not be necessary if all questions could be decided by the technicians of good governance developing the correct law or ideal method of administration. As with all techniques of good governance, anti-corruption campaigns can easily neglect the political realities of coalition- and consensus-building necessary to political life, seeking in effect to remove politics from government.

The anti-corruption mechanisms of Empire in Denial are not designed to strengthen trust in state institutions and inevitably weaken their public legitimacy. They are based not on engaging the public in the decision-making process or on making governing elites popularly accountable, but rather on legitimising external regulatory practices which seek to internationalise state institutions in the process of capacity-building them. These external mechanisms of regulation are at the same time designed to evade external political responsibility by posing regulation in terms of the depoliticised technical and administrative expertise of state-building, deemed necessary on the basis of the corrupt nature of politicians and the cultural incapacity of the societies being engaged with.

8
Techniques of Evasion (2)
The Rule of Law

Empire in Denial is drawn to the state-building techniques of the promotion and support of the rule of law. Rule of law promotion imposes an external agenda of regulation at the same time as denying political responsibility through presenting the legislative framework as strengthening the institutions of the state being capacity-built. External regulation is legitimised independently of the political process of the domestic state but is presented in the depoliticised terms of technical and administrative expertise. This approach has similar effects to the anti-corruption practices analysed in the previous chapter. In understanding legal or administrative solutions as a short cut to addressing political problems, it makes a fetish of the legal framework at the same time as marginalising the public sphere, producing state institutions which are internationalised but isolated from their societies.

This chapter draws on the discussion of the need for improved rule of law approaches in the wake of the instability following the war in Iraq. It demonstrates how external powers use the rule of law to deny their regulative agenda at the same time as attempting to impose their authority through the mechanisms of the internationalised domestic state; in this way, they seek to use the rule of law as a technique for evading the political responsibilities of empire. It will draw out the limitations of this technique and question the idea that the rule of law can be imposed from outside by focusing on three areas of legal activism in Bosnia: constitutional change; property return; and employment. Rather than coercive external involvement in the form of pressures for more legislation and better law enforcement, the experience of Bosnia highlights the need for greater levels of political legitimacy, a need which runs counter to the logic of the rule of law approach increasingly advocated in the 'lessons learned' approaches to state-building following recent international experiences.

FROM BOSNIA TO IRAQ

The problems of Empire in Denial can be seen in the crisis in Iraq under the 'fully sovereign' Iraqi interim government, which formally replaced the United States-led transitional administrative authority on 28 June 2004. The US initially attempted to recreate the Iraq state but in the process of overthrowing the old regime was working in a vacuum, as the Ba'athist regime left little room for alternative political movements to cohere, outside of the Kurd controlled north of the country. Unable to either engage with and mobilise Iraqi society in a process of renewal or take on the coercive costs and responsibilities of running Iraq, the US sought to deny its position of power and was forced to turn to the evasive practices of state-building in the attempt to empower an interim Iraqi administration with little connection to Iraqi society. The product of Empire in Denial is the existence of the phantom state of Iraq, which has formal independence and sovereign status, but whose government ministers cannot step outside the confines of the US protected green zone. The handover of formal sovereignty has, in effect, delayed Iraqi self-government, rather than facilitating it, merely attempting to conceal the mechanisms of external domination. The unwillingness of the US to hand over real power in Iraq was, in fact, one factor in the UN's refusal to take over the transitional administration.

Despite Iraq's formal sovereign status, the limited powers of the interim US-appointed government, headed by Prime Minister Ayad Allawi, were clear. The handover of sovereignty was driven by the US desire to escape political responsibility for the outcome of the war rather than any concern for the democratic rights of the Iraqi people. This was apparent in the fact that the US administrator, Paul Bremer, departed leaving 100 edicts that would continue to bind the new regime, while former US ambassador to the UN, John Negroponte, was installed as the US ambassador, then succeeded by Zalmay Khalilzad, presiding over the largest diplomatic mission in the world, with a staff of around a thousand policy advisers housed in Saddam Hussein's former palace compounds (Goldenberg, 2004). Dependent on US Special Forces for security protection, with the policy framework being developed by US 'advisers', and with US and other foreign occupation forces and private contractors having been granted legal immunities, there was little possibility that the Iraqi interim government could develop the independent basis necessary for establishing its legitimacy in Iraqi society.

Prior to the handover of sovereignty, growing security problems under the United States-led transitional administration, such as the August 2003 bombing of the United Nations headquarters in Baghdad, which caused the death of UN special representative Sergio Vieira de Mello, coupled with continuing problems in the repair of basic infrastructure, led to questions increasingly being raised about the coalition's postwar governance of Iraq. The *Observer*, for example, argued that 'Paul Bremer, America's proconsul in Iraq, should go. His autocratic rule has become a symbol of all that is wrong with the administration of the country' (*Observer*, 2003). According to many commentators in the UK and Europe, the alternative, or 'Plan B', was to replace Bremer with a UN appointee 'who has the backing of the international community' (*Observer*, 2003). However, in September 2003, talks in the UN Security Council aimed at ensuring broader support for postwar administration tasks broke down over the issue of whether the US would be willing to cede political authority to the UN.

There is little doubt that Bremer's legislative orders increased instability and uncertainty in Iraq. CPA Order No. 1, the 'de-Ba'athification' decree, which was issued on 15 May 2003, had the unintended effect of threatening tens of thousands of public sector Iraqi professionals in the education and health service sector with dismissal from their jobs because of their membership in the Ba'ath Party (CPA, 2003a). Given that belonging to the Ba'athist movement was a precondition for getting anywhere in Saddam Hussein's Iraq, Bremer's order reached far beyond the senior Ba'athist elite. Most skilled professionals were under threat of losing their livelihoods, contributing little to reconstruction or to winning over support from the Iraqi middle classes (Steele, 2003). CPA Order No. 2, issued one week later on 23 May, dissolved the Iraqi army, making thousands of militarily trained men unemployed and penniless, creating unrest and removing the one force best equipped for taking on the majority of security tasks (CPA, 2003b; Whitaker, 2003).

However, the chaos and destruction that followed the US defeat and removal of the Iraqi regime has generally been interpreted as revealing an important technical 'lesson to be learned' by the state-building advocates and institutional experts. These experts see instability in Iraq not as a political problem of the lack of any cohering political force which could tie Iraqi society together and give its citizens a stake in its future, but as a technical problem of the sequencing and management of post-conflict international administrations. Many critics of US policy and conduct, for example, argued that the United Nations should play a much larger role in the transition process and assist the US in developing a rule of law programme which could have prevented or ameliorated the violence and bloodshed (for example, Chesterman, 2004b: III; Dodge, 2004: 1).

While an Iraqi regime administered and advised by the UN might have been more popular with European governments, it is unlikely that greater UN involvement would have made much difference to the Iraqi people. US administrators have a monopoly neither on autocratic rule nor on imposing counter-productive measures. In fact, the rule of law practices of external state-building tend towards irrational and arbitrary forms of law-making precisely because the law-making process in the internationalised phantom states, which are the product of Empire in Denial, is separate from the domestic political process.

Whether the US ambassador runs Iraq indirectly from Washington with token aid from countries such as Britain or whether the UN begins to play a more substantial role in preparing legislation in Iraq is not really the important question. The desire to criticise the US actions in Iraq and distance the perspective of Europeans has led to a narrow focus on the institutional division of state-building tasks. What this ignores is the much more fundamental problem: that the rule of law cannot be implemented by external actors. For certain theorists, whether of liberal internationalist or neoconservative beliefs, it seems obvious that international bureaucrats can develop better laws than the people who live in post-conflict countries or their representatives. After all, they argue, these elites caused the misrule that 'forced' the internationals to take over, and the people did themselves few favours by voting such elites in or accepting their rule.

This understanding of the rule of law as a set of solutions that can be drawn up in Brussels, New York or Washington and then imposed with the help of NATO troops, UN peacekeepers or EU pen-pushers is a bureaucratic fiction, which attempts to legitimise the practices of Empire in Denial. As will be highlighted in the examples below, law that is disassociated from the political process of consensus-building and genuine social need is more a rhetorical statement of policy intent than a law of the land. Administrators of phantom states find it easy to issue laws and edicts, particularly when there is no need to gain the consent of elected or appointed representatives. For example, in 2003, Ashdown's office in Bosnia issued nearly 100 laws going against the will of elected representatives at state, entity and local levels – and this was eight years after the Bosnian conflict ended and seven years after the first internationally ratified elections were held (OHR, 2003).

The narrow understanding of both politics, which is dismissed as irrelevant to public needs, and of law, which is seen as an off-the-peg external solution, has little in common with the traditional liberal-democratic meaning of the rule of law. The rule of law has historically been understood in relation to the modern democratic framework and in contrast to the rule of bureaucratic regulation or authoritarian repression (Dicey, 1959: 202–3). The rule of law did not mean merely that there was a set of rules and regulations or laws, backed up by the military, police and the courts. It also meant that this framework was predicated on consent, the equality of rights and the autonomy of individuals. It is important to stress the qualitative difference between the liberal-democratic approach, which derives rights from self-governing human subjects, and the current rule of law approach of externally imposing a rights framework outside of the political process of debate and consensus-building.

The rule of law approach used by international administrators, as in Bosnia, attaches little importance to the political sphere and state institutions. The essence of the state-building approach is the belief that the rule of law can be developed and implemented separately from, and counter to, the political process. However, as E. H. Carr noted in his landmark study of international relations, the derivation of modern law from rights-bearing individuals is not merely of historical or philosophical importance:

Law is a function of a given political order, whose existence alone can make it binding ... Law cannot be self-contained; for the obligation to obey it must always rest on something outside itself. It is neither self-creating nor self-applying. 'There are men who govern', says a Chinese philosopher, 'but there are no laws that govern'. (Carr, 2001: 165)

While for Carr, 'the ultimate authority of law derives from politics', it is precisely the attempt to separate the sphere of law from that of politics which is the *sine qua non* of the rule of law approach in external state-building practices (Carr, 2001: 166). The attempt to impose externally the public interest through imposing the rule of law from the top-down, in fact, undermines the creation of any genuine public consensus from the bottom-up through the political process. Removing the process of engagement and participation in the political and legal process gives citizens no sense of ownership of these rights granted by the international administration. The product of this process is that the people of Bosnia may have a legal framework, which institutionalises their rights, but these imposed rights appear as an oppressive, alien and artificial creation. In the same way, the rights of Iraqi citizens, declared by the US–UK administration or their Iraqi successors, do not appear as rights but as alien impositions and are unlikely to bind society.

Not only does there appear to be no immediate connection between the number of laws developed and implemented by these internationalised state authorities and any strengthening of state capacities but also, it seems, the opposite relationship is in play. The focus on law rather than politics has been central to the regulative practices of Empire in Denial which seeks to appoint or empower others as law-givers in a demonstration that empire itself is not the location of power or therefore of responsibility. While passing laws written and devised by external advisers makes the phantom states appear to be legitimate actors, appearances can be deceptive.

The rule of law appears to be susceptible to international support and capacity-building as law is superficially the act of the law-giver, of an individual or small ruling elite. However, what this neglects is that law-making, as stated above, is a political act which relies on social power relations for either its acceptance or imposition. A government without social legitimacy or social regulatory control can pass edicts but these will not have the force or effect of law. The assumption that passing laws or making use of the legal process can address or resolve social or political questions therefore reverses the logic of the relationship between law and politics.

The attempt to use the technique of rule of law to evade the political responsibilities of empire can be seen clearly in postwar Iraq, for example, in the internationalised Iraqi state institutions' organisation of the Saddam Hussein trial. The October 2005 opening of the trial of Saddam Hussein, starting with the charge of killing 143 Shias from the village of Dujail in 1982, was held by many commentators to be a fundamental turning point for Iraq and its people. Apparently it marked the birth of a new post-Saddam Iraq, with the Iraqi government putting Saddam on trial for crimes largely committed against the Iraqi people. International advocates of the war made full use of the trial which allowed them to downplay the importance of the post-Saddam years in alleging that the main problem for the country was coming to terms with Saddam's legacy.

The relevance of Saddam to today's Iraq was exaggerated, and as a result the focus was shifted away from the consequences of the war and the international occupation (Cockburn, 2005; Hider, 2005). The *Independent*, for example, claimed that 'this trial is a necessary stage in the purging of Iraq's demons. Until the fate of Iraq's former dictator is resolved, it is hard to see how the country will be able to leave its past behind' (*Independent*, 2005; see also *Guardian*, 2005; *The Times*, 2005).

The trial increasingly assumed the central task previously claimed by the US-led occupation: the responsibility for leading Iraq's transition from Arab dictatorship to Western democracy. Commentators insisted on the importance of a fair trial, on 'justice being seen to be done', not so much for Saddam's benefit as for the political and educational benefit of the Iraqi people. Implicit in this discussion was the idea that Iraqi people could not move on without a thorough accounting for the past; that without this process they were not ready for the freedom their Western liberators offered them. Here responsibility for the chronic violence and instability of the Iraqi present was shifted away from the actions of the intervening powers and placed with the psychological immaturity of the Iraqi people.

More importantly, the fact that the Iraqi state was held to be enacting the rule of law led many commentators to argue that this was the first truly independent act of the provisional Iraqi government. *The Times* went so far as to say that 'attempting to internationalise the proceedings would seem an unwelcome foreign intervention to many Iraqis' (2005). In this respect, the widely publicised and internationally broadcast legal process was seen as an important part of the process, which started in June 2004, of 'handing back' Iraqi sovereignty. The fact that international human rights groups criticised the trial for not being internationally managed, and thereby being open to Iraqi political manipulation, merely added to the sense that the Iraqi government was now independent of the US (see, for example, HRW, 2005).

In fact, the appearance that the trial reflected the independence of the Iraqi government was an entirely fictional product of Empire in Denial. The relationship of dependency was highlighted by the trial itself, which had been scripted and stage-managed by the US and Britain – the opening speeches and format being laid down by the US and the British team training the Iraqi judges (*BBC*, 2005). Britain had, in fact, spent nearly £2 million on the trial in legal advice and training for the Iraqi judges, while the US Congress had provided £73 million for the tribunal's investigation and prosecution of former regime officials, and America's direct influence was apparent through the US-established Regime Crimes Liaison Office that played a leading role in the interrogation of high-value detainees (Tisdall, 2005). The rule of law clearly served a greater purpose in denying empire than in changing the political climate of Iraq. The Saddam trial had less to do with the Iraqi people overcoming their Saddam past than with the US and Britain distancing themselves from Iraq's post-Saddam present.

THE RULE OF LAW IN BOSNIA

In Bosnia, international High Representative Ashdown argued that his administration had 'the overriding priority ... of establishing the rule of law' (Ashdown, 2003c; see also 2003b). In its 2002 mission statement, *Jobs and Justice, Our Agenda*, the OHR lays out the mission of the rule of law as being the creation of a system of justice that operates in an equal, impartial and consistent manner across the whole of Bosnia, supported by a modernised system of governance and public administration and an efficient, effective and integrated law enforcement system capable of fighting crime and terrorism (OHR, 2002a). Ashdown attributed the slow progress made in Bosnia to the fact that, initially, the international administration focused on working with political representatives rather than on imposing a comprehensive legal framework: 'This, above all was the mistake we made in Bosnia ... It is much more important to establish the rule of law quickly than to establish democracy quickly. Because without the former, the latter is soon undermined. In Bosnia, we got these priorities the wrong way round' (Ashdown, 2003b). According to Ashdown, the international administrators were slow to learn that when it comes to state-building, 'the process is sequential'; a 'bitter price' was paid in failing to understand 'the paramount importance of establishing the rule of law as the foundation of democratic development' (2003b).

The argument for sequencing the rule of law before rolling back the authority of the international transitional administration is at the heart of calls for state-building reforms. The influential 2000 Brahimi panel report on UN peace operations suggested that: 'These missions' tasks would have been much easier if a common United Nations justice package had allowed them to apply an interim legal code to which mission personnel could have been pretrained while the final answer to the "applicable law" question was being worked out' (UN, 2000; see also Chandler, 2002a). Since then, other reports have concurred with the need for a rapid introduction of a judicial package supported by effective military forces that can quickly subdue armed opposition, perform basic constabulary tasks, and ensure that civilian law enforcement officers and administrative officials can perform their functions in an atmosphere of relative security (see IPA, 2002; CSDG, 2003).

There now appears to be a consensus among international policy-makers that state-building should be 'sequenced' with the rule of law establishing the basis for reconstruction and democratic elections. This 'more muscular' approach to state-building, held to be necessary to deal with criminalised or fragile states where social democratic forces have been marginalised through authoritarian rule, conflict and the privatisation or fragmentation of social networks, has been applied to Bosnia under Ashdown's administration (*Washington Post*, 2002). Ashdown argues that the rule of law only became the administration's number one priority in its sixth year, rather than in its first (2003b). However, the transition to the active imposition of legislation and rule of law activism can be dated back to the Bonn meeting of the Peace Implementation Council in December 1997 (PIC, 1997b).

This chapter argues that rule of law regulation through the prioritisation of law above the political sphere cannot compensate for, or overcome, the political problems involved in peace-building and postwar reconstruction. In Bosnia, international policy in this sphere has tended to marginalise the sphere of politics and has institutionalised the current ethnic and regional divides rather than overcoming them. Progress in the rule of law has been promoted by the OHR as demonstrating major improvements made under international administration, despite the continued political division of the small state. Here it is suggested that the gap between the internationally imposed laws and the politically expressed will of Bosnian society, at the heart of the justification for externally imposed legislation, creates a rule of law paradox. This paradox is drawn out below, in examples which illustrate that the attempt to privilege law above politics in fact weakens and discredits the rule of law rather than strengthening it. Firstly, while the new laws may appear to be very impressive achievements on paper, they do not necessarily reflect or encourage an improvement in practice. Secondly, and more importantly, the development of the rule of law through the external imposition of legislation undermines the process of consensus-building necessary to give post-conflict populations a stake in the peace-building or state-building process.

The following sections consider briefly three areas of legislation publicly justified as necessary to demonstrate the independence and authority of the Bosnian state and to build the capacity of the state institutions. In each of these cases the rule of law was developed and imposed over the opposition of Bosnian political representatives. The areas have been selected on the basis of their prominence in international reports on progress in the region. They are: firstly, the imposition of new constitutional changes which have sought to marginalise the governing influence of the main nationalist political parties; secondly, the imposition of housing legislation allowing refugees and displaced people to return to their prewar homes; and, thirdly, the imposition of public sector job allocations, particularly in the police force, in proportion to the 1991 census figures.

THE RULE OF LAW AND POLITICAL REPRESENTATION

In September 2000 the constitutional court of Bosnia ruled that the general principle of political equality of the three constituent peoples should hold throughout Bosnia and with regards to both political entities, the Bosnian Federation and the Serb-dominated Republika Srpska. This decision, which affected each entity's constitution, was pushed through by the court's three non-Bosnian, internationally appointed, judges but with the support of only the two Bosniak (Bosnian Muslim) judges. The two Serb and two Croat judges opposed the ruling.

Already clearly politically divisive, this general ruling on principle was then used by the international administration to reshape radically the political framework. In January 2001 the High Representative issued a decree creating two constitutional commissions, which met to discuss specific textual proposals for constitutional change, already drawn up by an international taskforce (OHR, 2001a; ESI, 2002a: 2). The Mrakovica–Sarajevo Agreement on the Implementation of the Constituent Peoples' Decision of the Constitutional Court of Bosnia and Herzegovina was finally imposed by the OHR in March 2002 (OHR, 2002b). Although it was signed by representatives of the United States and the European Union, the Agreement was not supported by Bosnian representatives despite its perceived constitutional importance as 'an addendum to the Dayton Agreement' (Bisenić,

2002). The new constitution was imposed by three decrees requiring constitutional changes in the two entities and reforming the election laws. According to the then High Representative, Wolfgang Petritsch, imposition was necessary:

I'm not going to allow ... nationalist parties ... to prevent them from taking effect. As a guarantor of the Mrakovica–Sarajevo Agreement, I simply cannot accept the continuing obstruction on the side of these nationalistic dinosaurs. I cannot allow the prospect that these ... parties could hold the citizens of this country hostage. (OHR, 2002c)

The implications for the governments of both political entities were extensive. Section II of the Agreement on Implementation of the Constituent Peoples' Decision, covering the distribution of key political posts, declares:

PM and Deputy Prime Ministers may not come from the same constituent people. Out of the following positions not more than 2 may be filled by representatives of any one constituent people or of the group of Others: 1) Prime Minister 2) Speaker of the House of Representatives/Republika Srpska National Assembly 3) Speaker of the House of Peoples/Council of Peoples 4) President of Supreme Court 5) President of Constitutional Court 6) Public Prosecutors. Presidents of Entities – the President shall have two Vice-Presidents coming from different constituent peoples. (OHR, 2002b)

Of the six most important positions in the RS only two, or one-third, could be held by Bosnian Serbs. This was hailed as a major step forward for democratising the Serb entity because the governing representatives would be dominated by non-Serbs. This was despite the fact that by far the majority of the current population are Serbian.

Section III of the Agreement covered in greater detail the 'minimum representation in the government of the Federation of Bosnia and Herzegovina and of the Republika Srpska', stating:

The RS Government (Prime Minister and 16 ministers) shall be composed of 8 Serb, 5 Bosniak and 3 Croat ministers. One 'Other' may be nominated by the Prime Minister from the quota of the largest constituent people. There shall be additionally a Prime Minister who shall have two Deputy Prime Ministers from different constituent peoples selected from among the Ministers; and the Federation Government (Prime Minister and 16 ministers) shall be composed of 8 Bosniak, 5 Croat and 3 Serb ministers. One 'Other' may be nominated by the Prime Minister from the quota of the largest constituent people. There shall be additionally a Prime Minister who shall have two Deputy Prime Ministers from different constituent peoples selected from among the Ministers. (OHR, 2002b)

The new framework radically transformed the governments of Bosnia, particularly in the RS. For Petritsch, the use of the law to implement drastic reforms to the peace settlement was immensely pleasing. He stressed that: 'never ever in the three years of my mandate in Bosnia and Herzegovina have I experienced a feeling of such profound relief and satisfaction' (OHR, 2002c). On paper the three main nationalist parties lost their power and control; governments at both the entity and state level are based on multi-ethnicity rather than votes. The October 2002 elections demonstrated the apparent necessity of adopting this strategy of using the law to reshape Bosnian politics. Representatives of the three main nationalist parties, the SDA (*Stranka Demokratska Akcija* – Party of Democratic Action), SDS and the HDZ won the Bosniak, Serb and Croat seats in the three-member Bosnian presidency. At the state level, and in the elections for the entity parliaments, the HDZ, SDS and SDA were the leading parties in their respective ethnic constituencies, yet they were restricted to minority positions in the ruling authorities.

The manipulation of election and constitutional laws, however, has produced a situation where the results of the elections have no relationship to the expressed will of Bosnia's citizens at the ballot box. Furthermore, it is not just at the level of entity governments that multi-ethnic political representation has been imposed from above, irrespective of the ethnic composition of the electorate. At the local level of municipal government and at cantonal level in the FBiH, the constitutional amendments have been used to break the hold of majority political parties elected to power where there is a clear ethnic majority. Representation on the basis of the population census of 1991, rather than on the basis of today's constituents, has meant that in some towns the representatives of the leading political party or even the town mayor may live not just outside the town, but in some cases many miles away, or even in another entity (ICG, 2002b: 26). This has heightened political tensions and raised questions over the legitimacy of policy made by people who do not have to live with the consequences of their decisions.

The imposition of these new constitutional arrangements, which have sought to ameliorate the influence of nationalist political parties, has done little to strengthen the Bosnian political framework. Institutions which are run by politicians elected on few votes and who have little connection to the people whose lives they are regulating have little political legitimacy and are unable to secure wider support for the political settlement. While the constitutional changes may produce governments which look good on paper, they institutionalise and perpetuate the problems which they seek to address. The fact that these institutions are dependent on international administrators to appoint them and oversee their operation means they perpetuate divisions and external dependencies. As long as the political settlement is dependent on external regulation, the questions of ethnic insecurity and uncertainty over the future remain. Rather than the nationalist parties losing credibility it would appear that their support is cemented by international manipulation of the political process (see, for example, Bieber, 2001; ICG, 2001). The use of the rule of law to reform the political process has merely resulted in the undermining of Bosnia's political institutions. With growing cynicism over the political process, there was little surprise that only just over half the population wished to vote in the elections of October 2002 (OHR, 2002f).

The Law on Property Return

Annex 7 of the Dayton agreement, Article 1(1), states that:

All refugees and displaced persons have the right freely to return to their homes of origin. They shall have the right to have restored to them property of which they were deprived in the course of hostilities since 1991 and to be compensated for any property that cannot be restored to them. (GFA, 1995)

The issue of property return to displaced people and refugees has been held to be a central part of the struggle to enforce the rule of law against the sectional interests of the main political parties. According to many international policy-makers, refugees and displaced people are up against the self-interest of political elites in two ways:

Bosnians wishing to return to areas where they will be a minority population face a double barrier. Nationalists in their former hometowns work to impede their return through administrative obstruction, intimidation and violence, more often than not with the connivance of local (and higher) authorities. Furthermore, the nationalist elites who rely on these deracinated populations as reservoirs of support also work to prevent their return. (DPI, 2002: 12)

For the international community, imposing the rule of law would mean 'squeezing' the 'opaque corrupt political and criminal networks' and 'helping uproot the deadwood that has no interest in Bosnia functioning for its citizens – of any ethnicity' (DPI, 2002: 12). In November 1998 the international community acted to impose legislation in the FBiH insisting that the right to repossess prewar property took precedence over any rights that local authorities had granted to the current occupant. In April 1999 similar laws were imposed in the RS (OHR, 1998; 1999b). These laws were later strengthened and harmonised by the High Representative and in 1999 no less than 38 separate acts of legislation were imposed by the High Representative in the field of Property Laws, Return of Displaced Persons and Refugees and Reconciliation (see OHR, 1999c). The implementation of property legislation met with resistance throughout Bosnia and entailed detailed regulation and enforcement by international agencies, including the UNHCR, the OHR, the OSCE and the UN Mission in Bosnia. The UN International Police Task Force has supervised local police to ensure that evictions take place and international officials have taken over the running of reluctant local housing offices, setting quotas to be resolved and overseeing their management on a day-by-day basis (ICG, 2002b: 9; OHR, 2002d). The High Representative has also used his 1997 Bonn–Petersburg powers to dismiss elected representatives and public employees, to sack over 30 mayors and other municipal officials held to have obstructed the implementation of property laws and the exercise of the right to return. Even with the international community effectively running local housing authorities and removing any scope for discretion, the solution is not straightforward. This is because property return is a political not a purely legal or administrative question.

Studies of the return situation and the imposition of property legislation suggest that the imposition of law is not the same as refugee return itself. On paper the more coercive international policy seems to be paying dividends. By the end of September 2002 it was reported that 150,000 people (62 per cent of applicants) had been successful in reclaiming their property (ICG, 2002b). However, forcing through property returns in a situation of uncertainty has merely resulted in the 'legally dubious but increasingly common practice of selling off property claims before they have been realised' or in the legally fine but politically counter-productive selling of property often to the former occupants (Heimerl, 2005).

Although the imposition of property legislation against the will of local authorities is promoted as a key example of where rule of law human rights protections and equal treatment have taken precedence over Bosnian political will, there is little accounting for the success of this policy on the ground. According to the International Crisis Group (ICG):

No international organisation or government agency has precise figures on how many Bosnians, after reclaiming their houses or flats – or receiving reconstruction assistance – then decide to sell or exchange them and relocate elsewhere. Both anecdotal evidence and classified advertisements in the newspapers suggest that the practice is widespread. (ICG, 2002b: 11)

In fact, the OHR has been happy to connive in the artificial conflation of 'law' and 'reality' in order to give the impression of progress. In July 2001 the High Representative decreed an end to the two-year moratorium on re-sale in the FBiH (OHR, 2001b). After the decree, applications for repossession from refugees shot up, the motivation being for sales rather than return (ICG, 2002b: 11). Along with not keeping figures distinguishing permanent return from selling or exchanging property, the High Representative seems willing to compromise on permanent return in order to boost the success of property law implementation.

The majority of the property law returns have been implemented for socially owned apartments in urban areas rather than private property in rural areas. This gives a misleading impression as it is precisely urban municipal properties that are most likely to be exchanged or sold. Permanent return is most often centred on villages because in the towns economic opportunities are scarce, while in the rural areas economic survival is helped through a reliance on subsistence agriculture (ICG, 2002b). Even if property sold or exchanged is excluded, many of the properties returned are not occupied by their legal owners and are either left vacant or rented out. Media in Sarajevo report that as many as 10,000 repossessed apartments in Sarajevo canton remain empty, representing half the properties repossessed in the canton (ICG, 2002b). In Dvar about 500 Serb owners of repossessed and privatised flats have signed rental agreements allowing displaced Croats to stay on. Similar arrangements exist in Foca where Bosniaks have repossessed their flats but have rented them out to displaced Serbs.

Often, even where property figures do represent actual returns, the level of return is only partial, and does not represent a return to prewar patterns of integration. In many cases where there is return to prewar housing, the figures are misleading as only part of the family returns, particularly older family members. Meanwhile, school-age children are likely to remain in or be sent back to their 'majority' areas (ICG, 2002b). In cities such as Prijedor and Sarajevo, survey results indicate that many people who have returned continue to commute to work in the places to where they were formerly displaced (ICG, 2002b).

The rule of law perspective, as imposed by international administrators, seeks its justification on the basis of the need to facilitate a return to the prewar situation. Yet, after four years of war and ten years of living apart, many people have naturally made new lives for themselves either in Western states, neighbouring states or in other parts of Bosnia. There have also been major demographic shifts brought about by the war and economic transformation which have little connection to concerns of being an ethnic minority. While the international community has provided support for the return of refugees, it has been left to municipal authorities to look after the needs of displaced persons who do not want to return to their prewar housing. This section of society is the most vulnerable group, with only tenuous rights to welfare and housing. The imposition of property laws has contributed to social and economic tensions, causing a secondary displacement of people on a large scale with more than 150,000 families vacating claimed property and another 100,000 facing eviction. Their care then falls to local authorities who are already under tremendous financial strains (ESI, 2002b).

However, from the perspective of the international administrators, any attempt to respond to the new needs created by population changes brought about by the war and economic and social transition is problematised and seen as preventing a return to the 1991 ethnic balance. Local authorities' attempts to address the needs of displaced people living within their area are perceived to be criminal actions designed to shore up the gains of ethnic cleansing. The distribution of building plots, construction materials, business premises and commercial estate to displaced persons is seen as problematic as this 'cements' ethnic cleansing, as does the provision of employment. This approach, whereby post-conflict legislators attempt to compensate victims and not perpetrators, forgets, as Rama Mani's comparative study notes, two crucial facts: firstly, that these two groups overlap each other; and, secondly, that post-conflict solutions depend not on the perpetuation of divisions but rather on the development of forward-looking approaches which focus on the 'community of survivors' (Mani, 2002).

Many local authorities have been building new housing, something which would normally be seen as positive in the postwar situation.

However, new construction is often seen as questionable because it inevitably reinforces the postwar status quo. In Pale, Sokolac, Srpska Ilidza and Srpsko Novo Sarajevo thousands of new houses and flats have been built to meet the needs of Serbs displaced from the FBiH. The RS municipalities previously linked to Sarajevo have been particularly active in building commercial enterprises – hotels, cafes and other businesses on socially owned land. Those involved in authorising and supplying these projects have been investigated by OHR staff. In April 2000 the OHR issued an edict banning the use of socially owned land without explicit OHR permission. In order to build on free land the authorities must petition the OHR for a waiver on the grounds that its use is 'non-discriminatory and in the best interests of the public' (OHR, 2000b). A year later, the OHR wrote to all municipal authorities informing them that the waiver system also applied retrospectively to all transactions since 6 April 1992, throwing into question 96 per cent of land transactions made since that time (ESI, 2002b: 3–9).

Petritsch and his successor Ashdown have sacked town mayors and other municipal officials for the crime of making land allocations without adequate permission (ICG, 2002b). Yet the OHR was ill-equipped to deal with the enormity of the new powers of decision-making it had awarded itself. It now covered 53 per cent of the country's territory, since all urban land, 90 per cent of forests and 10 per cent of agricultural land is socially owned (ESI, 2002b: 3). Even welfare policies, such as giving low-interest loans to war veterans and the families of those killed in order to purchase flats in new blocks, have been criticised. All these policies are held, by Bosnia's external rule of law advisers, to perpetuate current ethnic imbalances rather than encouraging the return to pre-war housing allocations (ICG, 2002b).

The gap between the Bosnia of 1991 and the Bosnia of today continually brings out the problematic nature of international rule of law enforcement. When elected representatives respond to the wishes of the electorate they are held to be pursuing criminal interests or to be 'cementing ethnic cleansing'. The biggest problem with the imposition of the rule of law and the focus on the imposed policy aims of the international administrators rather than political solutions negotiated by Bosnians themselves is that it is very difficult for society to move forward. There is an open threat that opposition to international regulation will be criminalised along with solutions aimed at enabling people to look forward and establish new lives.

Ashdown argues that 'we've invented a new human right here, the right to return after a war', by which he means not postwar return to one's country but to reclaim and return to one's own home (ICG, 2002b: 39). The 'human right' to put the pieces back together to the prewar status-quo is not one that has been decided upon by the people of postwar Bosnia. Nor is it one insisted upon by the Dayton agreement itself, which, under the constitutional rules of Annex 4, explicitly guarantees the 'right to liberty of movement and residence' (GFA, 1995). Across the political parties, regardless of ethnicity, there is a recognition that land allocation policies for displaced people are essential to facilitate returns and restore a sense of security to all ethnic groups (ESI, 2002b). To date, arguments for the rule of politics on behalf of those living in Bosnia rather than the rule of law on behalf of the international bureaucracy have been rejected by the international administration, and Bosnian calls for a new census to be held have been condemned as seeking to legitimise postwar population shifts.

The law on employment in public institutions

One of the most widely praised legal developments has been the Mrakovica–Sarajevo Agreement of March 2002, referred to above. Section IV of the Agreement covers 'proportionate representation in all public authorities, including courts' and states:

Constituent peoples and members of the group of Others shall be proportionately represented in public institutions in the Federation of BiH and Herzegovina and in Republika Srpska ... As a constitutional principle, such proportionate representation shall follow the 1991 census until Annex 7 is fully implemented. (GFA, 1995)

In this context, the figures and claims of success for multi-ethnic policing are particularly significant because Bosnia's police forces are the only public institution that the international community had systematically sought to integrate prior to the new constitutional ruling.

In restructuring agreements signed with the FBiH in 1996 and the Republika Srpska in 1998, the UN set down quotas for the recruitment of 'minority' officers. In the Federation, forces were meant to reflect the prewar national composition of each municipality; in the RS the quotas were less exacting (ICG, 2002a). As of March 2002 there were 307 non-Serb police officers in the RS and 633 Serbs and Others in the Federation. The RS police academy had 562 non-Serb cadets who had graduated or were in training and the Federation academy had 516 Serb cadets (ESI, 2002a: 5).

The UN Mission in Bosnia-Herzegovina was responsible for police reform until the end of December 2002 when the EU assumed responsibility. Former head of the UNMIBH, Jacques Klein, has argued that the police reforms made little difference:

Initially, it was assumed that the rule of law could be achieved solely by reforming the police. The thin slice of the international mandate given to UNMIBH in 1996 was confined to non-executive police reform and restructuring ... Consequently, there is an imbalance between the components of the rule of law. Local police and corrections personnel have reached a baseline of professionalism and democratic policing. All other elements, namely: courts, judges, prosecutors, legal codes, the rules of evidence and criminal procedure, and witness protection, still require radical reform and restructuring. (Klein, 2002)

Klein's comments indicate the limits of seeking to address the question of state-building through the imposition of new laws. The broader problems with the legal system in Bosnia reveal that the question of rights is intimately tied to broader questions of social, political and economic transformation which cannot be addressed by the swoop of the administrator's pen and sending round a few police officers (see, for example, Pugh, Cooper and Goodhand, 2003: Chapter 5).

However, it could be argued that even Klein exaggerates the achievements made in this area. The International Crisis Group argues that the numbers are misleading and that few of the ethnic minority police officers are experienced officers of a high rank (ICG, 2002b: 16). Those that do take employment in areas dominated by another nationality often end up marginalised and sidelined by not being issued with weapons or badges, prevented from participating in investigations, or being assigned to menial jobs such as parking attendant (ICG, 2002b: 17; 28). The ICG states:

The practice of not issuing firearms to 'minority' officers appears to be widespread. In Vlasenica, where there are 83 Serb police officers and four Bosniaks, none of the latter has received side arms. The RS MUP [Ministry of Internal Affairs] argues that this is due to lack of funds, but has rejected a suggestion by IPTF to rotate firearms among officers on duty. (ICG, 2002a: 41)

Studies into police reform in Bosnia suggest that the top-down imposition of ethnic quotas, while impressive on paper, may well not reflect any real establishment of a multi-ethnic force (see Celador, 2005).

Despite the problems with the high-profile restructuring of the police along the lines of ethnic proportionality, the international law advisers argue that they need to impose ethnic proportionality across the whole public sector. According to the OHR: 'For Republika Srpska, the Agreement states that Bosniaks, Croats and Others have to fill posts in the public administration, from the municipal level to the Entity level, according to the 1991 census. This means 45 per cent of all posts – tens of thousands of jobs' (Stiglmayer, 2002). The High Representative states that, following the Mrakovica-Sarajevo Agreement, in the RS: 'We have so many more opportunities now in the administration, in the judiciary. There are literally hundreds, if not thousands, of new jobs that are now being made available for Croats and for Bosniaks' (Petritsch, 2002).

The High Representative's claim that jobs in the public sector should be allocated on the basis of the 1991 census is clearly problematic. With unemployment officially at 40 per cent for Bosnia as a whole and a weak private sector (accounting for a mere 35 per cent of GDP), public institutions are the largest employers. Any redistribution of public sector jobs in this context will, as the International Crisis Group notes, 'prove difficult for both practical and political reasons' (ICG, 2002b: 38).

The motivation for the law based on the 1991 census is the argument that good governance and rule of law practices dictate that the current distribution of public sector posts needs to be challenged. However, the law is not necessarily the best mechanism to do this. In Višegrad, for example, the law insisted that 63 per cent of the posts in the municipal government and administration should be held by Bosniaks, despite the fact that they made up only around 3 per cent of the postwar population at that time. Further up the Drina valley the law stated that in Foca 52 per cent of the public sector jobs should go to the Bosniaks, though they constituted only 6 per cent of the population. On the lower Drina in Zvornik, the Bosniak population of 15 per cent was entitled to 59 per cent of government posts (ICG, 2002b: 38).

The 'public interest', as interpreted by international law-makers, is held to dictate that what is relevant for public sector employment is the population census of 1991 rather than the population situation today. When the rule of law insists that 63 per cent of public sector jobs or of government posts should be preserved for just 3 per cent of the local population, it is clear that either the law will only be imposed through increasing local antagonisms between ethnic groups or the law will be ignored, risking economic and political sanctions against the region concerned. Rather than the rule of law guaranteeing the basis for peace and reconstruction, it would appear that these laws, are simply statements of intent arising from the minds of international administrators rather than needs or interests of those affected by them.

THE RULE OF LAW?

Even the advocates of the rule of law realise that the external imposition of 'law' has been problematic in Bosnia. For example, the Democratization Policy Institute (DPI) suggests:

International experts are poorly poised to craft such sets of laws. The track record of internationals drafting laws for Bosnia is abysmal. Legal experts who parachute into Sarajevo on six-month contracts, have little grasp of the Bosnian context, no understanding of the language, and who don't have to live with the results of their work, have made a mess of attempts to reform Bosnian statutes ... The muddle resulting from internationals drafting detailed statutes leaves the Bosnian people understandably feeling like guinea pigs. (DPI, 2002: 15)

For the DPI and other policy think tanks the problem is a technical rather than a political one. Internationals involved in the drawing up of laws are too often more focused on 'high salaries, low expenses and a "per-diem rich environment"' resulting in bad laws (DPI, 2002: 15). The DPI recognises the gap between the laws imposed and the needs and sensitivities of the society in which they are meant to take effect and argues that this gap can be closed by giving selected Bosnians a larger role in the law-making process. They suggest that these Bosnians should be selected by international officials rather than by political representatives: 'Because the Bosnian political system is broken, OHR should not defer to it ... instead selecting the small group of Bosnians itself' (DPI, 2002: 15).

For this influential policy institute, laws should be drawn up by international experts and the OHR, after considerable consultation with local experts. But, they stress forcibly that 'politicians should be excluded' (DPI, 2002: 15). For the DPI the problem with external imposition of the law in the public interest is a technical not a political one. It is precisely this narrow understanding of both law and politics which is a problematic consequence of state-building practices which seek artificially to construct state institutions which are conduits for international policy prescriptions.

If there is any lesson from over ten years of international rule of Empire in Denial in Bosnia, it is that attempts to regulate through phantom states inevitably result in a crude prioritisation of the rule of law over the domestic political process. This has done little to help overcome insecurities and divisions, while undermining collective political bodies in which Serb, Croat and Bosniak representatives can negotiate solutions. The consequences for Iraq could be even more destabilising as security depends on isolating supporters of the insurgency and of inter-command violence which will be difficult as long as ruling institutions are seen as an illegitimate foreign imposition or bear little relationship to the needs of the society and are unable to engage the support of the citizens of Iraq.

CONCLUSION

The traditional understanding of the rule of law was the rule of constitutionality (see, for example, Jackson, 1990: 95–8). Law and justice were seen to result from autonomy and self-government. The focus on the rule of law by today's state-building administrators is very different from the post-1945 approach when the importance of state sovereignty vis-à-vis external rule was universally acknowledged. Today, the problematisation of the political process in many non-Western states and demands for international legislative action in the name of state capacity-building reflect the opposite trends, involving the internationalisation of governing mechanisms in states which are reduced to phantom, administrative shells.

The current doctrine of state-building posits the rule of law in opposition to self-government. Through viewing the political process as problematic, law appears as an external solution. In the areas considered above, the law has been imposed without it reflecting popular consent in the belief that the legal framework is the basis on which post-conflict reconstruction and nation-building can be shaped and guided. The experience of Bosnia would suggest that this legal idealism undermines the political process, the standing of the law and capacity for self-government.

As briefly described above, the imposition of the rule of law in order to enforce political consensus has merely served to discredit the political process rather than to give it greater authority, as intended. The lesson for Iraq is clear in the lack of popular support behind the Iraqis hand-picked to consult with the US and British administrations, and the lack of any possibility for locally accountable representatives to take responsibility for reconstruction. Similar unintended consequences have occurred with regard to the imposition of specific legalisation in Bosnia, which allegedly could not be left to Bosnian politicians. The advocates of the rule of law have criticised the slowness of political reform in Bosnia for producing 'façade democracy' but the edicts of the OHR demonstrate that the top-down imposition of the rule of law can be equally artificial, creating a legal façade of universality while in practice institutionalising ethnic division.

Finally, prioritising the rule of law above the political process runs the risk of unregulated and arbitrary power. This danger is all too apparent in Iraq where there is no constitutional process of appeal for wrongful detention (or torture), or capacity to challenge the rule of international administrators. Once the rule of law is separated from the democratic process it becomes the rule of tyranny rather than the rule of justice. In this respect, despite the language of empowerment and capacity-building, the rule of Empire in Denial is little different from the direct colonial rule of nineteenth-century empire.

9
Conclusion: Six Theses on Phantom States and Empire in Denial

State-building, despite its centrality to international relations, is an under-theorised issue. Perhaps one of the reasons for this is that, for many commentators, questions of state-building are narrow technical and administrative concerns; merely a matter of learning the lessons of previous experiences in international administrative assistance and external support in order to build the governance capacity of 'fragile' states. The material is mostly policy-led, designed to problem-solve – focused around empirical case studies and deriving fairly generic and idealistic sets of policy recommendations – rather than taking a step back to consider state-building in the broader context of international politics today.

This book has sought to consider state-building from a political perspective and, through a focus on the dynamics, practices and effects of external state-building, has raised a number of questions about the current practices and discourses of the international regulatory mechanisms of Empire in Denial. The central point that has struck me in my work in this area is the often problematic nature of the justifications for state-building projects.

Underneath the expressed concerns of democracy, human rights, security and development across the states of Africa, the Balkans, the Middle East and elsewhere, there appears to be a deeper concern of self-interest. Yet, this self-interest is not the one popularly imagined in security terms: the dark and dangerous threats from the 'black holes' that failed states could become (ICB, 2005: 38). The idea of failed states as a security threat is, I believe, an exaggerated one; the 9/11 bombers were educated and worked in the US and Europe, not Afghanistan. Terrorists, criminal masterminds and political extremists are not drawn to the parts of the world where law and order and public services are non-existent; money and ideas are made in urban centres not peripheries. It is the stuff of fiction to believe that the problems of drugs, crime, terrorism, etc. are manufactured in some strange exotic location and then exported to the West (see, for example, Dalby, 1997: 14–15).

The self-interest of Western state-builders is a much more complex and ambiguous one, that of the denial of power: the desire to avoid any investigation of their interests, of *their* capacities. State-building is the practice of denying empire. The problem with non-Western states from the Balkans to Africa is their subordination and weakness in relation to the Western powers. It is this subordination which raises awkward questions of policy responses and of political responsibilities and above all the question of Western political purpose: what does the West have to offer? This question is an unsettling one for Western governments and international institutions which acutely feel the lack of a sense of political purpose today and fear their inability to act in a way that openly projects their power.

Empire is drawn by the weakness of non-Western states, in the same way that nature abhors a vacuum, and empire is happy to make grand rhetorical statements of Western mission and sometimes to intervene coercively in the search for a sense of political purpose (see Laïdi, 1998; Chandler, 2003). Yet, as soon as policy action or intervention is undertaken, and costs have to be justified by justifications of political ends, denial becomes a central concern and policy practices attempt to shift responsibility and accountability onto the non-Western state itself. This process of the assertion of power and its denial sets up the contradictory dynamic of state-building, which is both highly interventionist and highly evasive. This book has sought to draw out in greater detail the largely neglected elements of denial and evasion and, in so doing, develop an explanation of how these aspects have shaped and influenced policy practices and also to develop a broader understanding of the negative and unintended effects of these practices.

This book has hopefully been the start of a project rather than its completion. It has sought to explore themes and practices which need, I believe, much greater theoretical and empirical consideration. Nevertheless, in conclusion, there are six theses that can be drawn from the chapters above. The first three theses relate to Empire in Denial: the difficulties which Western states and international institutions have in openly projecting their power in the international sphere. The second three theses relate to phantom states: the problematic effects of international state-building practices.

EMPIRE IN DENIAL

Empire?

New practices and forms of international regulation reflect Western economic and social power but it would be wrong to see these practices as a continuation of past forms of empire or of new forms of Foucauldian governmentality. In fact, the drive to extend these forms of regulation stems from the evasiveness brought about by the problems of legitimising power rather than the desire to exercise power more effectively. Empire in Denial therefore is neither a product of traditional material self-interests nor a reflection of changing state or international institutional identities as these concepts would be understood by either realist or social constructivist international relations theorists.

Foreign policy?

Foreign policy practices, manifested in the therapeutic state-building discourses of empowerment and capacity-building, are problematic not because they reflect power inequalities – this would be more of a tautology than a critique. They are problematic because they are driven not by the foreign subject of policy but by the desire to deny the power of empire. It is the self-orientated, one could say – with Ignatieff (1998: 95) – narcissistic, motivation behind state-building policy-making that leads its practitioners into generic 'codes of practice' and 'guidelines for action' for capacity-building. The concern is less with the problems of regulation, or even the needs and interests, of failed states than it is with the more central question of the evasion of political responsibility. This more inward-looking dynamic to policy formulation has made traditional foreign office staff increasingly marginal to policy concerns.

The ideology of power?

For traditional critics of empire the ideological discourses of empowerment and state capacity-building merely hide the interests of power. The interests of power stay fairly much the same while the ideological justifications and the nature of the division between 'us' and 'them', the 'friend/enemy' distinction, may be presented in a variety of keys. However, the rise of the discursive importance of the Other and the therapeutic practices of empowerment and capacity-building while being ideological denials of Western power on the one hand, on the other, also appear as necessary and real reflections of political changes at the level of the Western Self's capacity for projecting power internationally.

PHANTOM STATES

The state-building paradox?

The new regulative practices of state-building result in the weak and artificial state institutions of the phantom state. This may appear to be a paradox as the justification for these practices is the need for external support to enhance the legitimacy and capacity of these institutions. However, this is not a genuine paradox as the contradiction between the stated aims of state-building practices and their outcome merely reflects the contradiction between the external rule of empire and its denial. State-building seeks to capacity-build states but states without the genuine capacity for self-government.

Sovereignty?

In states subject to state-building practices, sovereignty no longer operates to demarcate the distinction between the inside and the outside of distinct political communities. Analysis of the core state institutions of southeast European accession and candidate states or those of poor or indebted states, which have been through the Highly Indebted Poor Country initiative and the process of World Bank poverty reduction strategies reveals that these institutions have been internationalised. Non-Western states increasingly lack even the formal capacity to formulate public policy independently of the requirements of international institutions. In effect, these states have been reduced to the administrative bodies of external power.

Governance without politics

In phantom states the political process which does exist is a hollow one, either subordinate to decisions made elsewhere or bypassing representative institutions and feeding directly into internationally managed policy processes through participatory consultative civil society forums. The dynamic of Empire in Denial is continually to undermine centres where social power exists in order to create artificial subjects to be empowered or capacity-built. This process can be seen in the participatory forms of legitimising 'country owned' poverty reduction strategies, which have tended to exclude socially organised groups and to favour the creation of ascriptive needs-based constituencies of individuals. It can also be seen in the regulatory frameworks of good governance, anti-corruption and the rule of law where group interests are often problematised as being sectional rather than those of the country as a whole.

CONCLUSION

Why should we be concerned about Empire in Denial? In engaging with formulating and defending the arguments presented in the chapters above I have been surprised by how many colleagues involved in this sphere of research have been generally supportive of the framework of therapeutic and empowering forms of exercising power which project administrative power over the domestic political process. For some of them this does not mean the end of politics but merely its reconstitution in new forms of local or needs-based participatory processes and public consultations. They argue that the larger policy questions are better off being considered at a higher institutional level, where policy decisions are likely to be better informed, and that in functional terms it is better for non-Western states to play a largely administrative role than have the poor management that seems to come with self-government (Lyon, 1993). But, is it really such a problem if representational politics and traditional frameworks of self-government are sacrificed for new forms of enlightened, externally managed good governance? It could be argued that the policy mechanisms may not be perfect, but that this should give cause for researchers to engage in the provision of problem-solving policy advice rather than preoccupying themselves with unproductive and potentially marginalising critique.

The answer to this question, I believe, depends on whether the answer is 'yes' or 'no' to a prior question: 'Is this it?' Why engage in a political understanding and critique of current practices of power and its denial if the political sphere has no better solutions for society than the administrative one does? This book has not focused on an administrative or problem-solving critique of the state-building practices of Empire in Denial. It is a political one: that the denial of power is a dishonest, reactionary and elitist perspective which seeks to argue that power is not important and that there is not much that power can do.

Progressive political movements have historically been based on an appreciation of political power and the possibilities this provides for marshalling the social power of society. For those with a social project the location of political sovereignty is important, for it is only by politically marshalling the social power of society that its resources can be directed towards consciously designed ends. Only those without a progressive social project would seek to deny their power and to obfuscate the location of sovereign power. In this regard, Empire in Denial is more reactionary and backward looking than empire at its formal zenith in the nineteenth and twentieth centuries. Both forms of empire might deny the capacity of subject populations to change things for themselves, only Empire in Denial seeks to deny the capacity for change and social progress entirely.

Empire in Denial promotes its practices of evasion as the solution to all things to all people and revels in its rhetorical claims to lack power and purpose beyond empowering the Other. It is surely necessary to challenge the consensus that asserts that power and self-interest are concepts to be shunned and avoided and that the best the majority of the people of the world can hope for is a good administration and gradual reductions in social exclusion and numbers in extreme poverty. Empire in Denial seeks to deny its own power and with it the possibility of social transformation and of a world where whole societies can be dragged out of relative poverty and underdevelopment and even societies in the West vastly improved.

This denial of power is based not on what is scientifically and socially possible today even given the application of existing levels of technological advance, but on Western elites' subjective lack of a political project capable of mobilising their societies. But this denial is a guilty and dishonest one; it is driven by the awareness that the only point of government is to advance society. If governments have no political project for social change then there is no point in the struggle for representation as the job would be purely one of administration. Government officials would then be chosen on the basis of technical proficiency rather than by popular vote.

To have the power of empire but not to have a social project makes the position of holding political power even more problematic. Empire in Denial seeks to take the easy way out, hiding behind the therapeutic codes of empowerment and the depoliticised regulations of law and administrative etiquette. The exhaustion of the Western political elite threatens to condemn the majority of the world to a future that is little different from the present and to pass the buck to others. In their lack of vision to mobilise the social and technical wealth at their command they reveal a historically unique lack of subjectivity. It is little wonder that they are in denial.

References

Abrahamsen, R. (2004) 'The Power of Partnerships in Global Governance', *Third World Quarterly*, Vol. 25, No. 8, pp. 1453–67.

Abrahamsen, R. (2005) 'Blair's Africa: The Politics of Securitization and Fear', *Alternatives*, No. 30, pp. 55–80.

Archibugi, D. and Held, D. (eds) (1995) *Cosmopolitan Democracy: An Agenda for a New World Order* (Cambridge: Polity Press).

Archibugi, D., Held, D. and Kohler, M. (eds) (1998) *Re-imagining Political Community: Studies in Cosmopolitan Democracy* (Cambridge: Polity Press).

Ashdown, P. (2002) 'Inaugural Speech by the New High Representative for Bosnia & Herzegovina', Bosnian State Parliament, 27 May. Available at: http://www.ohr.int/ohr-dept/presso/presssp/default.asp?content_id=8417.

Ashdown, P. (2003a) 'High Representative Comments on Resignation of Mirko Sarovic from BiH Presidency', 2 April, OHR Sarajevo. Available at: http://www.ohr.int/ohr-dept/presso/pressr/default.asp?content_id=29615.

Ashdown, P. (2003b) 'What Baghdad Can Learn from Bosnia', *Guardian*, 22 April.

Ashdown, P. (2003c) 'Broken Communities, Shattered Lives: Winning the Savage War of Peace', speech to the International Rescue Committee, London, 19 June. Available at: http://www.ohr.int/print/?content_id=30130.

Ashdown, P. (2004) 'International Humanitarian Law, Justice and Reconciliation in a Changing World', The Eighth Hauser Lecture on International Humanitarian Law, New York, 3 March. Available at: http://www.nyuhr.org/docs/lordpaddyashdown.pdf.

Ashdown, P. (2005) 'Remarks by the High Representative at the Press Conference on the Removal of President Covic', 29 March, OHR Sarajevo. Available at: http://www.ohr.int/ohr-dept/presso/pressb/default.asp?content_id=34399.

Bacevich, A. J. (2002) *American Empire: The Realities and Consequences of U.S. Diplomacy* (Cambridge, Mass.: Harvard University Press).

Bain, W. (2003) *Between Anarchy and Society: Trusteeship and the Obligations of Power* (Oxford: Oxford University Press).

Balkanologie (1999) Special issue, 'South-Eastern Europe: History, Concepts, Boundaries', *Balkanologie*, Vol. 3, No. 2, pp. 47–127.

Baudrillard, J. (1983) *In the Shadow of the Silent Majorities* (trans. P. Foss, J. Johnston and P. Patton) (New York: Columbia University/Semiotext(e)).

BBC (2000) 'Cigarette Smuggling "Costs £4bn"', *BBC News*, 27 November. Available at: http://news.bbc.co.uk.

BBC (2005) *BBC2 Newsnight*, 19 October.

BECM (2003) British Empire and Commonwealth Museum, 'Do You Remember Empire Day? Museum Asks Visitors to Share Their Memories as Part of This Year's Commonwealth Day Celebrations', Press Release, 3 March. Available at: http://www.empiremuseum.co.uk/pdfs/Commonwealth%20Day%20fk.pdf.

Ben-Ami, D. (2005) 'Postponing the "End of Poverty"', *Spiked-Online*, 6 May. Available at: http://www.spiked-online.com/Articles/0000000CAB08. htm.

Bendaňa, A. (2004) 'From Peace-building to State-building: One Step Forward and Two Backwards', presentation at 'Nation-building, State-building and International Intervention: Between Liberation and Symptom Relief', CERI, Paris, 15 October.

Benn, H. (2003) 'Africa: Are We Doing Enough?', Speech to Foreign Policy Centre fringe event at the 2003 Labour Party Conference, in *Africa: Are We Doing Enough?* (London: Foreign Policy Centre).

Benn, H. (2005) 'The Review of World Bank Conditionality: Statement by Hilary Benn, Secretary of State for International Development'. Available at: http://www.dfid.gov.uk/aboutdfid/dfidwork/conditionality-statement. pdf.

Bennett, C. and Knaus, G. (1999) 'Battling Corruption in the Balkans', *Global Beat Syndicate*, 27 August.

Bickerton, C. (2005a) 'Rebuilding States, Deconstructing State-building', paper presented at the SAID Workshop, University of Oxford, 28 April. Available at: http://www.said-workshop.org/Bickerton.paper.doc.

Bickerton, C. (2005b) '"Internationalized States" in the New Europe and the Impact of State-building on European Integration', paper presented at the British International Studies Association 30th Anniversary Conference, St Andrews, 19–21 December.

Bieber, F. (2001) 'Croat Self-government in Bosnia – A Challenge for Dayton', European Centre for Minority Issues, *ECMI Brief*, No. 5, May.

BiH DEI (2005) 'European Partnership for Bosnia and Herzegovina, Medium Term Priorities Realisation Programme'. Available at: http://www.dei.gov. ba/en/pdf/Complet_EP_PSP.pdf.

Bildt, C. (1996a) 'The Important Lessons of Bosnia', *Financial Times*, 3 April. Available at: http://www.ohr.int/articles/a960403a.htm.

Bildt, C. (1996b) 'Response to Henry Kissinger's Article in the Washington Post of 8 September Entitled, "In the Eye of a Hurricane", OHR Article by the High Representative', 14 September. Available at: http://www.ohr. int/articles/a960914a.htm.

Bildt, C. (1998) *Peace Journey: The Struggle for Peace in Bosnia* (London: Weidenfeld and Nicolson).

Bildt, C. (2000) 'Is the Peace a Success?', Remarks to the Peace Implementation Council, Brussels, 23 May. Available at: http://www.bildt.net/index. asp?artid=176.

Binyon, M. (1997) 'Cook Warns Bosnia Aid May Be Cut Off', *The Times*, 30 July.

Bisenić, D. (2002) 'Interview: Wolfgang Petritsch, the High Representative in Bosnia: "New Solutions Are Not Emergency Measures for Balkans"', *Danas*, 10 April. Available at: www.ohr.int/ohr-dept/presso/pressi/default. asp?content_id=7387.

Bøås, M. and Jennings, K. M. (2005) 'Insecurity and Development: The Rhetoric of the "Failed State"', *European Journal of Development Research*, Vol. 17, No. 3, pp. 385–95.

Booth, K. (1991) 'Security and Emancipation', *Review of International Studies*, Vol. 17, No. 4, pp. 313–26.

Booth, K. (ed.) (2005) *Critical Security Studies and World Politics* (Boulder, Colo.: Lynne Rienner).

Brown, D. (2004) 'Participation in Poverty Reduction Strategies: Democracy Strengthened or Democracy Undermined', in S. Hickey and G. Mohan (eds) *Participation: From Tyranny to Transformation?* (London: Zed Books).

Brown, G. (2006) 'Our Final Goal Must Be to Offer a Global New Deal', *Guardian*, 11 January.

Bull, H. (1995) *The Anarchical Society: A Study of Order in World Politics* (2nd edn) (Basingstoke: Palgrave).

Bunting, M. (2006) 'Last Year, the Politics of Global Inequality Finally Came of Age', *Guardian*, 2 January.

Bush, G. W. (2005) 'Inauguration Speech Transcript: "No Justice Without Freedom"', Washington, 20 January. Available at: http://www.cnn.com/2005/ALLPOLITICS/01/20/bush.transcript/.

Buzan, B. (1991) *People, States and Fear: An Agenda for International Security Studies in the Post-Cold War Era* (Harlow: Pearson Education).

Buzan, B., Wæver, O. and de Wilde, J. (1997) *Security: A New Framework for Analysis* (Boulder, Colo.: Lynne Rienner).

Campbell, D. (1998a) *Writing Security: United States Foreign Policy and the Politics of Identity* (Manchester: Manchester University Press).

Campbell, D. (1998b) *National Deconstruction: Violence, Identity and Justice in Bosnia* (Minneapolis: University of Minnesota Press).

Carr, E. H. (2001) *The Twenty Years' Crisis, 1919–1939: An Introduction to the Study of International Relations* (Basingstoke: Palgrave).

Cassese, A. (1998) 'Reflections on International Criminal Justice', *Modern Law Review*, Vol. 61, No. 1, pp. 1–10.

Celador, G. C. (2005) 'Police Reform: Peacebuilding through "Democratic Policing"?', *International Peacekeeping*, Vol. 12, No. 3, pp. 364–76.

CFA (2005) Commission for Africa, *Our Common Interest*, 11 March. Available at: http://www.commissionforafrica.org/english/report/introduction.html.

Chandler, D. (1999) *Bosnia: Faking Democracy after Dayton* (London: Pluto Press).

Chandler, D. (2000) 'International Justice', *New Left Review*, Vol. 2, No. 6, pp. 55–66.

Chandler, D. (2001) 'Bosnia: The Democracy Paradox', *Current History*, Vol. 100, No. 644, pp. 114–19.

Chandler, D. (2002a) *From Kosovo to Kabul: Human Rights and International Intervention* (London: Pluto Press).

Chandler, D. (2002b) 'Bosnia's New Colonial Governor', *Guardian*, 9 July.

Chandler, D. (2003) 'Rhetoric without Responsibility: The Attraction of "Ethical" Foreign Policy', *British Journal of Politics & International Relations*, Vol. 5, No. 3, pp. 295–316.

Chandler, D. (2004a) *Constructing Global Civil Society: Morality and Power in International Relations* (Basingstoke: Palgrave).

Chandler, D. (2004b) 'The Responsibility to Protect: Imposing the "Liberal Peace"?', *International Peacekeeping*, Vol. 11, No. 1, pp. 59–81.

Chandler, D. (ed.) (2005a) *Peace without Politics? Ten Years of International State-building in Bosnia* (London: Routledge).

Chandler, D. (2005b) 'From Dayton to Europe', *International Peacekeeping*, Vol. 12, No. 3, pp. 336–49.

Chesterman, S. (2002) *Just War or Just Peace? Humanitarian Intervention and International Law* (Oxford: Oxford University Press).

Chesterman, S. (2004a) *You, the People: The United Nations, Transitional Administration, and State-building* (Oxford: Oxford University Press).

Chesterman, S. (2004b) 'Bush, the United Nations and Nation-building', *Survival*, Vol. 40, No. 1, pp. 101–16.

Chesterman, S., Ignatieff, M. and Thakur, R. (eds) (2005a) *Making States Work: State Failure and the Crisis of Governance* (New York: United Nations University).

Chesterman, S., Ignatieff, M. and Thakur, R. (2005b) 'Introduction: Making States Work', in S. Chesterman, M. Ignatieff and R. Thakur (eds) *Making States Work: State Failure and the Crisis of Governance* (New York: United Nations University).

Chesterman, S., Ignatieff, M. and Thakur, R. (2005c) 'Conclusion: The Future of State-building', in S. Chesterman, M. Ignatieff and R. Thakur (eds) *Making States Work: State Failure and the Crisis of Governance* (New York: United Nations University).

Chopra, J. and Hohe, T. (2004) 'Participatory Intervention', *Global Governance*, Vol. 10, No. 3, pp. 289–305.

CILE (2000) 'Corruption and Anti-corruption Measures in the Federation of Bosnia and Herzegovina', *Final Report of the Commission of International Legal Experts*, 25 February.

Cockburn, P. (2005) 'As Saddam Faces His Judges, the Nation He Ruled for 35 Years Still Fears His Power', *Independent*, 19 October.

CoE (2000) Draft Report of the Special Delegation of Council of Europe Advisers on Minorities, 'The Promotion of Multi-ethnic Society and Democratic Citizenship in South Eastern Europe', Strasbourg, 1 February. Available at: http://www.greekhelsinki.gr/english/reports/stability-pact-1–2–2000.html.

Coker, C. (2001) 'The United States and the Ethics of Post-modern War', in K. E. Smith and M. Light (eds) *Ethics and Foreign Policy* (Cambridge: Cambridge University Press).

Columbo, A. (2004) 'Asymetrical Warfare or Asymetrical Society? The Changing Form of War and the Collapse of International Society', in A. Gobbicchi (ed.), *Globalization, Armed Conflicts and Security* (Rome: Cemiss-Rubbettino).

Cooper, R. (2002) 'The New Liberal Imperialism', Worldview Extra, *Observer*, 7 April. Available at: http://observer.guardian.co.uk/worldview/story/0,11581,680095,00.html.

Cooper, R. (2003) *The Breaking of Nations: Order and Chaos in the Twenty-first Century* (London: Atlantic Books).

Cousens, E. M. and Cater, C. (2001) *Towards Peace in Bosnia: Implementing the Dayton Accords* (Boulder, Colo.: International Peace Academy/Lynne Rienner).

Cousens, E. M. and Kumar, C. (eds) (2001) *Peacebuilding as Politics: Cultivating Peace in Fragile Societies* (Boulder, Colo.: Lynne Rienner).

Cox, R. W. (1981) 'Social Forces, States and World Orders: Beyond International Relations Theory', *Millennium: Journal of International Studies*, Vol. 10, pp. 126–55.

CPA (2003a) Coalition Provisional Authority, Order No. 1, 'De-Baathification of Iraqi Society', 15 May. Available at: www.cpa-iraq.org/regulations/CPAORD1.pdf.

CPA (2003b) Coalition Provisional Authority, Order No. 2, 'Dissolution of Entities', 23 May. Available at: http://www.cpa-iraq.org/regulations/CPAORD2.pdf.

Craig, D. and Porter, D. (2002) 'Poverty Reduction Strategy Papers: A New Convergence', draft, later published in *World Development*, Vol. 31, No. 1 (2003), pp. 53–69. Draft available at: http://www1.worldbank.org/wbiep/decentralization/afrlib/craig.pdf.

CRCM (2003) Commission for Reforming the City of Mostar, 'Recommendations of the Commission Report of the Chairman', 15 December. Available at: http://www.ohr.int/archive/report-mostar/pdf/Reforming%20Mostar-Report%20(EN).pdf.

CSDG (2003) Conflict, Security and Development Group, Kings College London, *A Review of Peace Operations: A Case for Change* (London: Kings College).

Cvijanovic, Z. (2001) 'Ivanic Bows to Western Pressure', *IWPR's Balkan Crisis Report*, No. 211, 22 January.

Dalby, S. (1997) 'Contesting an Essential Concept: Reading the Dilemmas in Contemporary Security Discourse', in K. Krause and M. C. Williams (eds) *Critical Security Studies: Concepts and Cases* (London: UCL Press).

Dean, M. (1999) *Governmentality, Power and Rule in Modern Society* (London: Sage).

Demmers, J. et al. (eds) (2004) *Good Governance in the Era of Global Neoliberalism: Conflict and Depolitisation in Latin America, Eastern Europe, Asia and Africa* (London: Routledge).

Denitch, B. (1996) 'Postscript', in *Ethnic Nationalism: The Tragic Death of Yugoslavia* (rev. edn.) (London: University of Minnesota Press).

Der Derian, J. (1995) 'The Value of Security: Hobbes, Marx, Nietzsche, and Baudrillard', in R. D. Lipschutz (ed.) *On Security* (New York: Columbia University Press).

Dervisbegovic, N. (2004) 'Nationalists Dominate Bosnia's Local Election', *Reuters*, 3 October.

DFID (2005) Department for International Development, *Partnerships for Poverty Reduction: Rethinking Conditionality: A UK Policy Paper*, March. Available at: http://www.dfid.gov.uk/pubs/files/conditionality.pdf.

Dicey, Albert. V. (1959) *Introduction to the Study of the Law of the Constitution* (London: Macmillan).

Divjak, B. (2000) 'Corruption in Bosnia and Herzegovina – The Iron Fist Channelled'. Available at: http://vrhinka.com/vrhinka/anti-corruption%20forum/clanek_3.htm.

Dlouhy, D. B. (1999) 'Director of the State Department's Office of Bosnia Implementation, David Dlouhy on Corruption in Bosnia-Herzegovina',

Statement to the House International Relations Committee, 15 September. Available at: http://www.usembassy.it/file9909/alia/99091711.htm.

Dobbins, J. et al. (2003) *America's Role in Nation-Building: From Germany to Iraq* (Santa Monica, CA: RAND Corporation). Available at: http://www.rand. org/publications/MR/MR1753/.

Dodge, T. (2004) 'Testimony to the US Senate Committee on Foreign Relations Hearing on "The Iraq Transition: Civil War or Civil Society"', Hart Senate Office Building, 20 April. Available at: http://www.senate.gov/~foreign/ testimony/2004/DodgeTestimony040420.pdf.

Doig, A. and Theobald, R. (2000) 'Introduction: Why Corruption?', in A. Doig and R. Theobald (eds) *Corruption and Democratisation* (London: Frank Cass).

Donev, J. (2003) 'Macedonia: A Promising Journey Interrupted?', in W. van Meurs (ed.) *Prospects and Risks Beyond EU Enlargement: Southeastern Europe: Weak States and Strong International Support* (Opladen: Leske & Budrich).

Dower, J. W. (1999) *Embracing Defeat: Japan in the Wake of World War II* (New York: W. W. Norton).

DPI (2002) Democratization Policy Institute, *An Agenda for Bosnia's Next High Representative*, 1 May. Available at: www.anonime.com/dpinstitute/europe/ balkans/Bosnia_and_hercegovina/20020501_Bosnia_agenda.pdf.

Duffield, M. (2001) *Global Governance and the New Wars* (London: Zed Books).

Duffield, M. (2003) 'Social Reconstruction and the Radicalization of Development: Aid as a Relation of Global Liberal Governance', in J. Milliken (ed.) *State Failure, Collapse and Reconstruction* (Oxford: Blackwell).

EC (2001a) 'The Stabilisation and Association Process and CARDS Assistance 2000 to 2006', European Commission paper for the Second Regional Conference for South East Europe. Available at: http://www.seerecon.org/ region/documents/ec/ec_sap_cards_2000–2006.pdf.

EC (2001b) 'Regional Strategy Paper 2002–2006: CARDS Assistance Programme to the Western Balkans', European Commission. Available at: http://www. europa.eu.int/comm/external_relations/see/docs/cards/sp02_06.pdf.

EC (2001c) Regular Report on Romania's Progress Towards Accession', Commission of the European Communities, Brussels, 13 November. Available at: http://europa.eu.int/comm/enlargement/report2001/ro_ en.pdf .

EC (2001d) 'Regular Report on Bulgaria's Progress Towards Accession', Commission of the European Communities, Brussels, 13 November. Available at: http://europa.eu.int/comm/enlargement/report2001/bu_ en.pdf.

EC (2002) 'The Stabilisation & Association Process: First Annual Report', European Commission, Brussels, April 4. Available at: http://www.europa. eu.int/comm/external_relations/see/sap/com02_163.pdf.

EC (2003a) 'The EU's Relations with Bosnia and Herzegovina', European Commission, June. Available at: http://europa.eu.int/comm/external_ relations/see/bosnie_herze/index.htm.

EC (2003b) 'Communication from the Commission to the Council and the European Parliament: The Western Balkans and European Integration,

COM(2003) 285 final, European Commission, Brussels, 21 May. Available at: http://europa.eu.int/comm/external_relations/see/2003.pdf.

EC (2003c) 'Report from the Commission to the Council on the Preparedness of Bosnia and Herzegovina to negotiate a Stabilisation and Association Agreement with the European Union', COM(2003) 692 final, European Commission, Brussels, 18 November. Available at: http://europa.eu.int/comm/external_relations/see/docs/com03_692_en.pdf.

EC (2004a) 'Commission Staff Working Paper: Bosnia and Herzegovina Stabilisation and Association Report 2004', SEC(2004) 375, European Commission, Brussels, no date. Available at: http://europa.eu.int/comm/external_relations/see/sap/rep3/cr_Bosnia.pdf.

EC (2004b) 'Council Decision on the Principles, Priorities and Conditions Contained in the European Partnership with Bosnia and Herzegovina', COM(2004) yyy final, European Commission, Brussels, no date. Available at: http://europa.eu.int/comm/external_relations/see/sap/rep3/part_Bosnia.pdf.

EC (2005a) 'Comprehensive Monitoring Report on the State of Preparedness for EU Membership of Bulgaria and Romania', Commission of the European Communities, Brussels, 25 October. Available at: http://europa.eu.int/comm/enlargement/report_2005/pdf/COM534_SUMMARY_PAPER_COLLEGE.pdf.

EC (2005b) 'Kosovo (under USCR 1244) Progress Report', European Commission, 9 November. Available at: http://europa.eu.int/comm/enlargement/report_2005/pdf/package/sec_1423_final_en_progress_report_ks.pdf.

EC (2006) 'European Commission: Enlargement: Candidate and Potential Candidate Countries'. Available at: http://europa.eu.int/comm/enlargement/intro/sap.htm.

ECZD (2000) 'Zagreb Summit, Final Declaration', 24 November. Available at: http://faq.macedonia.org/politics/eu/zagreb.summit.pdf.

Elliott, L. and Wintour, P. (2005) 'Biggest African Debt Rescue Saves Nigeria £17.3bn', *Guardian*, 1 July.

Emerson, M. and Whyte, N. (2001) 'Options for the Stability Pact', *Centre for European Policy Studies Commentary*, November. Available at: http://www.esiweb.org/.

ESI (1999) 'International Efforts to Combat Corruption in Bosnia and Herzegovina', *Background Paper* 4, October, European Stability Initiative Bosnia Project, Berlin/Sarajevo.

ESI (2001a) EastWest Institute and European Stability Initiative, 'Democracy, Security and the Future of the Stability Pact for South Eastern Europe: A Framework for Debate', April. Available at: http://www.esiweb.org/docs/printdocument.php?document_ID=15.

ESI (2001b) 'In Search of Politics: The Evolving International Role in Bosnia and Herzegovina', *European Stability Initiative Discussion Paper*, 1 November. Available at: http://www.esiweb.org.

ESI (2002a) 'Imposing Constitutional Reform? The Case for Ownership: A Discussion Paper', *ESI Bosnia Report*, No. 13, Berlin/Sarajevo, 20 March.

ESI (2002b) *From Dayton to Europe: Land, Development and the Future of Democratic Planning* (draft version for circulation to OHR only), Berlin/Sarajevo, 12 December.

ESI (2005) *The Helsinki Moment: European Member State Building in the Balkans*, 1 February. Available at: http://www.esiweb.org/pdf/esi_document_id_65.pdf.

Etzioni, A. (2004) 'A Self-restrained Approach to Nation-building by Foreign Powers', *International Affairs*, Vol. 80, No. 1, pp. 1–17.

EU (2001) 'Review of the Stabilisation and Association Process', European Union General Affairs Council Report. Available at: http://www.seerecon.org/Calendar/2001/Events/2536GA-Annex.pdf.

EUPM (2002) 'Council Joint Action of 11 March 2002 on the European Police Mission', *Official Journal of the European Communities*, Council of Europe. Available at: http://www.eupm.org/mission/bt/council1.pdf.

EUPM (2004) European Union Police Mission, 'Mission Statement'. Available at: http://www.eupm.org/mission/ms.htm.

EURM (2000) EU 'Road Map', reproduced in *Europa South-East Monitor*, Issue 11, May. Available at: http://www.ceps.be/files/ESF/Monitor11.php.

Evans, G. and Sahnoun, M. (2002), 'The Responsibility to Protect', *Foreign Affairs*, Vol. 81, No. 6, pp. 91–101.

Falk, R. (1995) *On Humane Governance* (Cambridge: Polity Press).

Fearon, J. D. and Laitin, D. D. (2004) 'Neotrusteeship and the Problem of Weak States', *International Security*, Vol. 28, No. 4, pp. 5–43.

Ferguson, N. (2003) 'America: An Empire in Denial', *Chronicle Review*, 28 March. Available at: http://chronicle.com/free/v49/i29/29b00701.htm.

Ferguson, N. (2004) *Colossus: The Rise and Fall of the American Empire* (London: Allen Lane).

Foucault, M. (1991) 'Governmentality', in G. Burchill, C. Gordon and P. Miller (eds) *The Foucault Effect: Studies in Governmentality* (Hemel Hempstead: Harvester Wheatsheaf).

Foucault, M. (2003) *Society Must be Defended: Lectures at the Collège de France 1975–76* (trans. D. Macey) (London: Allen Lane/Penguin).

Fraser, A. (2005) 'Poverty Reduction Strategy Papers: Now Who Calls the Shots?', *Review of African Political Economy*, No. 104/5, pp. 317–40.

Fudulu, P. (2003) 'The Weak Institutions Syndrome as the Effect of the Cultural-Institutional Gap', Indiana University Workshop Papers. Available at: http://www.indiana.edu/~workshop/papers/fudulu_041703.pdf.

Fukuyama, F. (1989) 'The End of History', *National Interest*, No. 16, pp. 3–18.

Fukuyama, F. (1995) *Trust* (New York: Free Press).

Fukuyama, F. (2004) *State-building: Governance and World Order in the Twenty-first Century* (London: Profile Books).

Gallagher, J. and Robinson, R. (1953) 'The Imperialism of Free Trade', *The Economic History Review*, second series, Vol. 6, No. 1. Available at: http://www.mtholyoke.edu/acad/intrel/ipe/gallagher.htm.

Gejdenson, S. (1999) 'Gejdenson on Corruption in Bosnia', International Relations Committee Democratic Staff Press Release, 15 September.

GFA (1995) *The General Framework Agreement for Peace in Bosnia and Herzegovina*. Available at: http://www.ohr.int/dpa/default.asp?content_id=380.

Ghani, A., Lockhart, C. and Carnahan, M. (2005) 'Closing the Sovereignty Gap: An Approach to State-building', *Overseas Development Institute Working*

Paper, No. 253, ODI, September. Available at: http://www.odi.org.uk/publications/working_papers/wp253.pdf.

Goldenberg, S. (2004) 'Experienced and Tough. But Bush's Man Will Still Have to Work Miracles', *Guardian*, 30 June.

Gould, J. and Ojanen, J. (2003) *'Merging in the Circle': The Politics of Tanzania's Poverty Reduction Strategy*, Institute of Development Studies, University of Helsinki Policy Papers. Available at: http://www.valt.helsinki.fi/kmi/policy/merging.pdf.

Gourevitch, A. (2004) 'The Unfailing of the State', *Journal of International Affairs*, Vol. 58, No. 1, pp. 255–60.

Gow, J. (1998) 'A Region of Eternal Conflict? The Balkans – Semantics and Security', in W. Park and G. W. Rees (eds) *Rethinking Security in Post-Cold War Europe* (London: Longman).

Grabbe, H. (2003) 'Europeanisation Goes East: Power and Uncertainty in the EU Accession Process', in K. Featherstone and C. M. Radaelli (eds) *The Politics of Europeanism* (Oxford: Oxford University Press).

Grigg, W. N. (2003) 'Rallying Round What Flag?', *New American*, Vol. 19, No. 8, 21 April.

Gryzymala-Busse, A. and Innes, A. (2003) 'Great Expectations: The EU and Domestic Political Competition in East Central Europe', *East European Politics and Societies*, Vol. 17, pp. 64–73.

Guardian (2005) 'Justice in Baghdad', editorial, *Guardian*, 19 October.

Gutman, R. and Rieff, D. (1999) 'Preface', in R. Gutman and D. Rieff (eds), *Crimes of War: What the Public Should Know* (New York: W. W. Norton).

Haass, R. N. (2003) 'Sovereignty: Existing Rights, Evolving Responsibilities', Remarks to the School of Foreign Service and the Mortara Center for International Studies, Georgetown University, Washington, DC, 14 January. Available at: http://www.state.gov/s/p/rem/2003/16648.htm.

Hardt, M. and Negri, A. (2001) *Empire* (New York: Harvard University Press).

Harrison, G. (2001) 'Post-conditionality Politics and Administrative Reform: Reflections on the Cases of Uganda and Tanzania', *Development and Change*, Vol. 32, No. 4, pp. 634–65.

Harrison, G. (2004) *The World Bank and Africa: The Construction of Governance States* (London: Routledge).

Harvey, D. (2003) *The New Imperialism* (Oxford: Oxford University Press).

Hatzopoulos, P. (2005) 'Non-nationalist Ideologies in the Balkans: The Interwar Years', unpublished thesis, London School of Economics.

Hedges, C. (1999) 'Leaders in Bosnia Are Said to Steal up to $1 Billion', *New York Times*, 17 August.

Heimerl, D. (2005) 'The Return of Refugees and Displaced Persons: From Coercion to Sustainability', *International Peacekeeping*, Vol. 12, No. 3, pp. 377–90.

Held, D. (1995) *Democracy and the Global Order: From the Modern State to Cosmopolitan Governance* (Cambridge: Polity Press).

Helman, G. B. and Ratner, S. R. (1993) 'Saving Failed States', *Foreign Policy*, No. 89, pp. 3–21.

Herbst, J. (2004) 'Let Them Fail: State Failure in Theory and Practice: Implications for Policy', in R. I. Rotberg (ed.) *When States Fail: Causes and Consequences* (Princeton: Princeton University Press).

Hertz, N. (2005) 'We Achieved Next to Nothing', *New Statesman*, 12 December, pp. 14–16.

Heywood, P. (1997) 'Political Corruption: Problems and Perspectives', *Political Studies*, Vol. 45, pp. 417–35.

Hider, J. (2005) 'Diehards Urged to Salute the Leader as He Faces Justice', *The Times*, 19 October.

Hobsbawm, E. (2005) 'The Dangers of Exporting Democracy', *Guardian*, 22 January.

Holbrooke, R. (1998) *To End a War: Sarajevo to Dayton: The Inside Story* (New York: Random House).

Holsti, K. (1996) *The State, War, and the State of War* (Cambridge: Cambridge University Press).

HRW (2005) 'The Former Iraqi Government on Trial: A Human Rights Watch Briefing Paper', 16 October. Available at: http://hrw.org/backgrounder/mena/iraq1005/.

Huntington, S. (1968) *Political Order in Changing Societies* (New Haven: Yale University Press).

ICB (2005) International Commission on the Balkans, *The Balkans in Europe's Future*. Available at: http://www.balkan-commission.org/activities/Report.pdf.

ICG (2001) International Crisis Group, 'Turning Strife to Advantage. A Blueprint to Integrate the Croats in Bosnia and Herzegovina', *ICG Balkans Report*, No. 106, Sarajevo/Brussels, 20 March.

ICG (2002a) International Crisis Group, 'Policing the Police in BiH: A Further Reform Agenda', *ICG Balkans Report*, No. 130, Sarajevo/Brussels, 10 May.

ICG (2002b) International Crisis Group, 'The Continuing Challenge of Refugee Return in Bosnia and Herzegovina', *ICG Balkans Report*, No. 137, Sarajevo/Brussels, 13 November.

ICG (2003) International Crisis Group, 'Thessaloniki and After II: The EU and Bosnia', *Balkans Briefing*, Sarajevo/Brussels, 20 June.

ICISS (2001a) International Commission on Intervention and State Sovereignty, *Responsibility to Protect* (Ottawa: International Development Research Centre).

ICISS (2001b) International Commission on Intervention and State Sovereignty, *The Responsibility to Protect: Research, Bibliography, Background* (Ottawa: International Development Research Centre).

Ignatieff, M. (1998) *Warrior's Honor: Ethnic War and the Modern Conscience* (London: Chatto & Windus).

Ignatieff, M. (2000) *Virtual War: Kosovo and Beyond* (London: Chatto & Windus).

Ignatieff, M. (2003) *Empire Lite: Nation-building in Bosnia, Kosovo and Afghanistan* (London: Vintage).

IICK (2001) Independent International Commission on Kosovo, *Why Conditional Independence: The Follow Up of the Kosovo Report* (Solna, Sweden: Tryckeriet Åsbrink Grafiska, 2001). Available at: http://kulturserver-hamburg.de/home/illyria/kosovocommission.org_report_english_2001.pdf.

Independent (2005), 'Saddam Hussein Is Not the Only One on Trial', editorial, *Independent*, 19 October.

IPA (2002) International Peace Academy, *You, the People: Transitional Administration, State-building and the United Nations* (New York: International Peace Academy).

Izetbegovic, A. (1999) 'The Goal of Article in the *New York Times* Is to Slander What Chris Hedges Calls Bosnian Government', *Dnevni Avaz*, Sarajevo, 18 August.

Izetbegovic, B. (1999) 'Bakir Izetbegvic Will Sue OHR', *Dnevni Avaz*, Sarajevo, 19 August.

Jackson, R. H. (1990) *Quasi-states: Sovereignty, International Relations and the Third World* (Cambridge: Cambridge University Press).

Jackson, R. H. (2000) *The Global Covenant: Human Conduct in a World of States* (Oxford: Oxford University Press).

Jenkins, S. (2005) 'To Say We Must Stay in Iraq to Save it from Chaos Is a Lie', *Guardian*, 21 September.

Johnson, H. J. (2000) 'Crime and Corruption Threaten Successful Implementation of the Dayton Peace Agreement', Statement of Harold J. Johnson, Associate Director, International Relations and Trade Issues, National Security and International Affairs Division, before the House of Representatives Committee on International Relations, 19 July. Accessed at: http://www.usis.it/file2000_07/alia/a0071906.html.

Jones, Dame P. Neville (2004) 'Rethinking the Dissolution of Yugoslavia', keynote conference speech, Senate House, Centre for South-East European Studies, School of Slavonic and East European Studies/University College London, 18 June.

Kaldor, M. (1997) 'One Year after Dayton', in *Dayton Continued in Bosnia Herzegovina (1)* (The Hague: Helsinki Citizens' Assembly Publication Series 11).

Kaldor, M. (1998) *New and Old Wars: Organized Violence in a Global Era* (Cambridge: Polity Press).

Kamm, O. (2005) *Anti-Totalitarianism: The Left-wing Case for a Neoconservative Foreign Policy* (London: Social Affairs Unit).

Karaboev, P. (2002) 'The Road to NATO Is More Important than Membership', *Dvenik*, 17 March. Available at: http://wire.tol.cz.

Keane, R. (2002) *Reconstituting Sovereignty: Post-Dayton Bosnia Uncovered* (Aldershot: Ashgate).

Kemp, I. and van Meurs, W. (2003) 'Europe Beyong EU Enlargement', in W. van Meurs (ed.) *Prospects and Risks Beyond EU Enlargement: Southeastern Europe: Weak States and Strong International Support* (Opladen: Leske & Budrich).

Keohane, R. (2002) 'Ironies of Sovereignty: The European Union and the United States', *Journal of Common Market Studies*, Vol. 40, No. 4, pp. 743–65.

Keohane, R. (2003) 'Political Authority after Intervention: Gradations in Sovereignty', in J. L. Holzgrefe and R. O. Keohane (eds) *Humanitarian Intervention: Ethical, Legal and Political Dilemmas* (Cambridge: Cambridge University Press).

Kiely, R. (2005) *Empire in the Age of Globalisation: US Hegemony and Neoliberal Disorder* (London: Pluto Press).

Klein, J. P. (2002) 'UN Security Council Briefing', 19 June. Personal communication.

Klein, N. (2005) 'Baghdad Year Zero', in N. Klein et al., *No War: America's Real Business in Iraq* (London Gibson Square Books).

Knaus, G. and Martin, F. (2003) 'Lessons from Bosnia and Herzegovina: Travails of the European Raj', *Journal of Democracy*, Vol. 14, No. 3, pp. 60–74.

Kovac, J. (2001) 'Bosnian Moderates Oust Nationalists', *IWPR's Balkan Crisis Report*, No. 211, 22 January.

Krasner, S. (1999) *Sovereignty: Organized Hypocrisy* (Princeton University Press).

Krasner, S. (2004) 'Sharing Sovereignty: New Institutions for Collapsing and Failing States', *International Security*, Vol. 29, No. 2, pp. 5–43.

Krasner, S. (2005) 'The Case for Shared Sovereignty', *Journal of Democracy*, Vol. 16, No. 1, pp. 69–83.

Krasner, S. and Pascual, C. (2005) 'Addressing State Failure', *Foreign Affairs*, Vol. 84, No. 4, pp. 153–63.

Krausse, K. and Williams, M. C. (eds) (1997) *Critical Security Studies* (London: UCL Press).

Kupchan, C. A. (2002) *The End of the American Era: U.S. Foreign Policy and the Geopolitics of the Twenty-first Century* (New York: Alfred A. Knopf).

Laïdi, Z. (1998) *A World without Meaning: The Crisis of Meaning in International Politics* (trans. J. Burnham and J. Coulon) (London: Routledge).

Léautier, F. A. and Madavo, C. (2004) 'Foreword', in B. Levy and S. Kpundeh (eds) *Building State Capacity in Africa: New Approaches, Emerging Lessons* (Washington, DC: IBRD/World Bank).

Leonard, M. (2005) *Why Europe Will Run the 21st Century* (London: Fourth Estate).

Lévinas, E. (1989) *The Lévinas Reader* (ed. S. Hand) (Oxford: Blackwell).

Linklater, A. (1998) *The Transformation of Political Community* (Cambridge: Polity).

Lund, M. (2003) 'What Kind of Peace is Being Built?: Taking Stock of Post-conflict Peacebuilding and Charting Future Directions', discussion paper for the International Development Research Centre, Ottawa, Canada, January. Available at: http://web.idrc.ca/uploads/user-S/10527469720lund_final_mar_20.pdf.

Lyon, P. (1993) 'The Rise and Fall and Possible Revival of International Trusteeship', in M. Twaddle (ed.) special issue, 'Decolonisation and the International Community', *Journal of Commonwealth and Comparative Politics*, Vol. 31, No. 1, pp. 96–110.

Maley, W., Sampford, C. and Thakur, R. (eds) (2003) *From Civil Strife to Civil Society: Civil and Military Responsibilities in Disrupted States* (New York: United Nations University).

Malone, D. M. (2005) 'Foreword', in S. Chesterman, M. Ignatieff and R. Thakur (eds) *Making States Work: State Failure and the Crisis of Governance* (New York: United Nations University).

Mani, R. (2002) *Beyond Retribution: Seeking Justice in the Shadows of War* (Cambridge: Polity Press).

Mann, M. (2003) *Incoherent Empire* (London: Verso).

Marquette, H. (2004) 'The Creeping Politicisation of the World Bank: The Case of Corruption', *Political Studies*, Vol. 52, pp. 413–30.

Marquis, C. and Gall, C. (2000) 'Congressional Report Says Corruption Is Stifling Bosnia', *New York Times*, 7 July.

Martin, S. T. (1999) 'Corruption Mars Bosnia Mission', *St. Petersburg Times*, 19 August.

Marx, K. (1954) *Capital: A Critique of Political Economy, Volume 1* (London: Lawrence & Wishart).

MCA (2005) 'The Millennium Challenge Account'. Available at: http://www.mca.gov/about_us/overview/index.shtml.

Meiksins Wood, E. (2003) *The Empire of Capital* (London: Verso).

Milliken, J. (ed.) (2003) *State Failure, Collapse and Reconstruction* (Oxford: Blackwell).

Minogue, K. (1995) *Politics: A Very Short Introduction* (Oxford: Oxford University Press).

Mirosavljevic, M. (2000) 'Corruption in Republika Srpska', *AIM Banja Luka*, 29 September.

Morgenthau, H. J. (1970) *Truth and Power: Essays of a Decade, 1960–1970* (New York: Praeger).

Morgenthau, H. J. (1993) *Politics among Nations: The Struggle for Power and Peace* (brief edn rev. by K. W. Thompson) (New York: McGraw Hill).

Mouffe, C. (2005) *On the Political* (London: Routledge).

Mungiu-Pippidi, A. (2003) 'Romania: The Eternal Candidate?', in W. van Meurs (ed.) *Prospects and Risks Beyond EU Enlargement: Southeastern Europe: Weak States and Strong International Support* (Opladen: Leske & Budrich).

New York Times (2003) 'Pentagon's Heart Not in New York's Ticker Tape Parade', *New York Times*, 5 May.

Nolan, J. L. (1998) *The Therapeutic State: Justifying Government at Century's End* (New York: New York University Press).

NSS (2002) *The National Security Strategy of the United States of America*. Available at: http://www.whitehouse.gov/nsc/nssall.html.

Observer (2003) 'Four Steps to Peace in Iraq', editorial, *Observer*, 7 September.

Observer (2005) 'Bush's New World View is Welcome', editorial, *Observer*, 23 January.

OECD (2005) *Principles for Good International Engagement in Fragile States*. OECD document DCD(2005)11/REV2. Available at: http://www.oecd.org/dataoecd/4/25/35238282.pdf (pp. 8–10).

OHR (1996) 'Report of the High Representative for Implementation of the Bosnian Peace Agreement to the Secretary-General of the United Nations', 1 October. Available at: http://www.ohr.int/other-doc/hr-reports/default.asp?content_id=3666.

OHR (1997) 'Report of the High Representative for Implementation of the Bosnian Peace Agreement to the Secretary-General of the United Nations', 11 July. Available at: http://www.ohr.int/reports/r970711a.htm.

OHR (1998) 'Decision Suspending Decision-making on Claims to Apartments in the Federation for which a Permanent Occupancy Right Was Issued After 30 April 1991, and Imposing a Moratorium on Sale of Apartments to Persons Who Acquired Their Occupancy Right After 30 April', Office of the High Representative, 5 November. Available at: www.ohr.int/decisions/plipdec/default.asp?content_id=151.

OHR (1999a) *A Comprehensive Anti-corruption Strategy for Bosnia and Herzegovina*, Anti-Fraud Unit, Economics Department, Office of the High Representative, Sarajevo, February.

OHR (1999b) 'Decision Cancelling All Permanent Occupancy Rights Issued in the RS During and After the War in Bosnia and Converting Them into Temporary Occupancy Rights', Office of the High Representative, 14 April. Available at: www.ohr.int/decisions/plipdec/default.asp?content_id=161.

OHR (1999c) 'High Representative's Decisions: Property Laws and Return, Displaced Persons and Refugees, 1999'. Available at: www.ohr.int/decisions/plipdec/archive.asp?m=&yr=1999.

OHR (2000a) 'OHR Launches 2nd Phase of Anti-corruption Campaign', OHR Press Release, 7 September. Available at: http://www.ohr.int/press/p20000907a.html.

OHR (2000b) 'Decision on Re-allocation of Socially Owned Land, Superseding the 26 May 1999 and 30 December 1999 Decisions', Office of the High Representative, 27 April. Available at: www.ohr.int/decisions/plipdec/default.asp?content_id=213.

OHR (2001a) 'Decision Establishing Interim Procedures to Protect Vital Interests of Constituent Peoples and Others, Including Freedom from Discrimination', Office of the High Representative, 11 January. Available at: www.ohr.int/decisions/statemattersdec/default.asp?content_id=365.

OHR (2001b) 'UN Security Council Supports High Representative, Condemns Attempt to Establish Croat Self-rule in Bosnia', Office of the High Representative Press Release, 26 March.

OHR (2001c) 'Bosnia and Herzegovina Media Round-up', Office of the High Representative, 26 March.

OHR (2002a) 'Office of the High Representative, Mission Statement, *Jobs and Justice, Our Agenda*'. Available at: http://www.ohr.int/pic/econ-rol-targets/pdf/jobs-and-justice.pdf.

OHR (2002b) 'Agreement on the Implementation of the Constituent Peoples' Decision of the Constitutional Court of Bosnia and Herzegovina', Office of the High Representative, 27 March. Available at: www.ohr.int/ohr-dept/legal/const/default.asp?content_id=7274.

OHR (2002c) 'Press Conference of the High Representative, Wolfgang Petritsch, on the Completion of the Constitutional Reform Process in Bosnia and Herzegovina's Entities', Office of the High Representative, 19 April. Available at: www.ohr.int/ohr-dept/presso/pressb/default.asp?content_id=7503.

OHR (2002d) 'A New Strategic Direction: Proposed Ways Ahead for Property Law Implementation in a Time of Decreasing IC Resources', Property Law Implementation Plan, 12 September. Available at: www.ohr.int/plip/key-doc/default.asp?content_id=27904.

OHR (2002e) 'Law on the Council of Ministers of Bosnia and Herzegovina', Office of the High Representative, 3 December. Available at: http://www.ohr.int/decisions/statemattersdec/default.asp?content_id=28609.

OHR (2002f) 'Report to the European Parliament by the OHR and EU Special Representative for Bosnia, July–December 2002', Office of the High

Representative, 23 December. Available at: www.ohr.int/archive/rep-eur-parl/default.asp?content_id=30140.

OHR (2003) 'High Representative's Decisions, 2003', Office of the High Representative. Available at: http://www.ohr.int/decisions/archive.asp?m=&yr=2003.

OHR (2004) 'Decision Enacting the Statute of the City of Mostar', Office of the High Representative, 28 January. Available at: http://www.ohr.int/decisions/mo-hncantdec/default.asp?content_id=31707.

OHR (2005) Archive of Decisions to Remove Officials or to Suspend Officials from Office. Available at: http://www.ohr.int/decisions/removalssdec/archive.asp.

OHRB (1996a) *Office of the High Representative Bulletin*, No. 17, 3 September. Available at: http://www.ohr.int/bulletins/b960903.htm.

OHRB (1996b) *Office of the High Representative Bulletin*, No. 28, 9 December. Available at: http://www.ohr.int/bulletins/b961209.htm.

OHRB (1997a) *Office of the High Representative Bulletin*, No. 56, 31 July. Available at: http://www.ohr.int/bulletins/b970731.htm.

OHRB (1997b) *Office of the High Representative Bulletin*, No. 59, 5 September. Available at: http://www.ohr.int/bulletins/b970905.htm.

OHRB (1997c) *Office of the High Representative Bulletin*, No. 62, 11 October. Available at: http://www.ohr.int/bulletins/b971011.htm.

OSCE (2000a) 'Citizen Outreach Campaign Anti-corruption Opinion Poll', OSCE Mission to Bosnia and Herzegovina. Available at: http://www.oscebih.org.

OSCE (2000b) 'Facts About Corruption', OSCE Mission to Bosnia and Herzegovina Public Information Office.

OSCE (2000c) 'Anti-corruption Campaign FAQs', OSCE Mission to Bosnia and Herzegovina Press Information.

OSCE (2000d) 'Civil Society Takes Part in Anti-corruption Campaign in Bosnia and Herzegovina', OSCE Mission to Bosnia and Herzegovina Press Release, 12 October.

Papic, Z. (2001) 'The General Situation in Bosnia-Herzegovina and International Support Policies', in *International Support Policies to South East European Countries – Lessons (Not) Learned in Bosnia-Herzegovina*. Available at: http://www.soros.org.ba/en/book/book.html.

Pardew, J. W. (2000) 'The Impact of Corruption in Bosnia, Statement before the House International Relations Committee', James W. Pardew, Principal Deputy Special Advisor to the President and the Secretary of State for Democracy in the Balkans, 19 July. Available at: http://osce.usia.co.at/bos19july00.html.

Paris, R. (2004) *At War's End: Building Peace after Civil Conflict* (Cambridge: Cambridge University Press).

Pender, J. (2005) 'Less Interests, More Influence: The Paradox of Poverty Reduction and the Redefinition of Development', paper presented at SAID international conference, 'Sovereignty in the 21st Century', Columbia University, New York, 1–2 December.

Perry, V. (2004) 'Quotas, Bridges, and Guarantees: The Politics and Process of Reforming Mostar', paper presented at the Institute for Strengthening Democracy in Bosnia and Herzegovina, Seventh International Seminar,

Democracy and Human Rights in Multiethnic Societies, Konjic, Bosnia, 12–17 July.

Petritsch, W. (2000) 'Speech by the High Representative, Wolfgang Petritsch', BiH Anti-Corruption and Transparency Conference, Sarajevo, 14 February. Available at: http://www.ohr.int/speeches/s20000214.html.

Petritsch, W. (2001a) 'The High Representative's TV Address on Dismissal of Mr Jelavic and Three Other HDZ Officials', Office of the High Representative Press Statement, 8 March. Available at: http://www.ohr.int/press/p20010307a.htm.

Petritsch, W. (2001b) 'Disappointing Progress of Bosnia and Herzegovina on the Path to Closer European Integration', Office of the High Representative Press Release, 28 June. Available at: http://www.ohr.int/print/?content_id=4469.

Petritsch, W. (2002) 'Press Conference of the High Representative, the Completion of the Constitutional Reform Process in Bosnia and Herzegovina's Entities', 19 April. Available at: http://www.ohr.int/ohr-dept/presso/pressb/default.asp?content_id=7503.

PIC (1995) 'Conclusions of the Peace Implementation Conference Held at Lancaster House, London', 8 December. Available at: http://www.ohr.int/pic/default.asp?content_id=5168.

PIC (1996a) 'PIC Chairman's Conclusions of the Peace Implementation Council', Florence, 13–14 June. Available at: http://www.ohr.int/docu/d960613.htm.

PIC (1996b) 'PIC Conclusions: Guiding Principles of the Civilian Consolidation Plan. Ministerial Meeting of the Peace Implementation Council Steering Board', Paris, 14 November. Available at: http://www.ohr.int/docu/d961114b.htm.

PIC (1997a) 'PIC Communique: Political Declaration from Ministerial Meeting of the Steering Board of the Peace Implementation Council', Sintra, 30 May. Available at: http://www.ohr.int/docu/d970530a.htm.

PIC (1997b) 'PIC Bonn Conclusions: Bosnia and Herzegovina 1998: Self-sustaining Structures', Bonn, 10 December. Available at: http://www.ohr.int/pic/default.asp?content_id=5182.

PIC (1998a) 'PIC Declaration of the Ministerial Meeting of the Steering Board of the Peace Implementation Council', Luxembourg, 9 June. Available at: http://www.ohr.int/pic/default.asp?content_id=5188.

PIC (1998b) 'PIC Declaration, Annex: The Peace Implementation Agenda, Reinforcing Peace in Bosnia and Herzegovina – The Way Ahead', Madrid, 16 December. Available at: http://www.ohr.int/pic/default.asp?content_id=5191.

PIC (2000) 'Annex to the PIC Declaration: Required Actions', Brussels, 24 May. Available at: http://www.ohr.int/print/?content_id=5201.

Poels, J. (1998) 'Bosnia and Herzegovina: A New "Neutral" Flag', *Flagmaster*, No. 98, pp. 9–12. Available at: http://www.flaginstitute.org/fibosnia.htm.

Pugh, M., Cooper, N. and Goodhand, D. (2003) *War Economies in a Regional Context: Challenges of Transformation* (Boulder, Colo.: Lynne Rienner).

Putnam, R. (2000) *Bowling Alone: The Collapse and Revival of American Community* (New York: Simon & Schuster).

Raik, K. (2004) 'EU Accession of Central and Eastern European Countries: Democracy and Integration as Conflicting Logics', *East European Politics and Societies*, Vol. 18, No. 4, pp. 567–594.

Reus-Smit, C. (2004) *American Power and World Order* (Cambridge: Polity Press).

Reuters (2000) 'Bosnian Nationalists Strong but Short of Majority', *Reuters*, 22 November.

Reuters (2001) '"Bosnia "Must Oust Nationalists to Keep US Help"', *Reuters*, Sarajevo, 14 January.

RFE/RL (2000) 'US Warns Bosnian Serbs on Karadzic Party', *RFE/RL Newsline*, Vol. 4, No. 240, Part II, 13 December.

Rice, C. (2005) 'The Promise of Democratic Peace: Why Promoting Freedom Is the Only Realistic Path to Security', *Washington Post*, 11 December.

Robinson, M. (1998) 'Corruption and Development: An Introduction', *European Journal of Development Research*, Vol. 10, No. 1, pp. 1–14.

Rodriguez, J. (1998) 'Our Man in Sarajevo', *El Pais*, 29 March (trans. Office of the High Representative).

Rosenau, J. N. and Czempiel, E. (eds) (1992) *Governance without Government: Order and Change in World Politics* (Cambridge: Cambridge University Press).

Rosenberg, J. (1994) *The Empire of Civil Society: A Critique of the Realist Theory of International Relations* (London: Verso).

Rotberg, R. I. (ed.) (2004a) *When States Fail: Causes and Consequences* (Princeton: Princeton University Press).

Rotberg, R. I. (2004b) 'The Failure and Collapse of Nation-states: Breakdown, Prevention and Repair', in R. I. Rotberg (ed.) *When States Fail: Causes and Consequences* (Princeton: Princeton University Press).

Rowden, R. and Irama, J. O. (2004) *Rethinking Participation: Questions for Civil Society about the Limits of Participation in PRSPs*, Action Aid USA/Action Aid Uganda Discussion Paper, Washington, DC, April. Available at: http://www.actionaidusa.org/pdf/rethinking_participation_april04.pdf.

Ruli, G. (2003) 'Albania: The Weakness of the State', in W. van Meurs (ed.) *Prospects and Risks Beyond EU Enlargement: Southeastern Europe: Weak States and Strong International Support* (Opladen: Leske & Budrich).

Sachs, J. (2005) *The End of Poverty: How We Can Make It Happen in Our Lifetime* (London: Penguin).

Sali-Terzić, S. (2001) 'Civil Society', in *International Support Policies to South East European Countries – Lessons (Not) Learned in Bosnia-Herzegovina*. Available at: http://www.soros.org.ba/en/book/book.html.

Schmitt, C. (1976) *The Concept of the Political* (New Brunswick: Rutgers University Press).

Sen, A. (1999) *Development as Freedom* (Oxford: Oxford University Press).

SGESC (2004) Study Group on Europe's Security Capabilities, *A Human Security Doctrine for Europe*, Barcelona, 15 September. Available at: http://www.lse.ac.uk/Depts/global/Human%20Security%20Report%20Full.pdf.

Shaw, M. (1994) *Global Society and International Relations: Sociological Concepts and Political Perspectives* (Cambridge: Polity Press).

Shaw, M. (2003) *War and Genocide: Organized Killing in Modern Society* (Cambridge: Polity Press).

Singer, P. W. (2000) 'Bosnia 2000: Phoenix or Flames?', *World Policy Journal*, Spring, pp. 31–7.

Smith, S. (2001) 'Reflectivist and Constructivist Approaches to International Relations', in J. Baylis and S. Smith (eds) *The Globalization of World Politics: An Introduction to International Relations* (2nd edn) (Oxford: Oxford University Press).

Solana, J. (2003) 'A Secure Europe in a Better World', European Council, Thessaloniki, 20 June. Available at: http://ue.eu.int/ueDocs/cms_Data/docs/pressdata/EN/reports/76255.pdf.

SPSEE (2002a) 'About the Stability Pact', Special Co-ordinator of the Stability Pact for South Eastern Europe. Available at: http://www.stabilitypact.org/stabilitypactcgi/catalog/cat_descr.cgi?prod_id=1806.

SPSEE (2002b) 'Parliamentary Co-operation', Special Co-ordinator of the Stability Pact for South Eastern Europe. Available at: http://www.stabilitypact.org/stabilitypactcgi/catalog/cat_descr.cgi?subcat=1&prod_id=7.

SPSEE (2002c) 'Good Governance', Special Co-ordinator of the Stability Pact for South Eastern Europe. Available at: http://www.stabilitypact.org/stabilitypactcgi/catalog/cat_descr.cgi?subcat=1&prod_id=3.

SPSEE (2006a) 'About the Stability Pact', Stability Pact for South Eastern Europe. Available at: http://www.stabilitypact.org/about/default.asp.

SPSEE (2006b) 'Anti-corruption Initiative', Stability Pact for South Eastern Europe. Available at: http://www.stabilitypact.org/anticorruption/default.asp.

Steele, J. (2003) 'US Decree Strips Thousands of Their Jobs', *Guardian*, 30 August.

Stiglmayer, A. (2002) 'Constitutional Reform in BiH: RS Is Becoming Multi-ethnic', editorial, *Jutarnje Novine*, 15 April. Available at: http://www.ohr.int/ohr-dept/presso/pressa/default.asp?content_id=7397.

Storey, H. (1995) 'Human Rights and the New Europe: Experience and Experiment', *Political Studies*, Vol. 43, Special Issue, pp. 131–51.

Straw, J. (2002a) 'Order Out of Chaos: The Challenge of Failed States', in M. Leonard (ed.) *Reordering the World* (London: Foreign Policy Centre).

Straw, J. (2002b) 'Failed and Failing States: Speech by the Foreign Secretary at the European Research Institute, University of Birmingham', 6 September. Available at: http://www.eri.bham.ac.uk/events/jstraw060902.pdf.

Stubbs, P. and Papic, Z. (1998) 'Part Four: Relationship between International Agencies and Local Non-governmental Organizations in Bosnia and Herzegovina', in *Local Non-governmental Organizations in Bosnia and Herzegovina: Problems, Analysis and Recommendations*, October (Sarajevo: Independent Bureau for Humanitarian Issues).

Szasz, P. (1996) 'Current Developments: The Protection of Human Rights Through the Dayton/Paris Peace Agreement on Bosnia', *American Journal of International Law*, Vol. 90, pp. 301–16.

Szeftel, M. (2000) 'Between Governance and Underdevelopment: Accumulation and Africa's "Catastrophic Corruption"', *Review of African Political Economy*, Vol. 27, No. 84, pp. 287–307.

Theobald, R. (2000) 'Conclusion: Prospects for Reform in a Globalised Economy', in A. Doig and R. Theobald (eds) *Corruption and Democratisation* (London: Frank Cass).

TI (2004) *National Integrity Systems Transparency International Country Study Report Bosnia and Herzegovina 2004* (Berlin: Transparency International).

Tilly, C. (1985) 'War Making and State Making as Organized Crime', in P. B. Evans, D. Rueschemeyer and T. Skocpol (eds) *Bringing the State Back In* (Cambridge: Cambridge University Press).

The Times (2005) 'Saddam on the Stand', editorial, *The Times*, 19 October.

Tisdall, S. (2005) 'A Chance for Justice, But Will it Be Seized?', *Guardian*, 19 October.

Tomiuc, E. (2001) '2001 in Review: A Tough Time for Romania on Road to EU Entry', *Radio Free Europe/Radio Liberty*, 14 December. Available at: http://www.rferl.org.

Tully, A. F. (2000) 'Bosnia: Clinton Administration Sees Hope in Fighting Corruption', *Radio Free Europe/Radio Liberty*, July.

UKSU (2005) UK Prime Minister's Strategy Unit Report, *Investing in Prevention – An International Strategy to Manage Risks of Instability and Improve Crisis Response*, February. Available at: http://www.strategy.gov.uk/downloads/work_areas/countries_at_risk/report/index.htm.

UN (1945) *The Charter of the United Nations*. Available at: http://www.un.org/aboutun/charter/.

UN (1960) 'Declaration on the Granting of Independence to Colonial Countries and Peoples'. Available at: http://www.unhchr.ch/html/menu3/b/c_coloni.htm.

UN (1970) 'Declaration on Principles of International Law Concerning Friendly Relations and Co-operation among States in Accordance with the Charter of the United Nations'. Available at: http://www.hku.edu/law/conlawhk/conlaw/outline/Outline4/2625.htm.

UN (2000) *Report of the Panel on UN Peace Operations* (Brahimi Report), A/55/305–S/2000/809. August. Available at: http://www.un.org/peace/reports/peace_operations/.

UN (2003) International Commission on Human Security, *Human Security Now* (New York: United Nations). Available at: http://www.humansecurity-chs.org/finalreport/English/FinalReport.pdf.

UN (2004) Report of the Secretary-General's High-level Panel on Threats, Challenges and Change, *A More Secure World: Our Shared Responsibility* (New York: United Nations, 2004). Available at: http://www.un.org/secureworld/.

UN (2005a) Report of the Secretary-General, *In Larger Freedom: Towards Development, Security and Human Rights For All*, 2005. Available at: http://www.un.org/largerfreedom/.

UN (2005b) '2005 World Summit Outcome', United Nations General Assembly, A/60/L.1, 15 September. Available at: http://daccessdds.un.org/doc/UNDOC/LTD/N05/511/30/PDF/N0551130.pdf?OpenElement.

UNDP (1994) United Nations Development Programme, *Human Development Report 1994* (Oxford: Oxford University Press).

UNMP (2005a) UN Millennium Project, 'Goals and Targets'. Available at: http://www.unmillenniumproject.org/reports/goals_targets.htm.

UNMP (2005b) UN Millennium Project, *Investing in Development: A Practical Plan to Achieve the Millennium Development Goals*. Available at: http://www.unmillenniumproject.org/reports/index_overview.htm.

US (1999) 'Final Report', 'A Global Forum on Fighting Corruption: Safeguarding Integrity Among Justice and Security Officials', Washington DC, 24–26 February. Available at: http://www.state.gov/www/global/narcotics_law/global_forum/global_forum_report.pdf.

USOCRS (2005) Office of the Coordinator for Reconstruction and Stabilization, US Department of State. Available at: http://www.state.gov/documents/organization/43429.pdf.

van Meurs, W. (ed.) (2003) *Prospects and Risks Beyond EU Enlargement: Southeastern Europe: Weak States and Strong International Support* (Opladen: Leske & Budrich).

van Meurs, W. and Weiss, S. (2005) 'Qualifying (for) Sovereignty: Kosovo's Post-status Status and the Status of EU Conditionality', Discussion Paper, 6 December (Guetersloh: Bertelsmann Stiftung).

Wallerstein, I. (1974) *The Modern World System: Capitalist Agriculture and the Origins of the European World Economy in the Sixteenth Century* (New York: Academic Press).

Waltz, K. (1979) *Theory of International Politics* (Reading, Mass.: Addison-Wesley).

Ward, L. (2005) 'Labour Claims 1.1m Fall in Number of Socially Excluded', *Guardian*, 29 November.

Washington Post (2002) 'After the War', editorial, *Washington Post*, 24 November.

Watt, N. (2003) 'Americans Raise Hackles by Flying Stars and Stripes in Iraq', *Guardian*, 22 March.

WB (1997) World Bank, *World Development Report 1997: The State in a Changing World* (Washington, DC: IBRD/World Bank). Available at: http://www.worldbank.org/html/extpb/wdr97/english/wdr97con.htm.

WB (2000) World Bank, *Reforming Public Institutions and Strengthening Governance: A World Bank Strategy* (Washington, DC: IBRD/World Bank). Available at: http://www1.worldbank.org/publicsector/Reforming.pdf.

Wendt, A. (1992) 'Anarchy Is What States Make of It', *International Organization*, Vol. 46, No. 2, pp. 394–419.

Westendorp, C. (1997) 'Interview with Carlos Westendorp', *Slobodna Bosna*, 30 November. Available at: http://www.ohr.int/press/i971130a.htm.

Wheeler, N.J. (2000) *Saving Strangers: Humanitarian Intervention in International Society* (Oxford: Oxford University Press).

Whitaker, B. (2003) 'Iraq's Fresh Start May Be Another False Dawn', *Guardian*, 5 September.

White, M. (2003) 'Downing Street Rules Out Victory Parade', *Guardian*, 10 May.

Wight, M. (1979) *Power Politics* (ed. H. Bull and C. Holbraad) (Harmondsworth: Penguin).

Wilkinson, T. (1998) 'Bureaucracy, Corruption Plague Foreign Investment in Bosnia', *Los Angeles Times*, 29 March.

Williams, R. (2000) 'Democracy, Development and Anti-corruption Strategies: Learning from the Australian Experience', in A. Doig and R. Theobald (eds) *Corruption and Democratisation* (London: Frank Cass).

Williams, W. A. (1964) *The Great Evasion: An Essay on the Contemporary Relevance of Karl Marx, & on the Wisdom of Admitting the Heretic into the Dialogue about America's Future* (Chicago: Quadrangle).

Williamson, D. G. (2001) *Germany from Defeat to Partition, 1945–1963* (London: Longman).

Wolfson, P. (1999) 'Bosnia Corruption', *Voice of America*, 15 September.

Wood, B. (1999) 'Bosnia Corruption', *Voice of America*, 20 August.

Yannis, A. (2002) 'The Concept of Suspended Sovereignty in International Law and its Implications in International Politics', *European Journal of International Law*, Vol. 13, No. 5, pp. 1037–52.

Zartman, I. W. (ed.) (1995) *Collapsed States: The Disintegration and Restoration of Legitimate Authority* (Boulder, Colo.: Lynne Rienner).

Zartman, I. W. (2005) 'Early and "Early Late" Prevention', in S. Chesterman, M. Ignatieff and R. Thakur (eds) *Making States Work: State Failure and the Crisis of Governance* (New York: United Nations University).

Zielonka, J. (1998) *Explaining Euro-paralysis: Why Europe Is Unable to Act in International Politics* (Basingstoke: Macmillan).

Index

Abrahamsen, Rita 16, 17
Action Aid 88
Afghanistan 4, 12, 13, 27, 30, 33, 40, 41, 44, 127, 189
Africa 2, 4, 16–18, 30, 33, 36, 76, 81, 84–95, 97, 189–90
  African leadership 9, 38, 73
  Commission for Africa 2, 3, 28, 36, 39, 83, 84–7
  New Partnership for Africa's Development (NEPAD) 84, 85
aid conditionality 29–30, 38, 85, 87
Al Qaeda 27
Albania 37, 98, 102, 105, 113, 114, 120
Allawi, Ayad 167
Amato, Giuliano 125
Annan, Kofi 60
Ashdown, Lord Paddy 53, 56, 138, 140–1, 145–7, 162, 169–70, 173–4, 182–3

Badinter Commission 66
Bain, William 68, 128
Balkans (*see also* South Eastern Europe) 23, 30, 37, 65, 78, 96, 98, 107, 126–7, 155, 162, 189–90
Baudrillard, Jean 92
Belarus 84
Bendaňa, Alejandro 56
Benn, Hilary 85
Bennett, Christopher 154
Bickerton, Christopher 106–7
Biden, Joseph 160–1
Bildt, Carl 130, 136
Blair, Tony 20, 64, 83
Bosnia-Herzegovina 4, 8, 13, 23–5, 27, 30, 33, 37, 44–6, 52–3, 65–9, 79, 111–12, 114, 116–17, 119, 120–1, 123–42, 143, 145–64, 166, 169–71, 173–88
  Bonn powers 134, 136, 138, 174, 179

Bosnian war 28, 124, 181
constitutional reform 166, 175–8
Council of Ministers (CoM) 52, 133, 137–8, 140
Croatian Democratic Community (HDZ) 161–2, 177
Customs and Fiscal Assistance Office (CAFAO) 153
Dayton peace agreement 41, 123–5, 127–32, 136–7, 149, 175, 178, 183
Directorate of European Integration (DEI) 23, 44, 137–8, 140–2
elections 131, 147, 149, 155–8, 160–1, 177, 178
employment law 166, 183–6
European Union policy 44–5, 66, 96, 98, 102, 105, 107, 123, 125–7, 128–30, 135–42
Federation (FBiH) 123, 146, 151, 152, 158, 161, 175–7, 179–80, 182–4
Federation Commission of International Legal Experts 152
flag design 44
Office of the High Representative (OHR) 23, 52–3, 57, 65, 107, 123, 128–30, 131–42, 145–9, 151, 153–9, 161–3, 169–70, 173–6, 179–80, 182, 185–6, 188
Organisation for Security and Cooperation in Europe (OSCE) policy 150, 156, 161, 179
Parliamentary Assembly 52, 134
Party of Democratic Action (SDA) 177
Party of Democratic Progress (PDP) 161
Peace Implementation Council (PIC) 57, 66, 98, 123, 125–6, 128–30, 131–5, 142, 148, 153–4, 174